The Mind Keys

To Transform Your Personal Destiny

Flick the Switch's, Transform, Change

and find your true self-path

FOR THE URGENT ADVANCEMENT OF HUMANITY TOWARDS PRO-CREATION

Copyright © 2022 Eric Martyn Addelsee

First published 2022

Cover Co-creator E.M. Addelsee

Co-creator Howarth McSwain designers

Cover image (adobe stock.com) 227490522/©

The right of Eric Martyn Addelsee to be identified as author of this work has been assured by him in accordance

With the copyright, designs, and patents act, 1988

The Mind Keys © 22022 by Eric Martyn Addelsee.

All rights reserved.

Copyright registered with copyright house.

London.

Registration id: 218973953

ISBN:9798362189556

Published by Amazon

Amazon publishing

410 Terry Ave, N Seattle.

WA 98109

USA

THE MIND KEYS
SWITCH
TRANSFORM
CHANGE

ERIC MARTYN ADDELSEE

In Loving Memory of my Dad

1940-2021

AN ACKNOWLEDGEMENT TO POSITIVE INFLUESNCES AND MENTORS WHO HELPED ME ON MY PATH OF SELF-ACTUALLISATION

June G Bletzer---The Psychic Encyclopaedic Dictionary

Richard Bandler---Co Founder-NLP

John Grinder---Co Founder –NLP

Anthony Beardsell---NLP Trainer-Excellence Assured

Anthony Robins—Awake the Giant Within

David Snyder---NLP Power

Jeffery Mitchlove---Thinking Aloud

Milton Ericson---Innovator of Hypnosis

J.R Sedel---Universal Cosmic Law "Hermetics"

Bruce Lipton---The Biology of Belief

Wallace Wattle---The Science of Getting rich

BSY Group-Holistic courses

Stephan Swartz—The seven Laws Of Change

CONTENTS

Introduction

Chapter One: **Parts and Ideas That Make Up Actuality** P:1

Chapter Two: **The Laws of the Universe** P:11

Chapter Three: **Three Levels of Unconscious Mind** P:18

Chapter Four: **Prime Directives of Unconscious Mind** P:30

Chapter Five: **The Mood Table** P:40

Chapter Six: **Understanding Meta- Programmes** P:44

Chapter Seven: **Brainwave frequencies and how we access them** P:54

Chapter Eight: **Thought, Value and Destiny Levels** P:62

Chapter Nine: **Combing Personality Traits, Meta Programmes and Values** P:72

Chapter Ten: **The Structure of Conversational Linguistics** P:78

Chapter Eleven: **How We Change Our Values and Change Our Reality** P:95

Chapter Twelve: **Chunking Up, Chunking Down, Chunking Across** P:110

Chapter Thirteen: **Perception Is Projection** P:132

Chapter Fourteen: **Quantum Physics and Esoteric Science** P:141

Chapter- Fifteen: **The Way Holographic Reality Defines Our Actuality** P:150

Chapter -Sixteen: **Timeline Explained** P:168

Chapter -Seventeen: **Hypnotic Suggestion and the Three Core Concepts** P:176

Chapter Eighteen: **The Principles of Hypnosis and Defining Your True Self-Path** P:191

Chapter --Nineteen: **Resourceful and Un-Resourceful Thoughts and Actions** P:210

Chapter -Twenty: **Affirmations and Afformations** P:234

Chapter -Twenty-One: **Examples of Inductions Deepeners, Suggestions And Cluster Scripts** P:246

Chapter -Twenty-Two: **Esoteric Influence** P:262

Chapter -Twenty-Three: **Inspirational Thought** P:273

Chapter-Twenty-Four: **Psychic self-defence from Destructive Brainwashing** P:284

INTRODUCTION

The bedrock of this book outside of Hypnosis and Neuro Linguistic Programming, is that there are Esoteric definitions which literally define the workings of the universe right down to our existences on Earth. The esoteric definitions describe the universal principles, infinite spirit, and the way everything in universe works by virtue of this. The point is over the years of study and experience. I can assert that these esoteric definitions do hold water so to speak, and when understood and applied can be life transforming. Over the years the main part my life was running like so many other people's on auto pilot; like a fixed loop, I decided to research why this was possible and found myself on a path to understanding what reality is and what causes it. Was it just fate? Or was there more to it than that; was life set in stone or changeable by choice? Do we have a destiny we can shape with our own intentions, or was it being shaped for us outside of our control? Social science would say born poor die poor, born rich die rich, was it possible to break out of this system; could we be born apparently destined to only have certain experiences and just enough? Or could we shift our lives up to other levels beyond just average wealth or health, way above and beyond; Essentially asking the question what makes things manifest? Was it coming from outside or inside? The answer as it turned out is both, internal and external messages/suggestion as well as some kind of action is what make things manifest. As it happened around that time, I came across what is known as the Seven Universal Principles, and later the twenty-one universal sub

INTRODUCTION

laws. which Understanding these turned out to be the bedrock/foundation of what we call manifestation. They became key to understanding the connection between conscious and subconscious communication, and what manifests is rooted to this understanding more than most people realise, especially the way everything in universe corresponds to everything else; It takes more than just knowing this to manifest what you want, the knowledge has to be applied, without this knowledge though the task becomes very difficult, and indeed this is the knowledge I didn't have when I was asking questions about what makes everything manifest. I wasn't religious so I found the answers as it turned out by studying that which is generally defined as esoteric. Hypnosis and Neuro Linguistic Programming became the main contributors to understanding and applying this, that said there was a pile of other stuff I studied that was also relevant and connected up the whole big picture so to speak; so I start with what the principles and sub-laws in this book as the bedrock/foundation to the rest of the book.

What we manifest, why and how; the way we manifest is built on solid ground and not sand, the things to apply and how they are all rooted back to understanding these principles; understanding that there are three absolute principles that shape and define who we are through a conscious hierarchy of perceptual filters. Discovering these things for myself became the turning point to further and deeper understanding which then became knowledge that can be applied; and yes, it does put our destiny and what happens to us as individuals in our own hands! we become able to be the masters of our own destiny. We are part of one overall unifying spirit/vital life force, defined by the first universal principles.

The all is mind, intelligent which connects us all, human, animal inanimate or otherwise, as a whole that we call Universe. We can connect and change our reality, actuality by applying these processes. Visualisation, hypnosis, Neuro linguistic programming, Meditation, ETP, and various other processes designed to improve our lives. Our mind is the most powerful tool and possession we have, and the least understood; century's or even decades ago very few people had any real idea about this, but now it is gradually becoming more mainstream, people will be spend time and energy understanding how to use a computer and to some extent how it

INTRODUCTION

works, or playing computer games yet none, or little time on how their own mind works and how to use it properly. We have the use of language possibly one of our greatest gifts, yet no understanding of the way to use it properly to re-organise our lives and, so called reality. We must first reorganise our mind, this is why around the world it seems like more people are living a life of lack than abundance. People focus on the physical objects, as though they are the things that matter the most, when in fact it is the mind that matters the most, without mind we have nothing and are nothing and this reflects across the globe, with so many people who literally have nothing, the root cause to this is their relationship to mind, money can be a useful to buy the things we like, however it is not, and never will be as important as our own mind. Mind over matter; something every single one of us has is mind and a connection to universe.

We are taught many things at school except the most important of all, indeed the first principle of the universe. "mind is all," and language is the doorway to our mind. If you can look at this and the rest of this book with an open mind, then you have found a pathway that will open up to you a life you may have thought, impossible; and will turn that which seemed impossible into possible; that which seemed unobtainable into obtainable. Where your life is now, can be switched by one degree of what it is, or the opposite of what it is if you will only take the time to look into you own mind and explore the possibilities that exist within mind, which is thought, linguistics, action, these three parts make up a system/process that creates our destined path, it's like another law of three, the universal ones being the overall absolute, and these subsets of absolutes, like the primary colours Red, Yellow, Blue, which make up the whole vast colour spectrum.

Thought, linguistics, action, makes up the whole manifestation spectrum, at least on our Human physical level in terms of what we perceive our physical reality as being in the here and now. Every external experience starts within the mind and is projected externally as experiences. Whenever we do a course in a subject, the course is always broken down into component parts, this is the same, I will say it's not just a matter of closing your eyes visualising every day and your world would change, it's not quite that easy or strait forward; visualisation just through mind's

INTRODUCTION

eye can and does work! however it is more than just that; it's deeper than that, and well worth digging down on the subject to gain the understanding and knowledge that creates change on a deeper level that's lasting, not temporary. I have come across many people who say they tried mind's eye visualisation and nothing happened, possibly because their first few attempts are way too big, you have to start small and get some history of success, also a person's mind-set and environment can affect visualisation if you have a real scarcity mind-set then you are probably going to have trouble manifesting a dream car or house, because you have to have and alignment between values, beliefs, desire intention and action, if you want to practice mind's eye visualisation I suggest start small, a jumper with a label or a jacket, then as you work on your beliefs and visualisation you start to create alignment, how much you do or don't value yourself is a major player in this, forget whether other people value you or not it always comes down to the self, self-esteem is not just about confidence. For many years, space agencies looked through telescopes for planets, they found some but not many; then they changed their perspective and turned to look for planets by observing dwarf stars and then seeing if there were planets orbiting dwarf stars, when they changed that perspective, they found probably hundreds of planets now because they changed Their Perspective. What I learned from Youth and seeing things now, is that then, everything was and seemed felt fated by virtue of attitude, fate that we had no hand in, what I discovered is it is like that when you believe that this book is about going from a fated lifestyle to one that's synchronised, and is personal destiny, from pre-fated to pre-destined.

CHAPTER ONE

PARTS AND IDEAS THAT MAKE ACTUALITY

When you put the component parts together and apply them, it's like putting the component parts of a car engine together, that creates the whole, an engine will move a vehicle, this book and the components that make the whole will transform not only your reality it will change your whole outlook on life. This book is not just about manifesting a couple of objects, or objectives, it's about creating a life/lifestyle that is, and feels abundant and whole. Like any book it's broken down into chapters, I try not to storyboard too much, just put down the whys and how to that create the results. some thing's you'll get strait off and some take "practice", "dedication" and some "patience", a lot of patience! it's worth the effort put in, and you will get out from this book by putting the effort in to understand the components properly, and applying them, "wisdom" comes from knowledge being applied, and to some degree trial and error getting there, but then before you know it you will be choosing your life decisions rather than your life chosen for you, you will be self-directing as opposed to being directed, self-dictating as opposed to being dictated to and know what self-esteem really is! I am going to reveal to you a "secret;" there are "no secrets" all the information you need is out there if you look for it. There is no forbidden knowledge only discernment of what knowledge you choose to learn or aspire two, there is no good or bad knowledge only the attitude of the person applying it. I will explain why your lives seemed to run by default "like Groundhog

Day" without you having the experiences and products you truly desired, I will tell you why this happened and more importantly how to change it with very simple procedures and maybe around an hour of your day, on a day-to-day basis. If you would give yourself 1 hours a day to completely transform your life to how you really wish it to be, then please continue to read, if not hey that auto pilot stuff isn't so bad. "Who you are kidding" life by conditioned default is not that great and you know it through poverty, illness, and an array of other things you may have gone on that you would rather not have gone on.

Before I proceed any further with this book, and before any of you become adept at mastering your destiny, I need to explain how personal return can backfire on you, if you don't fully understand the ramifications of what you're doing, you need to really understand almost literally "mind your own business", this is where a lot of people slip up before they even get started by putting all their focus on changing their friends, family and anyone else they come across who does not fit into their world view, which to a large degree defines co-dependency; the idea that we must control others to fit in with us, understand the concept of co-existence, letting go of relationships that fitted the old you, your old attitude, and start to draw in friends and maybe an extended type family or whatever, by just being yourself, but a self and a reality you actually know and understand and have influence over. In short to start with, anything you intend and act on that influences another person's life will have a return effect on your own, it's really important to understand this on the deepest level possible.

Wallace Wattle said in the science of getting rich, "it is not for you to want for another person, but you should want only for yourself" be minded of this; when you start trying to live other people's lives for them, you are on a slippery slope, Hypnosis and Neuro Linguist Programming should not be used to manipulate people against their will, I have read many books over the years on all sorts of subjects including casting spell's, and the same applies to this as to that; let's take a love spell for example, if you were to cast a love spell on an unsuspecting person, or use hypnotic suggestion, or an NLP technique, to bend someone's will to yours, or even put someone off going with someone their interested in, so they can gain their affections, then believe me, look out because the degree of manipulation and the effect you have through those actions toward someone, will be returned to you without them taking physical revenge, it will return the same in nature.

In fact it will return with far more intensity if they don't take revenge, "which is to some degree is forgiveness in itself" and worse than that it can't be reversed because you cannot protect yourself from your own personal returns. And any unpleasantness you caused them will be what you will receive, if you desire a relationship then focus on the type of person, personality, attributes, however not a specific people you know, and to some degree you also must have at least some of those personalities, and attributes to have an alikeness that will draw the relationship to you. If your intending to help someone, make sure they want that help, don't impose it on someone "no matter how well meaning," you must respect their free will to make their own choices, you must take no to mean no, no matter how good you become at what I'm showing you in this book, don't be tempted to try making other people's decisions for them, unless for some reason or another you have "their express consent".

Whether you're a practitioner, or someone who has mastered their own destiny, always make sure whether it's helping someone or a relationship of some sort, that you have their consent, without using manipulation, very, very important to get this, good relationships are "fairly give fairly take" not manipulate so you get everything, and they get nothing. There is a wisdom that is very ancient, I don't know who wrote it, or how far back in history it reaches, I don't think anyone does, the wisdom is this, "an it harm ye none do as thy will", the "ye" obviously refers to you, or the individual self, when you look at this in terms of personal return (you will reap as you sow) implies if you harm another it will return as harm, if you show a kindness then it will return as a kindness, because the intention and action comes back to you, the sender, always without exception, everything works in a cyclic manner, what goes around comes around. Keep what I have just said as your guidelines for applying what you will learn from this book, and you won't go far wrong; that wisdom definitely correlates to applying what is called law of attraction. You will make mistakes in life we all do, again without exception, if you apply that wisdom to your day-to-day undertakings, it will guide you away from harm and toward happiness, genuine happiness, which is after all what we all want, "happiness" which is an emotional (kinaesthetic) spin off return of what our desires, intentions and actions are. The seven universal principle's, and the twenty-one sub laws which are in the beginning of this book are effectively showing the same as I have just stated, so be minded if you go against this you are working against the nature of Universe, and the nature of Universe will always win, because is not competing, you are.

Be in alignment with the principles as best you can, and you will create a destiny and path for yourself in life that will give you more than you may believe possible at the moment. Work on the right side of the nature of Universe, and you will have the most powerful ally that exists on your side. Infinite spirit, or Universe, or whatever name you know it by has only one bias, toward pro-creation. Attitude is everything for a Human being, the rest of this book will show you how to change your attitude and change your reality, destiny.

Part of this book will show you how to communicate effectively, very effectively with your unconsciousness. I will explain this further on how to re- programme your attitude and reframe your destiny/life path, and you will soon see where I'm going with this, and why it's all relevant. When you follow this 'formula' if you like, it will give you full control over the steering wheel that guides your life, you will become the master of your own life experiences, on a day-to-day basis with absolute certainty. Conditioned mind-set and what it is, well this part I feel needs a fair bit of thought and understanding given to it, understanding this we operate our daily lives on one of eight thought/values levels each one can be worlds apart and generate eight different types of existence and subset existences within each level of value sets; unless you were brought up by parents who consciously brought you up knowing this you will be the same as me to start with externally conditioned values-sets or programmes if you like, and your life experience is one of manifestations from a generally conditioned egotistic way of thinking. It's not laying down laws, just the esoteric descriptions and the Universal ones, outside of that, there are no laws really, we all have free will even if we don't realise it, these are principles, live on the right side of them and your life can become bliss, live on the wrong side of them, and you'll face the corresponding consequences. when I first undertook looking, seeking answers to questions along the line of believing our lives and destiny are set in stone to be what we're being conditioned to believe with absolutely no way of changing it, or is there something more. That was the initial question I had in my mind.

  My life then was unremarkable the same old same old always playing out as my day to day experience, with a feeling of having no way out all I could do was be carried along with the same old daily grind as everyone else, I was in my teens in the 80s during an "era" when everything on the television oozed conditioning people to be full of fear, the threat of a nuclear holocaust seemed an inevitability my friends and myself all had the attitude that what's the point of studying or aspiring to be anything when most people believed that the bombs were going to drop at any minute, the proper-gander machine that was the news and newspapers were in their heyday, conditioned thoughts were rife and little literature on anything referring to reality shifting unless you read psychic books which were not as easy to locate as they are now.

  I remember my daily feelings being one of hopelessness, and what's the point when we're all going to get nuked soon, this was the stage, the platform that was my life then. So was I in tune with the universe did I have universal confidence then? Now my journey to the understanding that I have now started by meditating on like attracts like, I can still remember meditating on this, and realizing that what this was implying was big, really big and I had a sense that understanding this would open up doors in my life that had always been tight shut. The point to what I've just said is that my thoughts then were completely dominated by outside stimulus, I had no inner voice any intuitive thought used to be completely ignored, I felt doomed to a life I was told to expect, I believed then that those who were born poor stayed poor those who were born rich stayed rich and that was just the way it is. and my life pretty much stayed like that for a couple of decades except for one thing meditating on like attracts like had planted a seed in my mind that would grow into enlightened way of thinking and would show me that I can have the life, everything I desired, it was just a matter of figuring out a way to apply this. How, now that word 'how' to the main I would come to realise that I will show up that you want, I came to lean that 'how' is the domain of the sub-conscious, this is an important thing to remember and can make the difference between success or not.

The money, relationships, lifestyle I wanted never showed up, in part because I had the conditioned attitude of "how" it is going to turn up instead of the belief that it just would, then realising it doesn't just turn up you have to move towards it. The way our values, beliefs, attitude are, and that change starts from changing those three things. When we change our attitude, it becomes life transforming; shifting you literally from one reality to another, from when we are born our minds are under constant bombardment of what we should and should not believe and what we should and should not do, what is expected of us what we should expect to have or expect to be, cultural rules and codes that should be adhered to, if we do this others won't be pleased, if we don't do that others won't be happy with us, we are put under a constant bombardment of demands on our lives to the point that trying to focus on the self is made virtually imposable by people who impose this constant flow of conditioning and making us conform to how we should and should not think.

Too old to do this, too young to do that, too tall to fat to thin and all the other rubbish judgement calls, rather than focusing on self-responsibility and learning discernment. When we understand the way things manifest in our lives, then we have control over our own destiny, and when we stop allowing ourselves to be conditioned by the media and other negative stimuli, we then have a positive impact on the planet as a whole, because we are no longer giving all our thoughts to pushing against things thus creating more of what we were pushing against, the trend starts to reverse and become the opposite to the current affairs as thy are now, because when your just focusing on the salary waged job, in the scheme of things it will give a person a lifestyle which is orientated around their earnings and what they are left with after the mortgage and other bills the answer is to "find yourself to be yourself" and think above just that, in other words find your true passion in life, which is what I have done, part of

PARTS AND IDEAS THAT MAKE ACTUALITY

Which is authoring this book, it becomes a mission of being you and not trying to be someone else or make someone else be someone else then the knock-on effect is harmony amongst humanity, sure this isn't an overnight thing more of a gradual trend, but it starts with ignoring the negative influences, and opening ourselves up to the positive influences on focusing on what we are creating and manifesting.

Change for a lot of people isn't something they generally move toward, often people resist change because it's different/unknown or even scary, different often sparks a negative feeling like fear, fear of being ridiculed, laughed at or scorned on, but I will tell you something if your neighbours opinion, overrides your own then they make your decisions, when your opinion overrides theirs then your make your decisions, people don't become entrepreneurs by focusing on the criticisms of others they rise above them and focus on their success. Peoples desire to fit in is often a reason many never achieve any of their ambitions; and quite often have a mindset and path that takes them in the opposite direction to where they want to go in. Not only is this confusing for people it's dam right inconvenient, so why is it some seem to have a charmed life and others have just bearable or unbearable lives, well the cause of the difference is an "absolute science", and there is an answer and a set of components that when applied can turn anyone's life around, part of the answer is that we live in a universe that is holographic and systematic, and even manifestation follows a system rooted in cause and effect; every system has a process that runs it, and manifestation is no different to any other system. The way I have put this book together is designed to give the recourses to operate the system that controls their destiny.

There are two ways life works, one is it works by virtue of almost entirely outside beliefs and values, and the other way is through consciously choosing their beliefs, values and attitude which decide the experiences we have, and the emotions associated with them. I coach from a level of understanding of the etheric and human system that interact to cause our reality, from an understanding of universal principles, and from an understanding of our linguistics and what the makeup of words we use in everyday language are actually doing in terms of our life direction; from an understanding of why people make the decisions they make and do the things they do. And why change is viewed in general as hard and a struggle when it can be easy and with least effort, I coach from a level of being a qualified Hypnotherapist, Master Neuro linguistic Programmer, and Master NLP coach; I have also spent many years studying Esotericism/Parapsychology subjects which directly tie in with the whole structure of the resources needed to create successful change.

Each of the parts in this book cover a component prat of the whole system by the end of each chapter you will understand the components well enough to run the system, the chapters are orientated around and start to be more in control of what manifests in your reality; my point is there are things you aren't doing now that when you start doing them; change everything, mind-set and perspective, and believe me it's an awakening when things start moving in "synchronisation" as opposed to thinking it's all luck or chance, with what you actually want. Which as I will go into in more depth later happens through training the conscious mind to make the decisions and communicate it in a way to the unconscious mind, that the unconscious mind understands through understanding the way unconscious mind processes the information being transmitted by the conscious.

This book contains the principles of Hypnosis and NLP, with an esoteric backdrop which when applied becomes the subjective action required, because positive change follows from applying these strategies of Hypnosis and NLP. So was all this really a Secret well, no not really, there are certainly those who wouldn't share their knowledge of this, but the clues have been there for thousands of years it's just that in the main it wasn't presented or marketed until recently, there are metaphors that give us the clues if you follow the clues then you find the gem or treasure at the end of it. Most people that present this subject would probably all say they had done a fair bit of research (digging) before the really understood on a deeper level the idea that our experiences are a holographic reflection of our thoughts desires intentions and actions. Things like "affirmations" are a clue that habituated thoughts manifest and hypnosis one of the main focus areas in this book is obviously self-hypnosis creates habituated thoughts, when you put affirmations in a hypnotic suggestion's session together this kind of turbo boost's the intended suggestions to manifest. As opposed to repeating an affirmation thousands of times for weeks or months, you put it in a self- hypnosis session and it takes approx. thirty minutes a day, it may still take weeks or months to manifest, but you're more likely to stay the course having your headphones on and playing back a hypnosis session than repeat a statement tens of thousands of times a week. So basically, everything I have learned and used that works is in this book, and as you work through this it will become apparent reasonably quickly that we live in a multiverse that is connected. Everything corresponds to Everything else, therefore everything in universe is connected and communicating. Proven by quantum science, everything in Universe is entangled/connected.

The History of the Contents of This Book

The content of this book, which is Universal principles, Hypnosis, Neuro Linguistic Programming, and esotericism, goes back before the times of the Egyptian Pharos, and the Greek Hermes. Neuro Linguistic programming, and hypnosis are probably as esoteric in science and connected in nature as it gets; except for maybe herbalism, we know that the Pharos knew and practiced re-framing, and affirmations which means it's been around at least four thousand years. NLP, timeline work can be traced back to Shamanism, and Shamanism can be traced back at least 11,000 years. By Esoteric we mean working with mind, body and spirit, mainstream science like the pharmaceutical aspect is only mind and body not spirit, and to a large degree mainstream science see's us as just meat and brain, we are a lot more than just that, we are spirit in physical form which means there is a third missing if you like with some of the mainstream stuff. This shows up through the placebo effect where belief overrides the medicine, or sugar.

Hypnosis and Neuro Linguistic Programming can reframe and change beliefs values and strategies through process. An understanding of this process brings around the possibility of life transformation by process of applying subjective interventions that create or generate the change. Hypnosis and Neuro Linguistic Programming incorporate aspects of remote viewing and the concept of an empath. when practicing with others, in

Children's books that made the Wizards and Witch's, good or bad, different from everyone else, they knew and applied this, it was then the attitude of the witch or wizard that defined whether they were perceived as good or bad. So ever fancy being a Wizard or Witch from children's books or like Aladdin with a lamp? "Yes" then read on. The difference was they understood the connection between mind, body, spirit, they knew what the absolute universal principles where, and they knew how to manipulate the law of correspondence, which is like the anchor point between thought and vibration, which in turn manipulates thought and vibration.

The idea of any type of mental telepathy, incorporates the principle of universe is mind, intelligent, any type of telepathy in mainstream science is pretty much shut out; we could talk telepathy in hypnosis and neuro linguistic programming, communicating with conscious mind to unconscious mind, through spirit or superconscious mind, or telepathy on a more ESP level of one communicating with another without external audio linguistics, or sound, at least to human perception. The idea of any type of mental telepathy, incorporates the principle of universe is mind, intelligent, any type of telepathy in mainstream science is pretty much shut out; we could talk telepathy in hypnosis and neuro linguistic programming, communicating with conscious mind to unconscious mind, through spirit or superconscious mind, or telepathy on a more ESP level of one communicating with another without external audio linguistics, or sound, at least to human perception we are talking about the difference being communicating with physically perceived senses, and communicating with non-physical senses . the difference between someone talking information to you, and information coming let's say intuitively, one can be traced back to physical communication the other cannot be traced back to physical communication. As though one type of communication is physically transmitted and an-other one is transmitted through the Astral, or that which is considered non-physical like dark matter.

CHAPTER TWO

THE LAWS OF THE UNIVERSE

As humanity evolves the commentaries of the effect of the first three principles extend out to being called the twelve universal laws which are all in here, however it's worth pointing out that from four to twelve are commentary's, i.e. the first three are immutable/absolute "cause" and the others are the "effect" like the "law of attraction" is a commentary on the effect of the first three and as so is a variable as are the other eight. I have seen sites online that have twelve universal laws with correspondence as forth and the first three mixed around, the three absolutes are always first in this order. The first three principles are absolute truths, not variables; they are Mentalism/Mind, Correspondence/as above so below, Vibration, everything in universe is in movement, nothing rests. These first three principles are the three strands that weave the whole of universe together, the other principles are variables from the first three, this truth is absolute it has always been this way it will always be this way. Law of attraction is a variable of these three absolutes; it is these three absolutes working in unison that generates the law of attraction. Law of attraction isn't something that stands alone on its own; it is an effect of the three absolutes which are the cause of attraction. Universal principles define the origins of that which is absolute, cannot be changed and that which is variable, can be changed, which applies to everything that exists in Universe not just in humanity, nothing absolutely nothing escapes these principles. In general in nature there aren't that many absolutes, most things fall under polarity which defines dualism and variables, in most cases every truth is but a half-truth with the exception of these three principles "which are absolute colour spectrum Red, Yellow, Blue you can't just decide you want to lute truth", they will not vary, the same as primary colours that make up the colour spectrum Red, Yellow, Blue you can't just decide you want to change them to fit with you, you have to fit with them. In fact in pretty much every philosophy and religion, these three principles are appeared very heavily in metaphor; especially law of correspondence which is also one of the most miss-interpreted and least understood principles of the three absolute

The Three Absolute Principles

Mentalism: The First Universal Absolute. The All is Mind; The Universe is Mental; Universe is mind, mind is Universe; Totality. By Correspondence: The Crown Chakra and the Pituitary Gland; The first gland to appear in the Human Embryo; Associated closely with the rational; rational/irrational thinking, information, and Superconscious. This means that everything in Universe has varying degrees of intelligence, i.e. a rock knows it's a rock even though it doesn't communicate with language, it knows what it is and what its purpose is and has its own mental plane of existence. Mind: The term is used to acknowledge that mankind has access to another source of intelligence other than the physical brain. An invisible source of intelligence that flows through the brain; an ethereal vibrational frequency that contains an individual's Akashic records and present belief system; also called the subconscious mind/soul mind; Everything in universe has a consciousness varying only by degree; even a rock knows what it is even if it doesn't openly communicate or move; everything in universe is connected.2. Correspondence: As above, so below; as below, so above the way people's thoughts perspective and emotions project their physical reality. By Correspondence: The Brow Chakra and the Pineal Gland the Pineal gland produces "Melatonin" that controls the waking and sleeping cycles. Each person is a component/entity of; The All, Totality, "Send and return" Brings in the idea of illness caused, "subjectively" and can be removed, "subjectively." And that our entire destinies are created, formed, and transformed "subjectively." A persons reality corresponds to what they talk about in conversation the most, without being in an altered mind-state, hypnosis even casting a spell can cause change, how many of you thought change through conversation creates real physical change. As real as any change caused through hypnosis or casting a spell; correspondence out of the three absolutes is the one that has been overlooked the most, mainstream science and thinking incorporates the first and third principle but tends to ignore discredit or re-right it in some way. Holistic and Esoteric incorporates the first, second, and third principle.

This book works through the three absolute principles of, Universe and Consciousness. It is the bedrock/foundation of any personal transformation, understand these basic principles is to start to understand yourself and find who you are; by knowing the way beliefs and values are formed and if the ones you have fit with who you want to be, you could ask yourself a question, what beliefs would I have to have around this value or concept, to align my belief system that will manifest that version of value or concept by virtue of correspondence. Essentially correspondence with linguistics emphasise the power of symbolism, words and statements, the direction of "cause and effect" a subjective cause (conversation) with a physical effect or physical experience. The linguistic spin off being directly connected to the law of correspondence as an absolute. If you don't like someone or want their attention don't focus on them and interact as little as possible on them switch the focus to people you do want to associate with, which is what you do want, takes practice though.

When you like someone and wish to cultivate a relationship with them talk about them and show an interest in what's important to them; this defines repel and attract, you will either repel someone's interest in you or attract it, again all relationships are a mirror of attitude and alignment or non-alignment of variables like values and beliefs and even strategies of attaining goals and ambitions. There is Harmony and agreement between the several planes of manifestation, life being, this truth is an absolute truth, not a half truth, The universe is the all, everything that exists, exits it cannot not exist because it exists within the infinite, the all of universe, every emanates from the one source field, the same laws, principles and characteristics apply to each unit of combination of units of activity as each manifests its own phenomena upon its own plane. 3. Law of Vibration: The Third Absolute Principle. Nothing rests; everything moves; everything vibrates. By Correspondence: The Throat Chakra and the Thyroid Gland the Thyroid gland produces "Thyroxin" to convert oxygen and food into usable energy. Vibration of brainwave frequency's, Gamer, Beta, Alpha, Theta, Delta, Vibration associated emotion and feeling states and degrees

of conscious awareness. All that exists is in constant vibration and motion all of the universe is in constant vibration and motion. The all of the universe is pulsating and vibrating with life, energy and motion; there is no death anywhere in universe, except in the conceptualization of death by the human mind, which has no foundation or substance in reality, (unless you allow it to) when a person is able to bring this concept of life in the realm of their actual consciousness, not only to intellectual accept the fact but be able to feel and be conscious of the universal life activity in all aspects of reality, in other words you can accept something or accepts it's opposite or degree in between but whatever one you accept is your reality. We are infinite in nature but are sold the concept we are not.

Variable Principles/Commentary

4: Polarity, everything is Dual; everything has poles and degrees in-between everything has its pair of opposites like and unlike are the same; opposites are identical in nature, but different in degree; extremes meet; all truths are but half-truths; all paradoxes may be reconciled. By Correspondence: The Heart Chakra and the Thymus Gland the Thymus gland produces "T cells" for the immune system of the body. Information gathered through the senses and projected, creates a polarized reality; a spectrum covering a range from one to another polar opposite, the degrees in between. Everything is Dual; everything has poles; everything has its pair of opposites" like and unlike are the same; opposites are identical in nature, but different in degree; extremes meet; all truths are but half-truths; all paradoxes may be reconciled. The evidence of this principle is observed in the Polarity of planets and the various celestial bodies that includes our own earth, solar system, galaxy, and even the Universe. Everything has Polarity. Without the Principle of Polarity, light, heat, gravity, and electricity would not be possible.

When you view your automobile's battery, you can see the positive and negative terminals that make electricity possible - the Principle of Polarity is always at work in all things. 5: Rhythm (The Cycles) everything flows, out and in; everything has its tides; all things rise and fall; the pendulum-swing manifests in everything; the measure of the swing to the right is the measure of the swing to the left; rhythm compensates. By Correspondence: The Naval Chakra and the Adrenal Gland; The Adrenal gland produces "Hydrocortisone" that regulates the use of food and helps the body adjust to stress. Procession of cycles, i.e. four equinoxes to one yearly cycles; everything works in cycles but is mostly explained or defined in linier terms. 6: Cause and Effect; Every Cause has its Effect; every Effect has its Cause; By Correspondence: The Spleen Chakra and the Lydden or Spleen The Spleen produces "Macrophages" to cleanse the blood and is vital to the immune system of the body and a person's health. Everything happens according to the three absolute Laws; which together generate the principle of cause and effect; Chance is but a name for Law not yet recognized; there are many planes of causation, but nothing escapes the Law. 7: Gender. Gender is in everything; everything has its Masculine and Feminine Principles; Gender manifests on all planes. By Correspondence: The Root Chakra and the Sacral or Reproductive Glands of Male and Female in all Species.

The reproductive organs of "male and female" in all Life forms that exist. 8: Law of Action. The subjective and objective actions required. An action result from attention of thought and the nature of the action corresponds to the nature of the attention. Every thought produces an alchemical process in consciousness action is not homogenous, but contains three elements, the "thought" which conceives it, the "will" which finds the means of accomplishment, and the "union" of the two needed to bring the action to pass. 9: Law of Attraction. Law of attraction is an extended commentary from like attracts like, law of attraction is inclusive of the law of association. The electromagnetic sensitivity field that surrounds each atom either compatible with, or disturbed by, other atoms electromagnetic sensitivity field, surround, atoms of compatibility aggregate repeatedly with each other until matter that we perceive is formed. This makes it understandable how one draws to oneself, both experiences and a physical body, resulting in the nature of the atoms that emanate from mental activity. 10: Law of Inspired Action. Closely related to the law of attraction, the law of inspired action is all about taking those real, actual steps to invite what we want into our lives. Often the inspiration comes from within. "Inspired action is that gentle, internal nudge," says. "It's not always a plan of action." practicing this law is all about slowing down, getting quiet, and creating space for internal guidance. When we let go of our need to arrange and control how things will work out, and are instead open to all possibilities, it makes room for new ways of achieving our goals that we might not have considered otherwise. That intuitive nudge or an idea that pops in your head and then you act on it, and it produces positive outcomes, which from inspired action. 11: Law of Perpetual law of transmutation.

This law states that on an energetic level, everything in the universe is constantly evolving or fluctuating. Every action is preceded by a thought, with thoughts themselves having the power to eventually manifest in our physical reality. Ever been around a negative person and felt your own positivity depleting? That's one example, but it can also work the other way around: Higher frequencies transmute lower ones when applied with intention. Knowing this, we can actively seek to uplift negative energy around us with our thoughts and actions. 12: Law of Compensation. The law of compensation relates closely to the law of attraction and the law of correspondence. "You reap what you sow" is the main take-away; with the law stating your efforts will always come back to you positively. If you are seeking something, you must contribute in some way toward your goal. To work with this law in a manner that attracts (or compensates for) love and support, for example, ask yourself, "Where am I being called to serve and support others today" these are the principles by which we are all bound to, and our incarnations are defined by the way we relate to these principles and commentary's. We are what we think, do, and say. These principles help us understand how, why these things are possible

The 11 Eternal Principles

The First Eternal principle: Law of Totality: All people and all creatures are one, united with the Divine: The Second Eternal Principle: The Law of Karma. What you do and what happens to you is the result of your soul's choice to come to earth and learn the lessons it needs to learn. The Third Eternal Principle: The Law of Wisdom. Wisdom is knowledge of what you can and cannot change, accepting those limitations in this reality; and choosing to use your suffering as a tool for learning about yourself and growing spiritually.

The Forth Eternal Principle: The Law of Love. Pure, unconditional love heals our karma and our hatred and reminds us of our divine nature. The Fifth Eternal Principle: The Law of Harmony here is divine order in the universe, and we are meant to be in harmony with everyone and everything. The Sixth Eternal Principle: The Law of Abundance. Abundance is the energy state that manifests material wealth and other, more important forms of wealth. The Seventh Eternal Principle: The Law of Attraction. The Universe collaborates with us to bring us what we desire. The Eighth Eternal Principle: The Law of Evolution. God intends for us to continually evolve to a higher state of consciousness. The Ninth Eternal Principle: The Law of Manifestation. The power to manifest what we desire is our birth right, and we are constantly co-creating reality with the help of the Divine. The Tenth Eternal Principle: The Law of Destiny. We are flawed creatures, driven to unite ourselves with God/vital life force and end our suffering, and choose to take human form in order to purify our souls, rid ourselves of karma, and reunite with God for all eternity. The Eleventh Eternal Principle: The Law of Non-Locality. We can defy the laws of time and space, and participate in the co-creation, of the seemingly impossible. The definition of a principle is a fundamental truth or proposition that serves as the foundation for a system of belief or behaviour or for a chain of reason-ing.

The Universal principles serve as a Universal truth that these are the principles that define the system that is the Universe we all exist in, The Universe as I will explain further in the book is systematic, the definition of a system in general is three or more parts and it becomes a system, the three absolute principles of the Universe are essentially the three threads that weave the whole Universe together, they are separate principles, however entangled, connected in the same way as we are physical form and we separately from spirit in terms of planes of existence and purpose however we are connected we are spirit, vital life force and physical Human form. To be able, have the ability to transform your lifestyle, through changing values and beliefs it becomes essential to really have an inside out under-standing of these principles and what they imply, and believe me treat them as real because they understanding this takes things from thought-to-thought form. These principles mould what we call our incarnation. Understanding these principles and applying them will transform your life, by understanding that everything that comes in and out of our lives does so by virtue of the way we relate to Universe. Aspiring to live as best you can by the twenty-one Universal sub-laws or ignoring them and doing the opposite will produce two parallel life paths which are completely different to each other.

CHAPTER THREE

THE THREE LEVELS OF CONSCIOUS MIND

Three levels of consciousness; and aspiring to understand these levels of consciousness becomes psychic development; Superconscious, Subconscious/unconscious, Physical critical consciousness; Note, Sub-conscious and unconscious are the same thing, in the book I refer to it as unconscious but it is also sub-conscious. (Esoteric definition) 1; a primal, nebulous, invisible energy comprising all of totality, endowed with intelligence, energized with emotion; a forever changing energy with interaction between the brain (psychic senses), the soul mind (instinctual senses), and cosmic mind (preference sense); changes according to the awareness of knowing as each entity evolves, making matter for one's present life. 2; invisible matter made of free atoms, alive, endowed with energy and intelligence, subject to the thought and emotions of one's mind, using the law of polarity and vibration; various levels of matter correspond to levels of thought. 3: consciousness extends beyond time and space and is used in all kinds of "form" making reality of current thoughts; functions to constantly seek self-expression; 4: a total composite of what a person thinks, feels, and senses, accumulated from all that one has ever tasted, smelled, heard felt, and seen, and ones responses to this labelled "life. ."5: emotion is the activating force behind consciousness, and consciousness is the force behind all matter, in the physical, astral, etheric. planes what consciousness forms is always dependent on the emotion behind the consciousness; feeling is the energy of consciousness; conscious does not assume space. Unconscious/Subconscious (esoteric definition) 1: an invisible, ethereal energy field belonging to the physical body but vibrating faster than the physical body; has no counterpart in the physical body (as does the invisible astral body) but it's function is never separate from the brain area; 2: Structure is like a computer more complex than humans will ever make; this computer mind stores and holds in memory that which is given from conscious mind, the data processor; from each experience the individual goes through, the conscious mind forms an attitude.

A reaction, an idea, a concept, and feelings (mingled with outer stimuli of smells, tastes, sounds, sights, and touch feelings) The conscious mind stores the final judgement in the unconscious mind; the new data is orderly, compartmentalised, in the storage computer; new data that correlates with previously organized data adds to the total content of that data compartment. Increasing it in understanding and thus perfecting it; material can be fed to fast and be too foreign at one time. The objective is to perfect each compartment so change must come gradually; past data that corresponds to present activity and thought of the conscious mind surfaces automatically to help in the decision-making process. unconscious mind cannot make a decision on its own but takes data exactly as given from the conscious mind and doesn't lie in the return trip even if it has been stored from previous lives; 3: unconscious mind is the director of the sympathetic nerves system but subservient to the conscious ; having no decision making mechanism of its own; Superconscious (esoteric definition) 1: an ethereal energy field that brings knowledge and information of a higher source than the other two minds in the brain area; occurs spontaneously and intentionally; information and knowledge flow from the universal mind via the silver cord to the head and run along the spinal column in the kundalini; an infinite intellect.

2: the information bypasses the subconscious mind; therefore, the Subconscious belief system does not filter the data; the data is "pure".3: data and advice flow from the superconscious mind through the psychism called intuition clairsentience and hunch-ability data could not have been logically reasoned or figured out ahead of time; pure information;

because it flows through the spine, a physics remark, "I have a gut feeling or "I feel in my bones that I should not." Takes the same path as instinct and therefor is the only type of psychism that does not need to be willed; 4: superconscious mind knowledge flows through the psychism called inspirational thought, inspirational writing, inspirational art; this information was not learned in past education or past life experiences; knowledge is beyond the persons time period; a state of consciousness that geniuses are tuned into.

5: Mental brain programming- To logically reason with oncoming stimuli and information make a decision, react emotionally with the decision and drop in the subconscious mind (the computer the hardware); a normal function of the mental brain is to act like the software of the computer and programme the computer, occurs continually. "The conscious mind is telling the subconscious mind what to do even though one is functioning at a conscious level. Individual Unconscious mind is our personal hard drive of the three consciousness's it stores all personal memories and consequent memorised beliefs, habits, and the expression or effect of this is behaviour patterns; it is the persona of the person, and controls and produces emotion, feelings, unconscious mind It is like the middle man between conscious and superconscious mind, therefore it reflects both sides of the equation so to speak; it takes instruction from conscious mind but does not process negatives linguistically like conscious mind does, an example of don't think about the blue tree gets abstracted down to the blue tree, so the person will automatically think of a blue tree because that is what conscious mind has instructed it to focus on.

An understanding of unconscious mind and where their beliefs and behaviours are from Most people haven't got what they want because they were taught to chase what they want instead of drawing it in, the Chinese proverb goes like this, "if a horse makes a bolt for it, the harder you chase the horse the further away it goes, if you leave the horse be, it will probably come back of its own accord", what most people tend to do is chase what they want rather than apply ways to draw in what they want, which is actually a learned behaviour and it's learned by following value judgements which have come from outside opinion. Very few people in comparison focus on self-opinion, and are bound to compliance in order to fit in rather than self-assess their own values beliefs and the strategies their using, a lot of peoples values and beliefs are made up by lost performative statements, their too fat, their too thin, to young, to old, to thick, too smart for their own good, and the unsuspecting person accepts these judgements of them, the person giving those judgements is directing their opinion externally instead of internally, which effectively tells them they have to change in some way to fit in, and maybe face ridicule if they don't comply to the person or demand; however they may be perfectly accepting of themselves but feel they have to change to fit in, so we have to learn our self-opinion of ourselves includes us, which is self-empowering instead of being oppressed by negative outside opinion of us does not include us, which mirrors a lost performative statement, it's outside opinion attempting to be a dominant personality, and introvert the other. We learn to be our own dominant personality by focusing on self-belief and being happy with whom we are.

This new attitude changes behaviour and what returns to us, then things really begin to become a path of personal development and advancement which in turn builds confidence. One of the most important things to an individual is self-esteem, whether a person is directing their own life or not is largely down to whether they understand unconscious mind and the way unconscious mind processes language as soon as you tell someone don't do such and such what are they most likely to do? Exactly, what they were told not to do because of not understanding language processes of the unconscious. If someone were to say to me what one thing, they could do now to change their life, I would say learn what unconscious and subconscious are about. Part of what NLP coaches is, we have control over our own min, thoughts, and the way we direct them, but for the best part people believe they haven't got that on a level of control over their destiny, many believe everything runs by some kind of random luck or chance, and that belief produces that reality; So the more we understand about our own unconscious mind, the more we become our own dominant personality, because unconscious mind holds all the information that is our persona.

So the more we take control consciously of what we are allowing and declining in terms of opinion and beliefs, the more self-power we have over our decision making and what our reality evolves and shapes into, we have innate personal power, however for most people that has been lost to complying with conditioned and habituated ways of doing things, without challenging it from within.

So apart from our inherent genes that are absolute, hair colour, eye colour, skin colour, which were all rooted in climate region originally; bone structure which stay as absolutes in our incarnation everything else is a variable, which is or is not changed predominantly by how well we understand mind and whether we accept and apply the way mind processes language. I have read many times mind being related to the way a computer works; the screen is the projection of conscious physical reality, unconscious mind is the local hard drive subconscious mind is the RAM, the hard drive of all information that can be downloaded, the blocks of computer language are what makes the programmes work in a certain way, and the programmes can be changed by changing the instruction in the code. A computer has evolved into a direct reflection of the way mind works, three separate component parts that function as separate units hard wired together and used by language. The way we think, and talk will be influenced by our understanding or not understanding of what unconscious mind is about, and what its objectives are; someone who has a good understanding of unconscious mind will find this to be a valuable resource, someone who does not understand the workings of unconscious mind may view everything as fated or down to luck, or in the lap of the Gods.

When we understand the purpose of unconscious minds and the way it processes language then we have a conscious and unconscious relationship, we become consciously aware that everything that happens is coming from a deeper unconscious level, and if we consciously try to fathom all the how's we put up resistance to the unconscious and make things harder on ourselves not easier; when we look at the idea of words with power one word like abracadabra isn't going to give us what we want in an instant, but when we realise our collective words are often direct instructions to unconscious mind which always drops a negative, this knowledge gives us words with power, spoken or written that can and do cause an effect in our physical world. Ericson's model and the Meta model give us a solid foundation to the framework of the most effective way to apply language that causes manifestations (sends commands to the unconscious) it keeps, re-writes and changes habits and behaviour. The same as the principle of casting a spell to get more money or better health, but with the knowledge that the statements are being sent directly to unconscious/subconscious mind; "as command statements. When we talk or self-talk it shows just how powerful the receptive unconscious minds is, we are consciously receptive to the results of this through the experiences this produces; when these linguistic principles are applied a person's life can be completely transformed to something they may have been conditioned to believe would be impossible, achieve levels of health, wealth and happiness and other personal achievements they were conditioned to believe as impossible.

There is a conditioned way of thinking engrained into most of Humanity whereby people judge many things to be impossible to achieve or have because they cannot see how it could be possible, many who are Ill sadly cannot see how it could be possible for the body to heal itself, so this gives clear instruction to the unconscious mind, their focus on the illness they may have is so chronic that if there isn't a treatment trough medicine they would die.

There isn't an illness that the unconscious mind can't heal because it will always have the blueprint to perfect health, it has just been instructed by the persons beliefs not to automatically reverse a terminal illness and the persons feelings and emotions on the subject just echo that on every level of their being, and unconscious mind "accept" the instruction, when conscious mind instructs the unconscious mind to heal itself from any illness then it will follow the instruction and the person will heal; when the how will this happen is replaced with it will happen or has happened the doubt is taken out of the equation and then it becomes possible, so in short we have control of our destiny, when we realise what we are saying in daily conversation is being processed by unconscious mind as a command. There are Eight Billion humans beings on this planet in the here and now, here is the problem not the amount of people but if we take a statistic that probably averages about the same in most countries, only three percent of Americans are financially independent, so to be independent generally means that they are self-organising, which really equates to the other, ninety seven percent are in some way being organised by outside opinion and stimuli; which means that, that ninety seven percent of the populations unconscious minds are being programmed from the outside and not from within.

Which keeps them easy to organise and control, people chase the concept of the annual waged day job which generates a kind of comfort zone of financial security, but doesn't always give that and then only to some degree, a robot is programmed by a controller, an independent individual is controlled by themselves, because they consciously learned to be selective and discerning about what they believe, the majority of people can and are being herded by propaganda and "organisations" that are busy organising them. they have not got yet, the awareness that their unconscious filters are being programmed for them. When the internal representation of what is and isn't possible are changed then the reality associated with it changes! Mind stores memory by two separate parallels, timeline specific and non-timeline specific, one is changeable the other is not changeable a memory of a specific event is not changeable, a belief or value isn't timeline specific and is changeable, it may not be possible to change past events, but it is possible to re-frame past events and release any negative associations to it. Over the years of researching and learning mind over matter and hypnosis, I have come across many story's relating to unconscious mind. one such story is a man who had a pretty serious phobia which was causing him a great deal of anxiety and subsequent stress and inconvenience, he had seen several hypnotherapists to remove the phobia using clinical hypnosis technique's, none had any degree of success; desperate to remove the phobia he tried another hypnotherapist who used a different approach, instead of putting him in a hypnotic state and running a script, he put him in an hypnotic state and spoke directly to his unconscious mind, he created a channel between himself and the persons unconscious mind and the person spoke through the reply of his unconscious.

The person with the phobia had stated that they were mystified by the phobia and could not recall any reason or event which could have triggered it; the hypnotherapist asked the man in trance what had happened to cause the phobia the unconscious mind replied with what the event was, and that unconscious mind had created this state known as a phobia to keep him away from the potential threat that unconscious mind saw as a danger to him and to prevent that type of event from happening again, the hypnotherapist then negotiated with unconscious mind that this phobia was causing serious distress which was also a danger to him. There was no further reply, after the session was over the phobia had gone, the man kept the hypnotist informed of his progress and there was no further characteristics or signs of the phobia again.

So unconscious mind can repress memories to protect the person and in some cases what we know as phobias are the unconsciousness response to protect the person, these also sometimes manifest as panic attacks which are also the unconscious response perceived as protecting the person. Unconscious mind follows instruction the same as sub- conscious mind, the instruction from self-talk or believed outside opinion or stimuli. Why does unconscious mind maintain negative and destructive behaviour? Because at birth a child has not got a developed conscious mind, it is completely dependent for everything, so from birth to six everything in that child's conscious is a perspective of what life is and the memories are held in the unconscious, one of the child's way of perceiving what life is, comes from being taught directly and through assumptions, a child see's it's parents constantly arguing over money then the child assumes money is a problem and is hard to get.

Unconscious mind stores memories of habit formed behaviour so for example a toddler crawls to start with, then learns to walk by habitually trying to, the unconscious then remembers the memory of being able to walk and then walks without effort, so negative or destructive behaviour comes about in the same way, a good deal of negative or destructive behaviour is mimicked or learned in the years that most adults have not got many immediate memories of, say 0-6, so behaviour taken into adult life is to a larger degree leaned at this time, the problem often arises because the unconscious remembers and because there is no clear instruction to do things differently, children often take this behaviour right through their adult lives. So as an example if a child always got their own way when they throw a tantrum, then quite often this will manifest in adults expecting to get their own way by throwing a tantrum, which may escalate in adult life as threats if they don't' get their own way or violence. Because unconscious mind remembers always getting their own way when they trough a tantrum it thinks this tactic should still work because it has not been untaught or had that way of doing things erased and replaced with a new one, this is for the best part why unconscious mind maintains negative, disruptive, and destructive behaviour. Unconscious mind learns trough repetition, so when a child watches the same thing being done or repeats doing something unconscious mind adopts that and it becomes part of their behaviour pattern, part of a person's personality is held by unconscious mind, and most of their personality is mimicked from other people, so how many people know who they are? For most what they are is a collection of adopted behaviour both good and bad which filter out from values and beliefs that have been adopted, positive and negative from a range of other people including television and media and other outside stimuli.

So is it even possible for a person to actually be themselves if they have not got at least awareness of this, when unconscious mind stores negative emotions, it stores them in the body to be resolved at a later time, this can maintain negative effects in the body primarily disease; when we look at areas where terminal disease tend to occur we see that most if not all occur on around chakra points, which point to the probability that negative repressed emotions to are stored on or certainly of one of the seven energy chakra points these points distribute and convert energy the link is unconscious mind directs energy, and energy can be reduced severely when chakra points are blocked, all this points to a healthy or diseased body being that way mostly by thought patterns and beliefs. The brain is an alchemical laboratory; if a person feels good it is because the brain released a chemical to feel good in relation to what their emotions are. So any illness or damage can be reversed with the correct instruction to unconscious mind, if a person's belief is contrary to this then the body cannot heal or repair itself independently because the correct instruction has not been sent.

The use of hypnosis and Neuro Linguistic Programming is to open a communication channel with the intention to give unconscious mind commands essentially consciously connecting you to that which you may have felt disconnected from before, this will re-connect you. Even though technically you were not disconnected in the first place; Induction is a process most commonly known in hypnosis that heightens suggestibility and leads a person from beta state of consciousness to alpha and theta states of consciousness; which are known to be most effective for delivering suggestions to change behaviour, or to manifest desires and achieve goals, gain confidence, and remove phobias.

To induce trance usually a visualisation is used as a means to relax the person into a hypnotic/trance state, a bit like reading a story to a child at bedtime and they fall asleep, similar concept, except they are not asleep but in a hypnotic state; also with people who are more analytical an induction is used to give the conscious mind a task to do to suspend conscious activity while the suggestions are prescribed; such as counting down from one hundred to zero, the point of an induction is to reduce or remove conscious/critical mind interference; inductions range from instant under a minuet to fourteen to twenty minutes it's dependable of how suggestable the person is and what level of hypnosis is being induced, light-medium or deep hypnotic state.

Milton Ericson used linguistics to great effect; he created inductions for putting people in a hypnotic state that sounded like pure gibberish but embedded through the statements of gibberish were direct commands, you will be in trance, at the count of twenty; while the conscious mind was going frantic trying to work out the meaning of the gibberish, the command passed straight trough to unconscious/subconscious mind unhindered by the conscious mind, which was very busy. NLP doesn't use induction like hypnosis as such, it uses techniques to guide someone from associative to dissociative thinking. For example dissociative thinking. For example dissociating from a problem to associate to the solution, however "absorption" in the process can act as an induction high absorption of focus a typical example of absorption is, when reading a book you have got into after five to twenty minutes, you are so absorbed in the book that you are essentially in a light to medium hypnotic state, the point to being in a hypnotic state in the first place is to increase being open to suggestion, deep levels of absorption can shift you to an altered state,

THE THREE LEVELS OF CONSCIOUS MIND

advertisers know this and use it to great effect to make you prefer their product over their rivals product. Conscious mind references the self by requesting information from; unconscious mind which stores the references of self. Conscious mind, Creative processes 60-120 bits per sec, unconscious mind/ Receptive processes ten million bits per second.

CHAPTER FOUR

PRIME DIRECTIVES OF UNCONSCIOUS MIND

Prime Directives of Unconscious Mind: the way we think behave and talk will be influenced by our conscious understanding, or not understanding of what unconscious mind is about, and what its objectives and purpose is; someone who has a good understanding of unconscious mind will find this to be an invaluable resource, someone who does not understand the workings of unconscious mind may view everything as fated or down to luck, chance or in the lap of the Gods, and view everything as either physical matter or empty space, we have a constant dialogue between conscious and unconscious going on all day long, the only time conscious mind isn't self-referencing is when we are asleep, which may explain why hypnotherapists emphases the word sleep in instant inductions, the closer we are to theta and delta state the less influence critical conscious mind has essentially being temporarily suspended essentially theta or delta state being the deep to profound level of hypnosis put us back in the imprint period which is the period when we absorb information like a sponge. Children from birth to two years old are in a permanent delta state, whereas children from two to six or seven are in a permanent theta state while the conscious mind is forming, in other words they are not in a critical beta state like adults, so they take in all the information, suggestions without interference from a fully formed critical conscious. When we understand the purpose of unconscious mind and the way it processes language then we have a conscious and unconscious relationship with awareness that everything that happens is perceived and projected from a deeper unconscious level; and if we consciously try to fathom all the how's we put up resistance to the unconscious and make things harder on ourselves not easier. when we look at the idea of words with power, one word like abracadabra isn't going to give us what we want in an instant, but when we realise our collective words are direct instructions to unconscious mind, and that unconscious mind doesn't process a negative this knowledge gives us words with power, spoken or written that can and do cause an effect in our physical world we call reality, the reality is that, reality is unconscious we experience life from moment-to-moment actuality. Although we state conscious mind and unconscious mind as separate, they are connected and meshed together, they are part of the self they are the same but polar opposites; although the job of both conscious and unconscious is essentially to give us what we prefer or focus on the most and that's exactly what it does, so for those who are completely new to this way of thinking the unconscious is our other or better half.

Here is a list of the" prime directives" of unconscious mind.1: Stores memories, temporal (in relationship to time,) A temporal (not in relationship to time) Stores sub-modalities of the memory in different locations around the body, not stored in sense of being in a file in one location, stored as gestalts. 2: Is the domain of the emotions. Not in relationship to time, sorted of emotion generated, the timeline of this is stored somewhere else 3: organises all your memories (uses a timeline. Mechanics is the Gestalt) Gives the principle that if you can point to it, you can change it, can be pointed to physically or through visualisation, Imagination, interventions, through a timeline orientated process. 4: Represses memories with unresolved negative emotion.

The root of a lot of illnesses, phobias, panic-attacks are here, and this is the area NLP works on and why it has success reversing illness, phobias, and panic-attacks. 5: Presents repressed memories for resolution (to make rational and release emotions) have you ever been getting on with something quite happily when bam, a horrible memory of the past just seems to pop in your head, that is unconscious mind presenting something that needs resolution, if you make a note of these you may be able to resolve it on your own or, NLP timeline therapy usually succeeds in keeping the lesson but releasing the repressed emotions of resentment, fear, anger, hate, guilt, are generally the main negative emotions associated with a bad/negative experience, 6: May keep emotions repressed for protection, this can manifest as phobias, panic attack, PTSD, happens because unconscious mind may want to keep one or several lessons learned from the experience and will not let go so all the negative emotion associated with the event are kept as well.

The pharmaceutical tablet may help but will not release the negative emotion, it just puts the person in a position of suppressing the emotion even more and increase the likelihood of illness. 7: Runs the body has a blueprinted of body now, and of perfect health, the unconscious is the higher self. 8: Preserves the body maintains the integrity of the body, technically speaking our body does constantly re-generate itself, whether that regeneration produces illness in the body the body or a fitter healthier body depends on diet, exercise, mind-set/attitude.; Also controls the fight or flight mechanism which you generally have no say in consciously. 9: Enjoys serving needs clears orders to follow. Understanding the right use of linguistics, in the right mind state, will help you send clear coherent instruction to unconscious, the general rule is repetition! it will accept whatever command you give it, but you have to be working on your own values and beliefs even strategy's as well as just repeating statement in hypnosis or conscious affirmations, it's all part of forming an alignment you want you actually want, i.e. what would I have to believe for that to happen or manifest?

The timeline on changing beliefs and values through some form of repetition can be almost instantaneous but more often than not it may take a while for unconscious to accept the new belief or value depending on how deep rooted the old value or belief is. It works on a hierarchy system so the old belief or value isn't erased it goes down the hierarchy list and the new one takes top place in the hierarchy system. 10: Controls and maintains all "perceptions", regular/telepathic, we gain information through the five senses, but also from an extra sensory perception, such as intuition, remote viewing, mediumship, premonitions, any form of divining such as Tarot, dowsing comes under ESP. 11: Generates stores, distributes, and transmits, "energy" via the seven chakras 12: Maintains instincts, and generate habits, we have three basic instincts food, shelter, reproduction, habits are formed through repetition. 13. Needs repetition until a habit is installed 14. Is programmed to continually seek more and more there is always more to discover 15. Functions best as a whole integrated unit does not need parts to function 16. Is symbolic uses and responds to symbols 17. Takes everything personally. (The basis of Perception is Projection) 18. Works on the principle of least effort, Path of least resistance 19. Does not process negatives.

Unconscious mind is the hard drive of the consciousness's it stores all memories and consequent memorised beliefs, habits, and the expression or effect of this is behaviour patterns; it is the persona of the person, and controls and produces emotion and feelings. Therefore, it reflects both sides of the equation so to speak; it takes instruction from conscious mind but processes language in a different way to conscious mind; it does not process a negative, conscious mind does, the unconsciousness thinks don't repeated means do, it takes instruction from what's being focused on. For example don't think about a Red Balloon gets abstracted down to red balloon, so the person will automatically think of/picture a Red Balloon, because that is what conscious mind has instructed it to focus on. Our human mind is an integrated system of three separate units we use 100% of mind but only a small percentage involves conscious mind, the rest is unconscious, our intuition is a feeling or information that comes from unconscious and superconscious.

That which defines us is not what you might think; generally speaking, most people think these things define them and who they are, what other people think of you, your weight, likes and shares, past mistakes, your job, your age, grades and results, your struggles. The things that do define you and who you are, asking yourself what you want from life and what do you want your life to be, as opposed to what other people want for you and what they want your life to be, in other words creating your own big picture and moving toward strategy's. thoughts in line with actions for example create a self-hypnosis script that subjectively supports you outcome when you have subjective influencing the unconscious and actions to follow then the magic starts to click in. Most people haven't got what they want because they were taught to chase what they want instead of drawing it in, what most people tend to do is chase what they want rather than apply ways to draw in what they want, which is actually a learned behaviour and it's learned by following value judgements which have come from outside opinion. Very few people in comparison focus on self-opinion and are bound to compliance in- order to fit in, rather than self-assess their own beliefs and values. lots of people's values and beliefs are made reference's/representations of outside opinion; lost performative statements, there to fat, there to thin, to young, to old, to thick, too smart for their own good, and the unsuspecting person accepts these judgements of them, which effectively tells them they must change in some way to fit in and maybe face ridicule when they don't comply with the person or demand.

The more we take control consciously of what we are allowing and declining in terms of opinion and beliefs, the more self-power we have over our decision making and what our reality evolves and shapes into, we have innate personal power! But for most people that has been lost to complying with conditioned and habituated ways of doing things, without challenging it from within. Apart from our inherent genes that are absolute, hair colour, eye colour, skin colour which are rooted in climate region originally, bone structure which stay as absolutes in our incarnation everything else is a variable, which is or is not changed predominantly by how well we understand mind and whether we accept and apply the way mind processes language, I have read many times mind being related to the way a computer works; the screen is the projection of conscious physical reality, unconscious mind is the local hard drive, and the internet connection mirrors our connection to unconscious and superconscious; the blocks of computer language are what makes the programmes work in a certain way, and the programmes can be changed by changing the instruction in the block code, equivalent to our linguistics thought, written, or spoken.

A computer has evolved into a direct reflection of the way mind works, three separate component parts that function as separate units hard wired together and used by language. Ericson's model and the Meta model give us a sold foundations to the framework of the most effective way to apply language that causes manifestations and change in habits and behaviour, the same as the principle of casting a spell to get more money or better health, but with the knowledge that the statements are being sent directly to unconscious/subconscious mind; when we talk or self-talk it shows just how powerful the receptive unconscious and sub-conscious minds are; we are consciously receptive to the results of this through the experiences this produces; when these linguistic principles are applied a person's life can be completely transformed to something they may have been conditioned to believe would be impossible, achieve levels of health, wealth relationship happiness and other personal achievements they were conditioned to believe as impossible.

There is a conditioned way of thinking engrained into most of Humanity, whereby people judge many things to be impossible, to achieve or have because they cannot see how it could be possible, many who are I'll sadly cannot see how it could be possible for the body to heal itself, so this gives clear instruction to the unconscious mind, their focus on the illness they may have is so chronic that if there isn't a treatment trough medicine they would die, there isn't an illness that the unconscious mind can't heal because it will never forget the blueprint to perfect health, it has just been instructed by the persons beliefs not to automatically reverse a terminal illness, and the persons feelings and emotions on the subject just echo that on every level of their being, and unconscious mind accepts the instruction, when conscious mind instructs the unconscious mind to heal itself from any illness then it will follow the instruction and the person will heal, when the how will this happen is replaced with it will happen or has happened the doubt is taken out of the equation and then it becomes possible.

There are over eight billion humans beings on this planet here and now, here is the problem not the amount of people but if we take a statistic that probably rings true about the same in most countries, only 3% of Americans are financially independent, so to be independent generally means that they are self-organising/directing, which really equates to the other 97% as in some way being organised by outside opinion and stimuli; which means that, that 97% of the populations unconscious minds are being programmed from the outside and not from within, which keeps them on a level of thinking that unchecked will keep them bound to a metaphorical treadmill; many people stay on the same thought level for their entire adult life, they stay compliant to pre-programmed ways of thinking and doing things never looking outside the box or trying to move up the thought level process. A robot is programmed by a controller, an independent individual is directed by themselves because they consciously learned to be selective about what they believe most people can and are being herded by propaganda and organisations that are busy organising them. They have not got yet the awareness that their unconscious filters are being programmed for them.

When the internal representations of what is and isn't possible are changed then the reality associated with it changes; Belief of what's possible and impossible doesn't just affect finances but relationships and health. Over the years of researching and learning mind over matter, Neuro Linguistic Programming and hypnosis, I have come across many story's relating to unconscious mind; one such story is a man who had a pretty serious phobia which was causing him a great deal of anxiety and subsequent stress and inconvenience, he had seen several hypnotherapists to remove the phobia using clinical hypnosis technique's, none had any degree of success; desperate to remove the phobia he tried another hypnotherapist who used a different approach, instead of putting him in a hypnotic state and running a script, he put him in a hypnotic state and spoke directly to his unconscious mind, he created a channel between himself and the persons unconscious mind and the person spoke through the reply of his unconscious.

The person with the phobia had stated that they were mystified by the phobia and could not recall any reason or event which could have triggered it; the hypnotherapist asked the man in hypnosis what had happened to cause the phobia the unconscious mind replied with what the event was, and that unconscious mind had created this state known as a phobia to keep him away from the potential threat that unconscious mind saw as a danger to him and to prevent that type of event from happening again, the hypnotherapist then negotiated with unconscious mind that this phobia was causing serious distress which was also a threat to him, and that which had triggered the phobia in the first place was no longer a threat. There was no further reply, after the session was over the phobia had gone, the man kept the hypnotist informed of his progress and there was

PRIME DIRECTIVES OF UNCONSCIOUS MIND

no further characteristics or signs of the phobia again Unconscious mind can repress memories to protect the person and in some cases what we know as phobias are the unconsciousness response to protect the person, these also sometimes manifest as panic-attacks which are also the unconscious response perceived as protecting the person.

Unconscious mind follows instruction, the instruction from self-talk or believed outside opinion the things that form beliefs associated to a concept/value which can be changed internally by self or externally by outside stimuli, because at birth a child has not got a developed conscious mind, it is completely dependent for everything, so from birth to six everything in that child's conscious is a perspective of what life is and the memories are held in the unconscious, one of the child's way of perceiving what life is, comes from being taught directly and through assumptions, a "child" see's it's parents constantly arguing over money then the child's unconscious mind assumes money is a problem and is hard to get, the same with drinking or smoking, the child sees its parent drinking and smoking and unconscious mind assumes that drinking and smoking in some way benefits them, unconscious mind stores memories of habit formed behaviour.

So for example a toddler crawls to start with, then learns to walk by habitually trying to, the unconscious then remembers the memory of being able to walk and then walks without effort, so negative or destructive behaviour comes about in the same way. A good deal of negative or destructive behaviour is mimicked or learned in the years that most adults have not got many immediate memories of, around birth to six, so behaviour taken into adult life is to a larger degree leaned at this time, the problem often arises because the unconscious remembers and because there is no clear instruction to do things differently. Children often take this behaviour right through their adult lives. As an example, if a child always got their own way when they throw a tantrum then quite often this will manifest in adults expecting to get their own way by throwing a tantrum, which may escalate in adult life as threats if they don't' get their own way. Because unconscious mind remembers always getting their own way when they trough a tantrum it thinks this tactic should still work because it has not been un-taught or had that way of doing things erased and replaced with a new one; this is for the best part why unconscious mind maintains negative, disruptive, and destructive behaviour.

Unconscious mind learns trough repetition so when a child watches the same thing being done or repeats doing something unconscious mind adopts that and it becomes part of their behaviour pattern, so part of a person's personality are these types of representations unconscious mind then stores as strategy's beliefs and values most of their personality is mimicked from other people's behaviour i.e. People who are their roll-models or peers, so how many people actually know who they are? For most who they think they are a collection of adopted behaviour positive and negative from a range of other people including television, media, and other outside stimuli. When unconscious mind stores negative emotions it stores them in the body to be resolved at a later time, this can maintain negative effects in the body primarily disease; when we look at areas where terminal disease tend to occur we see that most if not all occur on or around Chakra points, which points to the probability that negative repressed emotions are stored on or certainly in the region of one of the seven energy Chakra points and around the nerves system; these points distribute and convert energy the link is unconscious mind directs energy.

All this points to a healthy or diseased body being that way mostly by thought patterns and beliefs; reality is a function of belief. The brain is an alchemical laboratory; if a person feels good it is because the brain released a chemical to feel good in relation to what their emotions are. Any illness or damage can be reversed with the correct command to unconscious mind, if a person's belief is contrary to this then the body cannot heal or repair itself independently, because the correct command has not been sent. So if anyone has tried to change or break a habit and found it very hard or impossible, then the reason maybe that unconscious mind has a memory that the habit in some way benefits them, the trick then is to change/switch preferences of what the habit is that doesn't benefit them to one that actually does, this can be done with hypnosis, NLP anchoring or swish patterns which switch one preference to another. We do so much unconsciously almost without thinking that understanding the function of our unconscious mind is very important and having techniques to send the right commands to unconscious in a way that unconscious mind will accept is also very important.

In referencing unconscious mind and sub-conscious mind are the same with the same prime directive, NLP, and Hypnosis in general refer to it as unconscious, you may come across other books, esoteric or example that refer to it as sub-conscious mind. Image metaphor, symbology, and day to day linguistics are the way we communicate with our unconscious with every second and every breath it is with us our own individual unconscious. It is an integrated part of the physical self, so like the physical self, it takes everything personally and is the root of perception is projection, so without a good understanding of what the unconscious mind is and what it's purpose is, and without understanding the Universal principles it becomes very difficult to advance or change in a way that gets positive outcomes or their perceptions will keep them in a metaphorical loop until they find the way out of it, people stay like pieces on a chess board or break out of the loop and then are not even on the chess board, they become masters of their own personal destiny, not stuck in a game they can't perceive themselves getting out off. There become an inherent need to create interventions to their unconscious such as self-hypnosis or Afformations and connect to themselves through learning to communicate with their own unconscious mind. The difference in processing speed can be compared to the difference between a quantum computer and a home pc. Basically no comparison, quantum computers and unconscious mind run at speed you just can't fathom.

CHAPTER FIVE

THE MOOD TABLE

The mood table reflects the vibrational physical plane we exist on by our mind-set/attitudinal thinking which creates our emotions. The two top moods categories, headed as, Enthusiasm and Interest, are ones to aspire to achieve these create the most feel-good emotions which manifest the most things to feel good about, they epitomise self-esteem, self-direction, self-belief. Being more in control of their own life because they take more notice of self-opinion than outside opinion, although not all outside opinion is ignored the best part comes from the self, they are aware of their intuitive self and have found their self, they know the difference between study of something because it actually interest them, or studying to gain respect from peers which leaves them with a metaphorical Achilles heel. Like being called to heel by his master without realising they are their own master. Existing in planes/moods below these too top ones brings the captain hook type characteristics into the Frey always lurking in the shadows trying to get a hook in and not seeing the magic of life like Peter Pan and Tinkerbelle. Outside the two top moods exists a conformist attitude right the way through and the effects of conforming or not, the degrees or percentage by which the outside opinions run their life in an automated way, the reason is we are free thinking beings with restricted thinking by outside opinion. Self-direction gives ultimate self-esteem because you are then creating who you are; the thing that keeps most people bound is conforming to the perceived idea that an annual waged day job is the only way money can come in, and the

THE MOOD TABLE

only way you can buy a house is to get a mortgage is an extremely delimiting view. For the best part most people are in some way conforming to what their being told they can or can't have be or do, the difference is telling yourself what you can have, be or do rather than conforming to outside opinion of whether it's possible or not. Free thought is what has been restricted here by the varying mind-sets attributed to mood levels under the top two; the more a person frees their thoughts the more the person discovers themselves.

The journey of self-discovery starts by aspiring to the top two mood planes on the table which are above that of getting others to conform or conforming yourself, the focus has to be on living your own life, not other people's otherwise it creates these complex masses of negative elemental-based reactions and responses. If everyone where to stop chasing and setting just physical tasks to achieve the how's, without any awareness of subjective influence, and just focused on already having what you want what do you think would happen? So how many unnecessary tasks do people set themselves because that's what their told to do? Everything comes from thought and matter corresponds to thought (mind over matter) Words and pictures are what direct thought and matter. The mood table is set like a GPS to some extent, also we can slip up and down the mood table throughout the day, but our attitude and mind-set at the time define in general being in one of these levels for the most part, we can stay stuck in each respective mood or shift to another.

Obviously being generally set on one mood level influences personal behaviour and the way we respond or react to events. 1: Enthusiasm: Cheerfulness, a light-hearted soul with a free mind, flexible, a winner, creates own success. 2: Interest: Amusement, actively, interested in subjects related to survival and advancement, doing well. 3: Conservationism: Contentment, the conformist, doesn't rock the boat, resists changes, not too many problems and stops progress. 4: Boredom: The spectator, all the worlds a stage and they are the audience, either committed or discontented, endures things, purposeless, careless not interested. 5: Antagonism: The debater loves to argue, blunt, honest, tactless, poor sport. 6: Anger: Chronic Pain: distemper, blames, holds grudges, threatens, demands obedience. Touchy, irritable, scattered, sticking at source of pain

7: No Sympathy: Cold fish, unfeeling, suppresses violent anger, cruel, calm, resourceful. acidly polite. 8: Covert Hostility: The cheerful hypocrite, gossip, an actor, often likes puns and practical jokes, seeks to introvert others, Nervous laughter, or constant smile. 9: Fear: Coward. Anxious, suppositious, Worried, Running, Defending, or caught in indecision 10: Sympathy: Obsessive agreement, afraid of hurting others, Collects the downers, sometimes wobbles between complacent tenderness and tears. Always saying their sorry.11: Propitiation: Appeasement, do-gooder, doing favours to protect themselves from bad effects, Intention is to stop growth or progress; Tenderness and tears. 12: Grief: The whiner, collects grievances and mementos, dwells in the past, feels betrayed, everything painful. 12: Making Amends: The yes man who will do anything to get sympathy or help blind loyalty, a mop the floor with me tone; 13: Apathy: Given up, turned off and dissociated, Suicidal, addict, alcoholic, gambler, fatalist, may pretend they have found peace.

The mood table reflects our overall attitude toward ourselves and other people, it defines whether we are co-dependent or co-creating, whether we take responsibility for our own actions or look to blame everyone else, Interest and enthusiasm are the two we should be aspiring to, although not easy you have to look at these and be honest with yourself, this is part of the whole knowing yourself, if you can't be honest with yourself then you're going to struggle to find balance. There are two levels to this, we have a general fixed mood which defines the way we behave overall toward our self and others, and the daily changes in mood according to events and environment, a bit like the values table one to eight, to get to the top ones we have to pull ourselves up through the other ones level by level, so we aim for the top ones, and work out what we need to do to get there.

For example if you're stuck in a day job you hate (we've all been there) then look at what you could do with enthusiasm and interest, that will pull you up the table, like letting go of past grievances, by focusing on "success" instead of revenge, we can all moan about not having enough money or all your relationships are rubbish, whatever it is drop it, it does not benefit you or anyone else, and start to look at what you can do that will benefit you, and others, without causing harm that could also lead into generating an income doing something you love, and have an interest and enthusiasm in. If what you want to do means quitting the day job and studying for a diploma or degree, or doing an apprenticeship of some sort, but when you have finished that you would be able to do something you would love to do then do it, and look on it as moving toward actions, or it might be you have already mastered something and want to turn professional, you can look for an excuse or a way to do it, (without causing harm) if you are almost in a position to do something you love then keep pushing for that until you achieve it, listen to yourself not others, because everything you do reflects on you, so decide to be more self-reliant, self-directing and self-motivating. There is no better feeling than putting something together yourself and knowing you got there from your own efforts, yes it takes courage, yes it takes patience, yes it takes dedication, but think how much do you want what you say you want, it's probably not going to come from a lottery win, it's not going to come by expecting others to do it for you, it's going to come from your own efforts, but the outcome will be better than a lottery win because it's not going to be a one off, but a continuous income from your own efforts.

CHAPTER SIX

UNDERSTANDING META-PROGRAMMES

This next part leads into what is known in NLP as Basic meta-programmes/perceptual filters, it's the basis of psychological profiling, of your-self and others, it essentially defines behaviour traits, from internal representations and the beliefs and values you were brought up with. When you sit down quietly on your own working on your big picture, (what you want your life and life style to be) you can go through these traits, first look at the ones that define you the most, again as with the mood table, there are traits that are constant and some change through the day, but the main ones stay constant, for example if your introvert then that will be constant although you may find extrovert traits there as generally no one is 100% introvert or extrovert we tend to have a 50%-50% or 80%-20% and so on; when you have defined where you are in the here and now look at your big picture and ask yourself, are there any traits you can change that will bring you more into alignment with your big picture. The way to change these are further on in the book but for now just focus on the traits you have now and the ones you would like to change to, maybe you always seek outside validation, and would like to be more self-validating, or always find yourself in group participation but would like to also do things on you own. write down the ones you want to change, how it is relevant to your big picture, in other words the purpose of the change, this is part of the whole know yourself process. Some of the personality traits may be adopted from mimicking of modelling from other people; they serve you well or hold you back only you can decide that really, the best way to use this chapter is to be very honest with yourself and pick the traits that best fit you, you can also ask family and friends which ones best define you at present, although you don't have to, you can do it on your own it's your choice. Then think of the things you would like to do, and the type of person/personality you would like to be and write those out as well, I will show you in this book how to move toward changing the personality traits to something that will serve you in the things you want to accomplish and achieve, also there is in NLP something called in-time and through time, which means, In-time is having the past and future laid out before you. Through-time is having the past behind and the future out in front, I cover this more in the book. Basic meta programmes although they may feel very set in stone and absolute, they are variables which means they can be changed and are not set in stone, often we switch personality traits during the day to fit with different people environments and events, like personality masks, however they are not set in stone, but in general we have a fixed traits, that can stay the same of be changed again, it's up to you which ones you want to keep and which ones you want to change; called re-framing.

Understanding the self and Personality traits

Before we look at the personality traits as I have been studying researching and practicing this subject, it has become obvious that there are two biases which directly affect personality and behaviour, environment is one thing that influences this, also reptile and hive mind-set which is in everyone, the balance between these two mind-sets directly influences personality; reptile mind for example more self relates to reptile, more group relates to hive, the more linier thinking the more hive the more self-sufficient thinking the more reptile, so as you go through the traits you will find they relate to reptile mind-set and hive mind-set, and the balance between more self or more group. The way we express ourselves externally and how others may see us, we are generally not one hundred percent one or the other as in one hundred percent introvert, or sensor, however we may have a very high bias toward one and a much smaller bias

THE MIND KEYS

toward the other or be in the middle, like an ambivert is an even bias between the too. The Myers Briggs personality traits are four sets of personality traits; Introvert---Extrovert; this corresponds to confidence, internal/external biased. Sensor---Intuiter; this corresponds to the way we process information. Thinker---Feeler; this corresponds to emotions, kinaesthetic. Judger---Perceiver; this corresponds to "in-time through time," (see timeline chapter on how to change timeline and what timeline is.) Introvert: Internally focussed, good listener, Sit in background, alone, Few Close Relationships, Internal validation, non-Huggers, one thing at a time, think then speak. Extrovert: More than one thing at a time, lots of friends, Party Organisers, speak then think later, Huggers, outside validation, Group Participation. Sensor: Facts figures data, Tangible results, read magazines cover to cover, task at hand, don't tend to fantasize, in the now, finer detail. Intuiter: Relationship of ideas, how things relate/work, Abstract, likes puzzles, Ideas/theory, chunked up, future orientated, how does it all fit together? Thinker: Dissociated, enjoy clarification, easy decisions, fair and truthful, Ad, Logic, Objective, firm minded, tell people when they disagree. Feeler: Go with the flow, Kinaesthetic, Feelings Gentle Hearted, extend themselves for others, Judger: Order/sequence, fixed pattern, don't like surprises to schedule, Organised, on time, need closure, Make the world fit them, like to make lists. Perceiver: Love to explore unknown territories, high options keep options open, play it by ear, Punctuality less important, easily distracted, change to fit the context creative and spontaneous, Plans are not important. So now you have looked this do you feel you are starting to get to know yourself? You are starting to empower yourself and become the new you, and what you have just done is a moving toward big picture action, so now you're on your way, your train has left the station. In short, our meta- programmes portray/project our internal representations i.e. the way we see ourselves and others.

The self and the world outside and are our pre-programmed strategies that organise who we are as a person and the way we do things, essentially what this means in real terms is that there are parts about you that are absolute, height (bone structure), eye, skin, and hair colour, pretty much everything else is known as a variable and can be changed if you choose

UNDERSTANDING META-PROGRAMMES

to. A good question to ask yourself in terms of achieving your desires is what values and beliefs would I ned to have for that to be true? In other words, to have the things you would like to have in life and do the things you would like to do, what would you have to believe for that to become actualised? How you see yourself and how would other people see you. For example you want to be more extrovert than what would you have to believe to be more extrovert, maybe you would say more confident, so being more confident comes from having a higher self-esteem, so the area you would need to work on is self-esteem, as you go through the book you will naturally have a higher self-esteem through understanding yourself better, that doesn't automatically equate introverted people as having a low self-esteem this is just a basic example. So where do self-beliefs that are our meta-programmes come from?

Well, they come from your Mother, Father, and other family members, teachers, anyone who has in some way influenced your values, beliefs, and most importantly the way you see yourself. You are not necessarily a hereditary product of your Mother and Father, who you are what you do and why you do it stem from these meta-programmes. How confident or insecure you may or may not be, whether you do things with certainty of have a lot of self-doubt are defined by these programmes, essentially where you're at now if you have never looked at these are the consequence of what we call outside stimuli, in essence you are what you have been told you are, your behaviour reflects who you have been told you are. An example can be if as a child you were constantly told you where clumsy or stupid then that would reflect in your behaviour, if you were told you are clever and competent then that will have reflected in your behaviour, essentially you are what you were told you are, which may have been very negative, very positive or somewhere in between, you have a belief system of what you may believe in terms of religion or no religion, and wealthy background poor background which tiles down into how intelligent you think you are or not.

What foods you may or may not like are all influenced by these programmes, a lot of your meta-programmes will come from a period you don't remember much about i.e. your childhood. What you believe you can and can't do, what you believe is possible or impossible, were you constantly criticised or constantly encouraged, these things all became the building blocks of who you are and where you are now. Where you brought up in a fearful environment or happy environment, were there a lot of drink or drugs or both, or sober and no drugs, This defines what your meta-programmes are, which also define the habits you may or may not have; what part of the world you were brought up in environment plays a big part, who your inner and outer circle was in terms of family and friends, and media, anything that essentially stuck in your mind is a meta-programme. Obviously understanding your own behaviour is a vital part of being able to change; all behaviour is a consequence of representations we have of the world around us, and ourselves, as perception is projection.

Complex Meta-Programmes

Essentially advanced meta-programmes are directional, our basic beliefs and values formed through suggestion, experience, imagination, and the five scenes: self-perspective, self-identity, sense of importance; why people do the things they do and make the decisions they make comes down to the basic meta-programmes each individual is running. They cover a person's overall destiny from moment to moment, lifestyle, thought levels, moods, occupation," perceived" level of intelligence, health, financial independence, and relationships. Complex meta-programmes are the way we function on a day-to-day basis, our personality traits, in-time, or through-time, they define our strategy's for doing things, our self-perspective the way our values and beliefs are set up, all entangled and working together simultaneously. These meta-programmes can stay unchanged or are changed/re-programmed or relearned they are in a general sense formed through repetition. What make up a large part of our pre-suppositions from suggestions come from what our meta-programmes are running as, change the pre-supposition and change the reality associated with it, in literal terms, you can create new suggestions and create new pre-suppositions to override old ones. Inner and outer orientation, why you should look at each orientation and which ones are best for particular circumstances; or achieving outcomes, Inner-orientated; "I the self, outer orientated; we/outside self. Where do we fit in, we'll go with there is always and exception to the rule, but in general no one is a hundred percent inner or outer we just have a higher bias toward one or the other. Self or group directing, Self or group, confidence, Self, or group, actualised. Self-discipleship: to become a student or follower of one's own inner feelings and directions regardless of comments of friends, family, and other cultural systems.

This effectively puts you in a position where you can pick and choose levels of self and outside so you have a balance of self and outside that works for your lifestyle and gives you plenty of flexibility to do the things you want to; rather than the things you were told you're supposed to, you can switch your life to choose to, not supposed to! In fact most of your reality/actuality so far has been your choice, you just weren't aware you were making choices that cause an outcome that's been working away on auto pilot in line with what your beliefs, values and strategies were; overall perspective where up to this point the spoken perspective is the perception that projects back. In other words we talk in our reality, at least for the best part. When self-perspective starts to be added to what for most people has been an predominantly outside orientated especially where information coming in was concerned, for example television, adverts contain Visual, Audio, and Kinaesthetic anchors in them, designed to "influence" an unsuspecting mind, judging by the billions spent on marketing each year I'd say it works very well, think of all the potential ways there are that are getting information into your subconscious to be held as beliefs, how much of what you believe is from outside information bombardment. When you get this, you can start to shut out negative or manipulative outside "influence" because you'll see them for what they are, rather than seeing them as a consumer. People are very easy to influence in general because if it's something they want to be true they become less discerning, i.e. this aftershave will make you more attractive, that type of advertising that's just superficial and very misdirecting. Following the guidance of these principles can make getting to the path and direction in life it is that we desire and intend most, and integrating these sub-laws in with the way we do thinks starts to create more positive change through self-direction. And developing independent ways of thinking and doing.

The 21 Universal Sub-Laws/ Positive human characteristics

Aspire to Positive human characteristics and generate a more positive lifestyle, the Buddhists state that the way we relate to universe is the way it relates back to us, your reality reflects the way you relate to it. Which pretty much defines the law of correspondence in action, which in essence states we manifest our reality by a large part in the conversations that states the way a person is viewing themselves and their reality, which then forces what's being stated to re-manifest, as in, "history repeats itself", and it does so in relation to our levels of thought and our values and beliefs, we are essentially casting spells every day, and we do it through our conversation and the spells are all manifesting!

Part of what his book is about and the way to transform our lives is to change the root attitude, essentially "attitudinal healing", part of changing attitude is to look at the sub-laws and define which ones we are practicing, and the ones were not, and to aspire to and to move toward following these sub-laws which in turn help us become more positive in attitude, and then our attitude becomes our protection from what the negative opposite implications and outcomes are, say having a hateful attitude as opposed to a loving one, or a jealous attitude as opposed to creating our own life and not looking at what everyone else has and is doing; our reality is in effect is being manifested by virtue of our overall attitude. Essentially law of attraction is saying if you are constantly jealous or hateful of others then that is what you are giving out and that is what you will attract back, and you have no protection from that because it follows the law of personal return, so, what you cause for others is what you cause for yourself, essentially cause and effect, that is the way it works like it or not. Those that cause hurt, will get hurt there is no escaping this law it is rooted in the three absolutes. Personal return is often not always instant sometimes it may take some time, but it will return with absolute certainty. This is reiterated in a Chinese proverb.

"If you poison the well of another person then your well will get poisoned also," you cannot send something out to another good or bad without it returning the same in nature. There is a correspondence when you look at people who appear to be on seven to eight though/values levels, having greater association to the positive twenty-one human characteristics, and also brainwave frequency association of more alpha to low beta, as opposed to other thought/values levels being higher beta, which is also a contributing factor where health is concerned. It may not be easy to be this virtuous and we are human beings with emotions not unfeeling robots, however we can at least aspire to these so called sub-laws and start to create positive personal change in all areas of life, again you probably won't notice any changes instantly although you might do, but stick with it or stay the course as they say, and you will notice after time a gradual change and shift to more positive outcomes, the negative opposites to these sub-laws are obvious, and will only return a negative, you cannot give negative and expect positive returns, you cannot give out positive and expect negative returns, this is the nature of the Universe we have our existence in, what you direct at another person you direct to yourself. Also talking of expectations, as far as you can go into each day without expectation of any particular outcome just try to allow the desired outcomes to unfold without chasing them, go easy on yourself anything that is worth having taken practice and patience.

The twenty-one Universal sub-laws are. 1: Aspiration to a higher intelligence: Unconscious superconscious mind is the higher self, so the more you work on understanding just what unconscious and superconscious are, and the way we consciously connect with them, is aspiring to higher intelligence, also to learn however to learn subjects you are drawn to as opposed to learning subjects you're not drawn to look good for so called peers. 2: Charity: An action of giving without expecting to get anything back. 3: Compassion: Empathy between the self and others understanding, the self and why Humans behave the way they do, in other words what causes certain behaviour, any why people make the decisions they make. 4: Courage: To be yourself and want to be yourself, courage to not be selfish but to not take on the burdens of others. 5: Dedication: To apply yourself to goals or ambitions and essentially your personal big picture, a process of create and move towards actions.

6: Faith: In the self-first, always the self-first, that everything in universe is connected by a divine oneness. 7: Forgiveness: To not take an action of physical revenge but to allow universal balance to do just that, balance through personal return. 8: Generosity: To give freely where chosen time and energy, but not give less to you and all to others, more an attitude of fairly give fairly take. 9: Grace: To have the good grace not to rain on someone else's parade, not to be a stick in the mud or wet blanket when someone else has good fortune. 10: Honesty: Self responsibility to keep in a position where telling a lie is not necessary. 11: Hope: To not allow oneself to fall into a mind state of despair or despondency always be hopeful of a positive outcome. 12: Joy: The joy of moving toward actions not just gaining the outcome of living the big picture you're moving towards. 13: Kindness: We are all of one kind "Human beings" so the way we treat each other returns in kind or unkind.

As above so below, like attracts like, including kind action. 14: Leadership: From practicing self-responsibility, developing a good attitude for others to want to follow in the first place, leading by example. 15: Non-interference: mind your own affairs, you are no required to take on the burdens of everyone else, but to focus on being the best you can be yourself. 16: Patience: More haste less speed, keep your energy's focused we can multitask to some degree, but when we try to multitask to many things at once then we scatter our energies and cause ourselves unnecessary stress, working at a pace that fits you, gets more done, when you set yourself reasonable timelines to achieve the desired outcome, you are more likely to succeed and find it easier, the joy in the doing as well as the efforts/actions when you get there. 17: Praise: To express appreciation of another's ability's.18: Responsibility: Ability to respond. 19: Self-Love: Find the things you love about yourself that include the things you love doing. 20: Thankfulness: Expressing gratitude, appreciation, to yourself and other, for food shelter.21: Unconditional Love: Love is the highest feeling and expression. The more we aspire to adopt these characteristics in our lives, the better people we become, the more positive our lives will become, the more self-protecting our attitude will be, obviously when we aspire to be more loving as a person instead of hateful, this will make a difference in what returns to us in our reality/actual waking state; depending on our upbringing or environment we live in how hard or easy this is, is different for different people but when we aspire to be more patient, hopeful, etc. then our personal returns will change this is a key point to remember when we are looking at ways we can change our reality for the better. I have discovered personally that when we focus with hope on a positive outcome, it is far more positive in what returns than with expectation that something may go wrong, "negative what ifs,) when we focus on being hopeful of becoming healthier it becomes the prelude or prerequisite of being healthier, it makes a difference, it's not just about closing our eyes for several minutes every day and visualising our dream life or though that is part of it, we have to put conscious effort into changing the way we think and do things as well, or nothing really changes. As you work through this book you will find the keys to real transformation, these characteristics are one of those keys, and as you become more adept at using these keys your beliefs will change, your reality/actuality will change with absolute certainty. It does take patience and practice, but when you look at the list of things you really want you have to ask yourself how much do I want this, enough to change the way you think and do things? Or you could say well practicing this is hard and takes quite a lot of effort, but like learning to ride a bike, it gets easier with practice and the outcomes are worth the practice.

It does take effort and actions but would staying the same make your life easier or harder; self-mastery is the outcome of all this, and any type of mastery, takes practice and effort. As you change, your relationships will change, people you used to be drawn to you may no longer be drawn to, you will lose some friends and gain new ones through this process of changing your thoughts and actions. What you have to remember about change is it is different, sometimes dam right unsettling, this is all part of moving toward your big picture; through which are all the things you actually want as part of the new you, the new lifestyle you desire so much. So, take another good look at these characteristics and write down the sort of things you can do that will put you more in line with them, and stick to it! you can re-evaluate it as you go along but at least make the effort to make the difference, you don't have to give loads of money to charity, just little charitable acts, like helping an old person across the road. Understanding meta-programmes enables you to drop old limiting beliefs and switch them to new self-empowering ones.

CHAPTER SEVEN

BRAINWAVE FREQUENCIES AND HOW WE ACCESS THEM

Brain wave patterns are lines drawn on a graph paper made by brainwave activity that is amplified by an EEG instrument; these lines vary in length and depth, and behave similarly for long enough intervals that they form a phase or groupings of mental brain activity; these lines are made by the amplification, through the electroencephalograph, the ergs of energy that constantly emanate from ones brain; electros are placed on various areas of the head, and then attached to a wire and jack, so the person can be hooked up to the EEG instrument; these outside lines are found to be affected by outside stimuli, reaction of the five senses, and change in emotions and thoughts; it has been found that a Man or a Woman makes four definite universal patterns, and recently it has been discovered that there is a fifth pattern that appears to be interacting with or entangled with the other four. The brain produces four main types of brainwave which are shown by EEG readings. Each type of brainwave produces the listed effects at specific frequencies: Name: Gamma Brain Waves, supporting role for other brain patterns: Frequency: (30—100 HZ cycles per second) Characteristics: association and corresponds to superconscious, unifies thought processes and brings

BRAINWAVE FREQUENCIES AND HOW WE ACCESS THEM

perception together into coherent picture. 'In the zone' peak performance Induction /Entertainment: Binary beats, meditation and yoga, benefits feelings of one-ness, compassion, and happiness. May improve information processing; Caution: Not much is yet known about the Gamma state. Take care when "experimenting." Maximizing the results of meditation practice Improving memory, recall, and focus, stimulating whole-brain thinking, Enhancing intuition, increasing intelligence and mental abilities, overcoming mental distress, several studies find disturbing effects when a person lacks or has abnormal gamma states, including Panic attacks, Insomnia, Anxiety, Depression, Epilepsy, Alzheimer's disease. The lack of gamma brain frequencies found in people who suffer from these conditions, suggests that activating these brainwave patterns might assist in healing or controlling the symptoms of these disorders. This lack of Gamma states may well be because of being in a near constant high Beta state from awake to sleep every day. Name: Beta brain waves Frequency: (13-30 HZ cycles per second) Characteristics: associates and corresponds to physical conscious, the fastest physical frequency, representing the most intense state of alertness; the result of heightened mental activity; Maximum mind power; all five external senses, logical mind, memory from the five senses & logical thinking.

Name: Beta Brain Waves. Benefits: Focused, analytical, rational, wide awake, alert awareness; concentrated, focused mind, heightened sensory perception, emotional stability, visual acuity, cognitive control of motor activity Beta is a 'fast' higher frequency bandwidth typically associated with outward awareness, full alertness, and rapid thought generation. Clinical studies of beta link it to full awareness of self and surroundings, energy, alertness, activity, increased mental ability and focus, peak states of concentration, motivation and possibly, visual acuity. It's also been associated with IQ increase, perhaps in an equivalent manner to 'smart drugs' or nootropics, by stimulating overall brain activity. Beta activity often produces the overactive "chatterbox/ monkey-mind" that prevents us from sleeping.

Those with 'slow wave' conditions like ADD, ADHD and depression typically exhibit low waking beta wave activity and may be prescribed stimulants to increase daytime beta activity and/or block slower frequencies. The beta range falls into three classifications: Beta 1 (~12.5 Hz – 15 Hz): Slow or Low Beta wave activity. Beta 2 (~ 15 Hz – 23 Hz): This mid-range beta is frequently used by clinicians. Some consider 18.5 Hz in particular to be an optimal frequency for focus and concentration. Beta 3 (~ 23 Hz – 40 Hz): This fast beta activity, especially in its higher range has been associated with hyper-arousal/hyper-vigilance, anxiety, stress, paranoia, excessive energy, and 'burnout'.

In clinical applications, Beta 1 and 2 brainwave stimulation has been used to promote wakefulness and alertness, focus, mood elevation, general cognitive performance and for assistance with depression and ADHD. The highest portion of the population operate almost entirely on beta, and not any other ranges outside of going to sleep and awaking, the beta frequency deals with information and problem solving and works quickly to get the job done. The over activity of the beta frequency is a sign of the times and is prevalent because of the constant stresses of a rushed life. Although beta is very useful when it comes to getting stuff done on a practical level, it is also the brainwave frequency most associated with three very common ailments in our world: stress, anxiety, and exhaustion.

We seem to live in a feedback loop of overactive stress which is a repetitious re-run of high beta states. The only time we tend to dip into the more relaxed frequencies of the mind seems to be when we sleep and even that is a struggle for a lot of people, with over a quarter of people reportedly not getting enough sleep in the US, and 10% suffering from full blown insomnia. In other words, millions of people are unable to slow their minds down to get some rest. Our ancestors it would be expected, spent a great deal more time on alpha frequencies (as is common when you spend a lot of time in nature) and in theta frequencies, as is common in shamanic trance, meditation, vision quests, and other spiritual ventures. With so many people unable to 'switch off' their busy brains, understanding your brainwaves is more important than ever. Name: Alpha Brain Waves Frequency: (8 to 12H HZ cycles per second: Characteristics: associates and corresponds to physical conscious this brain wave indicates a relaxed state of mind, State of relaxed alertness, good for inspiration and learning facts fast, a meditative mind, In this state tap into

BRAINWAVE FREQUENCIES AND HOW WE ACCESS THEM

internal "antenna" like qualities, visions, powerful ideas, mindless creation of the incredible, Internal feeling and sensations.

Relaxed but waking state, most prevalent upon waking or just before sleep. Calm and at ease, mental functioning in a zen-like state. Information absorbed with less barriers, which lends itself to affirmations and visualizations. More prevalent in practitioners of meditation/self-hypnosis, who can remain calm during chaos; Brainwave entrainment of alpha helps you to achieve a more relaxed and enjoyable state of mind, switch off after a hard day, or get more critical problem solving and information processing, Lower levels are more relaxed focus, while higher levels can mean stress, anxiety, and mental overdrive, help to improve brain functioning in logical areas such as maths, reading, and writing. Improve concentration and mental focus, especially useful for those with attention issues or ADHD. Most people run on high beta too often, so brainwave entrainment on this level is not recommended unless you feel you cannot motivate yourself Induction; /Entrainment: Fully awake. Binary beats Benefits: Information processing; relaxed, tranquil consciousness and inward awareness; creative flow states; the coalescence of different frequencies; improved HRV, serotonin production, memory, and dream recall; reactivity to disturbing noises in sleep.

Alpha activity begins at around the age of six years old. In adults it produces a characteristic calm, creative 'flow-state' when we close our eyes and begin to withdraw from external sensory stimulation such as when 'daydreaming'. It's often referred to as the bridge between waking and sleeping. Alpha activity may be more pronounced in creative, artistic, and entrepreneurial people. It has been linked with the inspired experience of creative insight and 'out of the box' thinking. EEG monitoring of Alfred Einstein showed he produced consistent alpha-band activity while solving complex mathematical tasks. Studies suggest that while upper or mid-range alpha may assist with these kinds of activities, its lower range may be counterproductive for highly attentive, focused critical thinking or technical, detail orientated work. Alpha stimulation has a long and successful history of clinical applications for stress, anxiety, drug and alcohol addiction, depression, ADHD, Autism, PTSD (thought to block alpha activity), peak performance and headache relief. At or close to 10.2 Hz, it has proven helpful for seniors (who usually experience a slowing of alpha frequencies as they age) and facilitating memory in both younger and older adults. Alpha stimulation has also been shown to as emotional stability reductions in cortisol (a major stress hormone) serotonin production and significant improvement in heart rate variability (HRV). Other studies suggest frequencies at the alpha, theta threshold promote the most cerebral blood flow. Name: Theta Brain Waves; Frequency: (4 to 8 HZ cycles per second) Characteristics: Upper theta associates and corresponds with physical conscious, lower theta associates and corresponds to unconscious, deep meditation.

Deep inward thought. This is associated with life-like imagination; high state of mental concentration; a magical mind, internal pictures/visualisation, Intuition, inner guidance, access to unconscious material, dreaming this is the realms of your subconscious mind, usually most dominant during REM sleep and dreaming. Waking experience of theta is a dreamy, visual, abstract, and highly creative one. Trance and deep meditative states may arise in theta; can be used for extreme relaxation, and as an aid for sleep. Entrainment: at the theta level is usually used for meditation, lucid dreaming, trance, and affirmation type work, can bypass subconscious mind, making theta a super-learning state when combined with higher knowledge or affirmations; Increases insight and creativity. Entrainment: Binary beats Benefits: Memory consolidation; creativity, imagery, and visualization; free-flowing lucid thought; spatial navigation tasks; inspiration and intuition; REM; processing of new (episodic) information; emotional processing and heightened suggestibility. Theta production begins at around two years of age. Arising from the right hemisphere and the deeper subcortical regions of the brain, theta frequencies have long been considered the 'doorway to the unconscious.

These sleep inducing, low-frequency brainwaves have been associated with deep relaxation, creativity, memory consolidation, emotional processing, vivid imagery, extrasensory perception, intuitive insights, REM states and a great deal of other subconscious activity and phenomena. Hypnotherapists, consider theta-which is associated with the highly suggestible 'hypnagogic trance'-to be the optimal state for accessing the right hemisphere and changing unwanted subconscious behaviours and programs, the reception of information beyond normal waking consciousness, and the gateway for learning and memory. Deeply suppressed emotional material and childhood memories appear to be most readily accessed and released in theta, under expert guidance. Dominant in very deep meditation, prayer, hypnotic trance and REM states, and theta is also associated with enhanced immune function and neurochemicals including vasopressin and catecholamine.

Pronounced theta activity while awake during the day however is considered abnormal in healthy adults and may be indicative of slow wave conditions like depression, ADHD, and PTSD. Nonetheless, it's perfectly normal in young children from two to six where it facilitates their rapid learning abilities and vivid, creative imaginations. It's during their highly suggestible 'theta years' that a child's fundamental, life-shaping beliefs, experiences and assumptions about the world are 'programmed' into their subconscious. That's why loving, positive early parenting and safe, supportive environments are absolutely vital for their best future-and ours! The theta bandwidth is used extensively in our deep relaxation and sleep protocols; Name: Delta Brain Waves Frequency: (0.5 to 4 HZ cycles per second) Characteristics: deep dreamless sleep, deep relaxation, State of oneness, whole body feeling, pure being and will. The deepest and slowest frequency that humans usually exhibit and associated with being flat out in a dreamless sleep, functioning is minimal, basic bodily systems slow down, consciousness is lost. Body enters this state naturally to activate cell healing, release growth hormone, and reset your internal clock. Most often used to get straight to sleep, very useful for insomniacs. Use for deep body healing, can be used for very deep levels of meditation, but practice will be needed, as the frequency is more likely to put you to sleep; Entrainment: Binary beats; Benefits:

When the body switches to deep dreamless healing state, deep dreamless sleep, immunity, regeneration, and healing; anti-ageing hormones, cortisol reduction and pituitary release of H.G.H.; extremely deep relaxation; Delta waves are present at birth and are known to persist in the waking state of children to around five years. Both delta and sub-delta are vital for deep, restorative sleep and its many associated benefits; during production of this very low frequency, high amplitude brainwaves we're usually completely unconscious and catatonic in non-REM sleep stages 3 and 4. However, brain scans have shown that some advanced meditators, such as yogis and monks, can enter delta states and remain there with full conscious awareness.

Delta has been associated with physical/emotional healing and immune functioning, memory consolidation, the production of anti-ageing hormones including DHEA and melatonin, significant stress reduction (calming of the limbic system) and the lowering of cortisol. It has also been linked to pituitary release of trace amounts of human growth hormone (H.G.H) gamma-hydroxybutyric acid (G.H.B) and of course the many essential benefits of a good night's sleep - which include accelerated muscle repair and optimal fat burning. Delta production typically declines with age, and, by adolescence, levels may decrease by about 25%. Seniors and the elderly may produce very little delta activity during sleep. Studies suggest delta is typically under-produced in chronic stress or sleep conditions (including those who choose voluntarily sleep curtailment), and that a lack of this frequency may play a role in Parkinson's disease, diabetes, and schizophrenia. Not surprisingly, the clinical use of delta and sub-delta brainwave stimulation is primarily used for stress and sleep related issues like insomnia, as it is with. Diet and herbal matrixes, reduction of simple sugars have been shown to balance out the body and supply the brain with nutrients, iron, zinc, which enable the brain to be at it's optimum, excess sugar especially simple sugars, which prevent the liver sending omega fats to the brain and instead the brain is feed sugars which effectively work on the brain like a corrosive. Understanding brainwave frequencies helps us to build better understanding of ourselves, the way we process information, and shift through different states throughout the day, when in deep concentration we are in a conscious theta state, and concentration can be helped by playing binary beats in relation to theta state.

Binary beats can be very useful, there are literally hundreds on you tube, good if you're interested in chakra healing, sleep, meditation, and self-hypnosis, use Alpha, theta, or delta depending on the depth of hypnotic state you require, using Alpha binary beats when stressed or after a long day can bring you quickly out of high beta state. Just doing that at

BRAINWAVE FREQUENCIES AND HOW WE ACCESS THEM

the end of a day twenty minutes listening to Alpha binary beats will improve health possibly very significantly, ways to improve health and generally wellbeing that you may not have been aware of before. What these frequencies and the association to various states while operating on these frequencies shows us, is that we are part of a massive Universal communication network, matrix in which everything is communicating we are not just skin bones muscle and brain we are an integrated transmission unit. With unlimited potential, and whether or not our full potential is ever realised comes down to the parts that make up a system called our attitude.

This also corresponds directly to the Universal absolute principle of Vibration, Emotions and feelings, are the realm of brainwave frequencies which means we can affect our own mind state and moods by understanding the role of brainwave frequencies gives us access to tools like binary beats, forms of meditation, help us take control of our mind state by being able after practice change you frequency levels at will, these are very powerful tools for personal development that most people are just not aware of so their going through life say hitting bouts of depression that we can will ourselves out of quite easily and one way to do this is to change brainwave frequencies with these tools they become an essential tool for self-transformation and development and pulling yourself out of bad moods quickly and not just spending three months sulking about things but bring yourself back to a good feeling state..

CHAPTER EIGHT

THOUGHT, VALUE'S, AND DESTINY LEVELS

Again similar to the mood table, there is a level that we are at overall, (like a set GPS position) in general though there can be degrees of entanglement, The values define the beliefs as in the beliefs correlate around the value, so part of changing beliefs is to look at the value and change the value, what level do you aspire to be at once you have defined the level you are generally at. If you're at four and want to be seven then what would you have to believe to shift the values level you're operating from, the one to eight definitions are a guide, in general it is generally not possible to jump more than one level at a time because we learn lessons from all these levels, as we go up, for example a level three. may aspire to be level five, by earing money in a legitimate way instead of just focusing on money and not caring if it hurts or kills others, they may get to level five but hold onto some of the level three values. Values levels can also define degrees of limiting beliefs, which can lead to self-sabotage. Self-sabotage is generally unconscious and relates to self-esteem or lack of, and form studying and applying these values levels I can assert from experience as well as book knowledge that these values levels should be viewed as being like different planes of existence from one to eight by virtue of they do define a person's lifestyle, the other big thing to get that defines lifestyle is whether you come under the umbrella term of dependant on salary waged income or studying for that, or are in the mind-set of more entrepreneurial, interdependent; self-actualised, self-sufficient or at least that to a large degree more able to take responsibility for one's own destiny.

If you look through the levels of thinking and the traits associated to each level again some areas are more self-internal, some more outside; I and we; that can also help you decide the types of self and outside you want as influences and to operate from. When you have assessed what thought level, you're on now, then you only have to aspire to be on higher thought levels to start the metaphorical ball rolling, and then say you want to be operating from a seven-thought level, the best answer to that is seek out people on that level as mentors, you won't get to level seven. if all your mentors are level seven; it doesn't work in the sense of being able to leap frog from one to eight in one jump, there may be the odd person that has done that, but not generally, for the simple reason the different levels represent evolving mind-set and the level they have evolved to so far, however putting some time in to study and practice changing though levels will return immeasurably more than just putting everything down to chance, or bad luck, they are just descriptor words that describe intention, action and personal return. Synchronicity, everything in someone's life is synchronised by their levels of thinking, responding/reacting, and the best way to approach this is to come at it with an attitude of, gradual progression. Create your big picture then look at where you are now, then ask yourself what can you do in the here and now that becomes a moving toward action and continue focusing on evolving up through the different levels until you at where you want to be, it's important to practice keeping some focus on thought levels and linguistics this really is one of the main platforms of the cause of what manifests as personal reality; set values have set beliefs that associate to the value.

You can't go back and try to remember all the information you absorbed from the imprint period birth to six you can repeat the modelling period though seven to fourteen, by choosing who you aspire to, and choose to have mentors, from the perspective of living your big picture as here and now, which becomes about looking at what associations are in line with what you want, and what associations are out of line with what you want. This creates developing a mind-set that is not only in line with what you want, it's supporting having what you want; effectively creating a coping system for the reality you want to actualise, there are many statistics about people who have come into large amounts of money in the windfall sense of the word, and the percentage is massively higher of people who within two years where back at pretty much where they started, in most cases in more debt than before, and this is the reason they had the money, they did not have the mind-set and the thought level they were on when the money came will be the level they end up back at because they were still using the same linguistics thinking reacting and responding in the same way.

The only difference is they had money and that's not enough when their mind-set doesn't support having it, to walk the walk so to speak you really must be thinking from that level first. Life starts to become less hard and much easier the more your levels of thinking are in line with your desired outcomes, the whole thing sounds a bit like going up to higher levels in computer games, the principles the same in as much as you pick up resources on one level that you can take up to and use in the next level, whilst simultaneously letting go of the previous level to experience the next one. If you find your at level four and you want to be free of working for someone else and do your own thing then start looking at level five thinkers be selective though it's all very well thinking you want to be a CEO of your own company, the question is would you be able to cope with having a large staff dependency, if your just looking for more independence which is probably most people then look at level five traits that represent independence, in a way that gives service or add to people who will be your customers or clients in a positive way, say like a hypnotherapist, or NLP practitioner helps you remove an addiction or phobia and they charge the person the going rate for the sessions, have they done their client out of money and the answer no, the opposite from the perspective of the client which has a greater value, the money they paid or the addiction being removed.

The practitioner has given them greater value than an amount of money and has added value to the other person's life experience; if you want to start a business to make money then check that the way your business makes money isn't going to backfire on you, by taking cash but not giving added value back in a way that genuinely gives value or service to the other person.

The point is think about who you want to be as a person as well as the things you want to have, it will turn out to be far more productive to work some things out beforehand, that's to say, right I'm going to fly into this and find yourself completely overwhelmed, not really having what you want because you scattered your focus to far and wide to end up burned out and overburdened. Decide what you want, then stack all the things you may have to do into seven metaphorical cups, so each cup has say two or three or three main areas of focus, then when that set of things are complete move onto the next set, a lot of people do get to exited to start with and try working on all the tasks at the same time, and it doesn't take them long to realise that they can't cope, the best way to cope with change you are bringing about for yourself is to do it gradually, and constantly evaluate what you're doing and why and is it in line with the outcome you desire; also seriously focus in a way that's about solutions, not problems, sounds obvious though lot of people get stuck on focusing on problems and not solution, when you make a decision your happy with, don't let yourself or others get you thinking negative what ifs, it has a "speak of the devil and he's sure to appear" outcome! when you focus on negative what ifs, then what you focus on expands and the what ifs are bound to show up, keep your objective side in check it's good to be objective in some areas, however don't lose sight of the subjective imagination work, not just completely objective, working with Universal laws and law of attraction are as much about balance as anything else, doing things that are subjective and objective, combing self and outside so you have balance.

Rather than being a self that is completely directed from outside, you want to be self-directing and selective of what you let in from the outside; if it doesn't fit in with where you're directing yourself then don't focus on it. As I said earlier about modelling look outside your usual circle for people who are already out their doing the sort of things you want to do and who are way ahead of you, if you ask someone down the pub who's in a similar job or situation what to do their not going to have the answers or the mind-set to model from, for most people their modelling period seven to fourteen was made up of mentors who were family, teachers, etc. but not people you had actively sought out to learn from. The values levels are generally viewed as eight, however there would be a ninth level if you were to consider the possibility of hybrid human, however this level is little known about so for most of us one to eight is fine, however the system of three there would apply if there were nine levels as three separate and integrated matrix systems. Which effectively makes the first three a system that corresponds closely with each integrated level, and tiles on from that, four to six and seven to nine?

Values Level One: Survival: Food, Shelter, and Reproduction: Imprint Period: Sick: Homeless: Dependent: i.e. at birth and childhood. People who live off the Grid, (In the Wilderness) Values level one represents primary survival, instincts a basic example as an analogy would be if you were outside sick, and a crocodile your body's survival instinct will kick in and rather than the body focusing on healing the body from the sickness all the energy will be put into running away from the crocodile, then the body will switch back to trying to heal the sickness.

On this level we are the same as the rest of the animal kingdom in terms of an instinctual primary response, which is controlled by what we call reptile mind, which is the body's automated fight or flight system, its other function is to move away from pain and toward pleasure. The imprint period also mentioned elsewhere in this book is when a child is totally dependent on parents for survival, it is also the period when a child starts developing beliefs and values the child at this point is in delta and theta state until around six to seven, so are not able to make full beta conscious rational decisions, although they can absorb information like a sponge. so this really is a values level of survival at the most basic level; also when sick or in an accident we become dependent on medicine, healers, or surgery, so outside influence and internal instincts play a big part at this level, this is also the level of poverty, Values Level Two: Modelling Period: Cults: Tribal: Luck, Chance, The Unknown: Mysteries: The Occult: Witchcraft: Energy Healing: Chrystal's: Objects with Energy: Everything has Consciousness: Superstitions: May Aspire to Being Level

THOUGHT, VALUE'S, AND DESTINY LEVELS

eights. Values level two is about the modelling period when from around seven to fourteen which is when we model off so called role models, peers, teachers, pop stars. it is when we develop and attain full alpha and beta states of consciousness. When we start to join cults, tribes, or groups, and may look at universal mysteries, when we are curious and no, we don't know it all and want to learn more and understand more, become more expressive as opposed to level one which can be single minded on just surviving, we ask questions and may ponder the meaning of life, as well as becoming more social as a person. It's the period when we define what direction we may be going in life.

We may see everything as luck, chance, or destiny being set in stone. Also a point when we are developing our internal representations and view of the world; and also pick up limiting or empowering beliefs of ourselves. Level three: and four are predominately defined by experiences and beliefs adopted during imprint and modelling period the environment we were brought up in have a big influence on whether going into adulthood, note these can be changed, but if someone doesn't focus on change or doing things differently then they may well stay on three or four their entire lives. Three and four are also connected to socialisation period fourteen to twenty-one, Me, me, me, Gangsters: No guilt; No remorse, Football crowds: Loyalty: Immediate pleasure, (Sensory) Will not hesitate to kill; Influenced by environment: Can't take embarrassment: Egotistic: Keep them busy: Revenge: Head of the family (The Boss) Road rage: Bellow those who lay down the Law: Not Interested in the Consequences; Feelings of not Fitting in In: Demand respect:

Level Three: are a mix of get rich quick schemes,(which normally backfire and are more like get poorer schemes) or get you beaten up shot or in prison; these are the gangsters and drug dealers terrorists, were their role models, if these types of people are the ones you aspire to be like then you need to re-model your role models and fast re-modelling techniques are further on in the book" they're the kids in ghettos with guns, they're the head of gangs, they only respect the people in their gang or the people who support the same football team, they have their own codes, they put money before human life they have no value for life at all except their own; they have no respect for Universal law or manmade law, only the ones they make up for themselves known as the code, they want power and money and don't care about whose heads they tread on to get it, they think only of themselves and not others, it may not be their fault they find themselves on this level but it is their responsibility to get out of it, the first step would be to chunk up to level four.

Values Level four: Mainstream: Keyworkers, Police, Army, Nurses, Teachers: Can't do: Government's: Uniforms: Seek Peers Approval: Externally validating: Chunked down: Details: Already know it all: There way is the Only Way: Closed off: Compliance: Church, Religion: Tunnel visioned: Lies: Desire Respect: Need to fit In: Belonging: Want to help others (Even if they don't want to be helped) Guilt Trips: Love Insurances: Support Groups for Problems: Judgemental. Level four, these are more outer orientated, they will put others first which can be a dilemma for them as they will try to please everyone else, but not focus on what they want, they can be easy to manipulate and are the medias and advertises dream, they are the go to church get married get a mortgage and have kids, they are following a pre-defined script, their intelligence is defined by their day job, in fact their relationships and pretty much why they make the decisions they make are defined by their day job, and the way they look at themselves and others, following this value infrastructure will get them degrees of wealth and happiness, not generally above what is defined as financial independence which is around 70,000 a year, if you ask them what they really want from life they will give you a blank look or say what. They don't know what they really want because they are focussed on what everyone else wants, which can technically give them a metaphorical Achilles heel, they need to apply a more balanced "self" and others attitude, the danger is switching completely to self and ending up in level three or juggling three with four like the corrupt policeman politician: They want to chunk up to five values.

Values Level five: Associates to age 21-28, the Development Period: Start Thinking Out of the Box; Seek Coaches and Mentors: Taking Control of Own Destiny: Want to Be Independent (Own Boss) Thinking more as an entrepreneur: Financial gains, big picture: Moving toward success: Done with the day Job: Goal orientated: Competitive: Professors: Destroy planet for gain: Profits, profits, profits. These are the entrepreneurs, self-made wealth, presidents of a company or at the higher levels within a company/cooperation, or born into wealth, they can be level 4's who worked their way up the ladder or level threes who got there from attaining money in level 3 ways, or postgraduates, they have a big picture and move toward it, and will seek out mentors and coach's to get there, which can be books, lectures on you tube, courses or meeting the person. To some degree the social science concept of a class system exists within levels three to five, three would be more associated with working class, level four would be more associated with working and middle class, and five would be more associated with middle to upper class, moving out of and up to six and eight, generally starts to take you out of the class system. Values Level Six: Group causes, Conservation of the planet, Ban the bomb and Save the whale: Being on time doesn't matter: Peace and harmony: Judgemental: Guilt: Care for all creatures: Reject level fives values: Suspicious of sevens Values: Good/Bad vibes; Question having Leaders: Working in Groups; Preservation of humanity, in fact all life is Precious; Meditation: Love everyone who loves them.

Everyone's equal. Level Six's are compassionate; they will accept responsibly for their actions and expect everyone else to do the same, in tune with nature, everything is in balance, they are suspicious of level seven, but aspire to be level eight, level six values perceives the so called system of the class system and see's it is real for those with associated values, but that system exists the whole salary waged job and intelligence being gauged on the level of earnings, but they don't have to exist in that system, there are other systems associated with six to eight, which bring a person at least in the realms of becoming far more self-sufficient in all areas of life and a lifestyle they want, as opposed to a lifestyle their salary allows them.

Operate outside of the class system and reject the concept of a class system. Values Level Seven: Know themselves know their craft: Nothing to Prove to others: Compete with compassion: Good degree of Self-sufficiency: Integrated self: Self-actualised; do That which benefits the Self and others: Ethics, Intellectual connections; Self directing; Self-motivated; Well-earned self-esteem: Done with one to six values, but can operate on any level; Ability to evaluate commitments: Love complex thinking: Every problem Has a Solution: Functional flow; A master but do not think they know It all, There is always something to learn. Now life starts to get interesting in a good way, the concept of an integrated-self where you have come up through all the levels and learned valuable lessons along the way, mastered your craft and know yourself, even if you were thrown back to survival you be able to get back to this level fairly quickly, by knowing the right and wrong way of doing things, there are still many things to learn (there is always something to learn) but you have gotten over the idea that you know it all, you can work on your own or in a group quite happily in fact probably balance the two in your day-to-day life, you understand the concept of self and others, not just self and not just others, you may come across problems, but always focus on the solution rather than being drowned in the problem.

They have adopted good ethics and do what you do without needing to intend or cause harm to others i.e. mastered the rede (an it harm ye none do as thy will) and know this to be the true wisdom to living a free willed life without the need of man-made law; you have learned that you don't need to compete and look for people to compete with, because you create your own destiny not trying to compete with others destiny, you have functional flow, and can help others attain being at this level, you understand the difference between co-depend and co-create, and your relationships in all areas reflect this, and that other people's negative behaviour is a reflection on them not you. They now look at both sides of the coin before making a firm commitment, they know that life events aren't luck or chance, but synchronised personal returns, they are curious not assuming. Values Level Eight; Holistic thinking: At one with Universe/Vital life force: Synergy of all life: Evolution is the mission: We are All connected; Re-evaluation of Level two Values. Vales level eight: has possibly dropped religion and exchanged it for a more philosophical or para-psychological approach, knowing there is one vital life fore that connects everything in universe, (infinite spirit which permeates the whole of Universe) this is how telepathy, remote viewing/interaction and other psychic ability's including premonitions work.

Healing is more than just energy, it is subjective intervention, life transformation is not just objective but subjective and objective, illness can be caused subjectively therefore can be removed subjectively. Esoteric science is the true science above just mainstream, mind, body, and spirit, not just mind, body; differing from level two who maybe starting on a psychic development path wondering if this works, level eights know this works they have the personal history of success. When you are big picture building theses values levels are real in the way that they play out, so take a good look at what each level implies and the type of life experience you get from living of each of the values levels, their environment what important to them, also look at family and friends and work out which values level they are on mainly, remember we attract by likeness so if you were aspiring to get to seven or eight in values sets, then take into account that if all your friends and associates and family are all level four values then somewhere along the line your relationship landscape will change.

Level seven values represent the mind-set of real success through creative not competitive thinking, it's not true that no man is an island, we can be, we can be far more self-sufficient and less dependent in general, independent but able to operate on all levels though in general are done with operating on one to six levels. So as you build the mind's eye big picture of your destiny, things to consider are, purpose and meaning to the things you want, in other words start to build criteria and association with what you want, people who literally started from scratch following these principles and understanding the thing I have put in this book are doing certain things in a certain way that cause positive personal change, some general key traits that these people adopt and associate to are, self-direction, self-assured, self-reliant, creative, innovative, balance perceiver and judger to become discerning; self-direction is probably the most important one to focus on initially, and not just self-direction, scattering energies or multi-tasking to ridiculous levels will keep you in a loop forever, it is far more effective to focus on smaller amounts of things first, in order of what really takes priority, you are more likely to succeed if you have say three projects going at the same time as opposed to twenty-three.

CHAPTER NINE

COMBINING PERSONALITY TRAITS META-PROGGRAMMES AND VALUES LEVELS

Combining our personality traits, basic and complex meta-programmes, values levels, and the way this creates our perception of what our life appears to be, this process will help you understand what your perceptual filters are, as photosynthesis defines what we are seeing as what colour it is, perceptual filters define what we see as our reality/actuality. So when we take the modelling period if all your role models turned out to be pretty negative, you can re-do the modelling period, drop the old negative ones and seek out new ones, this time around you get to choose your mentors not have them chosen for you, and you start to become more aware and accepting that your destiny is your choice, which to be fair can take a little getting used to if you've been told all your life that your destiny is set in stone and can't be changed, there is some degree of truth in destiny being set in stone but only in as much as personal intention, action, personal return, which changes when your mind-set changes, reality shifting to the degree of noticeable change comes from changing paradigms, when your paradigms change your reality/actuality changes with absolute certainty! Which is what this whole book is about, not courage to change but knowledge of how to change. Doing things or appearing to be different can take some courage, but then you think well do I want to stay where they are, because sameness doesn't get different. Which also becomes another trade off of, how much of your life if any do you want to stay the same, and how much of your life do you want to be different and are there any parts of this that might cause inner conflict in as much as pulling you in two separate directions at the same time, and find yourself in a kind of tug of war between same and different, successful outcomes need to have coherence, you can't drive along a road and when you come to a fork in the road go down both roads at the same time, you would be amazed by the amount of people I have come across that try to do exactly that, and the outcome to that is called stuck in a rut. Some people get the notion that it's just about closing their eyes and everything's just going to manifest, mind's eye does work visualisation does work it is one component part though, you can have the clearest visualisation, but you must have work going on around mind-set orientations, then if you manifest something through a mind's eye visualisation, you may have the thing or experience but with the same mind-set, which will eventually pull you back to where you started from.

What I discovered with moving up through the thought levels is you tend to be thinking from that level first, then the more you think from that level the more you start to walk the walk so to speak. Although for many the idea of getting a millionaire mind-set first, then getting the millions sounds alien or the wrong way around, the statistics of people who come into money first without a mind-set of having the money first are, the ones that lose it all, believe me mind-set rules, so it stands to reason if you're modelling off someone that does what they love doing, has the millions and keeps them, then they have the mind-set to support it. Sameness doesn't get different, and that applies very much where mind-sets concerned. It's fair enough to think well I can think and do this differently, get the life I want then stick with keeping that the same, thinking different is chucking up and when you start chunking up you start thinking outside of problems and outside of the box. You start seeing there are levels above where you are that you can access, whereas before you may have thought anything you thought was above you would be inaccessible to you, any reality you want to have is accessible when you view it from levels of thinking. If you find yourself getting overwhelmed at any point, then just chunk down a little and focus a little more on objective or detail or find something that's familiar for a bit.

An example would be if you were more group orientated before and you've been doing a lot of self-stuff and it feels a bit much, then do something in a group for a bit and go back to what you were doing for self, no one feels comfortable riding a bike for the first time, because it's unfamiliar, it's different, then after a while you don't even think about it, that pretty much sums up what change is. If you have always done things in groups then doing things by yourself it will feel a bit like riding a bike for the first time, then after a while it becomes second nature, and the same if your used to doing everything by yourself and you start to work in a group, like riding the bike you have the desire to ride the bike so you will. That is basically why assessing honestly what thought level you're on, and how much self and others you have in your life, then deciding what level you're aspiring to and why and how much self and outside you want your different or new lifestyle to be will make thing's much easier in the long run, rather than just jumping in without any real evaluation of outcomes.

Also fear of being or doing different, leads us into the oldest part of our mind which is known as reptile mind, the job of reptile mind is to keep you alive, it generates the instinctive response of fight or flight, it's not like a belief or value that can be changed so you have to understand what it is, and what it does, and how that impacts on your life, if you look at early humanity and even those who still live undiscovered in rainforests, they are at level one to two survival and tribe, so the difference between the way reptile mind operates for people in that environment and modern civilisation environment is, in civilisation reptile mind will move away from doing different for fear of ridicule or being laughed at, in an off the grid environment reptile mind will move away from a snake for fear it will kill you, being laughed at won't kill you, being bitten by a snake might well do, reptile mind has evolved the same as humans from instinctual food, shelter, reproduction, fight or flight outside of something that maybe a threat; to moving toward pleasure and away from pain. An example of this is say your level four and you're all set to move up to seven or eight, this is where understanding reptile mind becomes very helpful, if you think that everyone else you know is going to wish you well when you tell them, then I'll give you fair warning, most of them won't, your more than likely find they try to make a joke of you, insult you, or tell you what your decisions and choices should be, don't let them, don't let the reptile move you away from where you want to go which would give you pleasure, I found this out through personal experience so this isn't really being pessimistic it's just being honest about the thought level their reacting/responding from, believe me some of them will through all the what ifs they can muster, ignore them and learn to trust your own judgement, or they will hold you back forever, if you find they are closed off to applying these techniques, I'll tell you about people who are closed off to your way of thinking and doing things, you will waste the rest of your life trying to convince them, I know more people that stayed level four their whole lives than I could wave a stick at, and they will keep you stuck there to if you give them half the chance. I'm a Hypnotherapist and Master NLP practitioner and life coach.

I would not waste my time cold calling for clients then try to convince them different if they were obviously closed off and have no interest in it. It also fits in line with the type of people you want to attract in your life, do you want a bunch of closed of doubting Thomas's, which mock your way of life, or do you want a bunch of people who think believe and do similar to you, which one will give you pleasure which one will give you a proverbial pain in the neck. This is what I mean by as you go up through the levels your social circle will change it has to, it doesn't mean disown your family because their all level four just be aware of what level four are about, and to a large degree it's not actually their fault for their behaviour and comments because they may be operating from an almost entirely outside programmed mind-set, it makes it easier to deal with when you understand this, I didn't have this awareness of thought levels when I first started studying hypnosis and working on my big picture, so I can tell you this from bitter experience, fortunately I was aware of natural justice so I didn't embark on tit for tat or revenge. I just let it go and let their own personal return for their intentions and actions towards me take care of it, also known as Karma. Getting back to self-hypnosis for a moment, this is another area that can be hugely beneficial and save a lot of time wasting, create statements or scripts of suggestion that affirm to being and thinking on a higher level first, you may still have to do some of the old ways of doing things for a bit, like a day job while your sorting things out, or a certification course of some sort. There will be degrees of physical action to get up the levels, it's much more likely to turn out successfully if you are working on beliefs, values, mind-set alongside the mundane stuff, then when you have the certifications or whatever the recourses are you need, you'll be thinking and have the mind-set of the next level even if your only just starting to walk it, as I said trying to do all the physical stuff to get up to higher levels, and not work on mind-set; well that's probably why 90% of businesses in the UK fail in their first year, they haven't got the mind-set to support it, and no doubt rely far too heavily on luck and chance, rather than designed outcome.

I can't overstate the advantage self-hypnosis will give you in achieving the life you want; Self-esteem levels are defined by this, creative draws things in, competitive chases things away, defining whether something is a moving toward or moving away from action, is the difference between whether the motivation is creative or competitive. Subjective/creative or Objective/competitive, that which defines the direction of our destiny lies within the extreme side or degree in-between a person's belief and values are orientated for the best part. Desire intention repetition, go into things without expectation of the outcome, you can have a preferred outcome your hopeful of and although it's not easy to start with, and takes practice to get out of the habit of expecting a certain outcome, and into the habit of being hopeful of the of the preferred outcome; Parents biggest flaw with children younger or older is they put far too much expectation on the child performing well or whatever it is, the child does the best they can, they didn't let the parent down the parent put too much expectation into the equation and the parent felt let down, children have so much pressure put on them by parent's, teacher's and society in general, that you have youngsters hitting burn out and even committing suicide because of this unreasonable expectations built around them, the pressure on them is simply too much. Quantum mechanics essentially defines the idea that the universe is systematic which leads into the three absolute universal principle being real, one is singular two is dualistic three is a system, and that you cannot have quantum mechanics without consciousness being in the equation. It is also now being said amongst some of our greatest scientific minds that, in relation to the split light experiment, that it was not observation or measurement, that caused a wave to collapse but interaction, if any of you are familiar with remote viewing, it takes away the idea of viewing and replaces it with interaction, should we now consider remote viewing to be remote interaction; it certainly seems to make more sense and better describe remote viewing for what it is, a series of interaction.

This comes at a time when Quantum entanglement has been proved as real in nature by a series of complex experiments with almost zero margin for error, Einstein postulated that Quantum entanglement was impossible, now we find not only is it possible but real in nature, what does this mean? That Everything in universe is connected, that anything is possible, that possible or impossible is the way we interact, and that the Universe is systematic, that universe does not measure itself but interacts with itself. It also leads into the idea that when scientist conducts experiment's expectation plays a role in the outcome. So, Expectation is pretty much the opposite of Hope and is there a difference in outcome when someone is hopeful of their preferred outcome or expectant of the preferred outcome, many experiments in science have been conducted and the outcome was "not" what they expected. When you refer to the twenty-one Universal sub-laws or positive Human characteristics hope is there, and expectation is not. Could expectation be putting a negative twist on potential outcomes and behave like a negative elemental in the same way as Hate, or Jealousy. we can do our own self-validating experiments without being egg head quantum physicists. If we consciously focus on something, an outcome with expectation and consciously focus on something else with hope which yields the most positive outcome, will the outcome be the same or different, this is also the way I have put this book together so when you work through it and apply what I'm saying, the outcome will be self-validating.

CHAPTER TEN

THE STRUCTURE OF CONVERSATIONAL LINGUISTICS

Words with power; words are a thought that become animated, our vocabulary with letters making words are like an egg yolk in cooking used to bind the ingredients together; our words can and do crystallise thought and bring it into physical being, the problem for most people is they fire off words all day long and essentially take absolutely no notice, or rather have no awareness of what their words are actually doing when saying them, and that words as statements people are repeating are actually forming their reality/actuality, fortunately for us we realise this but you have to feel pity for those who don't, or who cast off the idea that reality works in this way, a brief example, I read a statement on an online forum where a person was describing a craft he enjoyed doing, making pendants, now a craft you enjoy doing puts you in the highest level on the mood table of interest and enthusiasm,

However here is the problem, he then stated that it takes his mind off his anxiety and depression, written as "my anxiety and depression," which brought him backsliding down to associating to anxiety and depression, to release yourself from anxiety and depression you have to find ways of taking your mind off it, that parts right and then stay dissociated from it. So I would re-frame the statement as I am interested and enthusiastic about making pendants/jewellery because it's something I enjoy doing, that is what I call overlaying a negative or counterintuitive statement with a positive one. That kind of statement works on more than one level, it states having in the here and now/acceptance, it states that it is a part of him, which then creates potentially a permanent attachment to the condition that is being associate with, I couldn't define a statement of moving away from any better if I tried it just sums up the power in self-talk, hence the conditional statement, the statement contains conditions which in this instance are anxiety and depression, which in essence is sending a command to unconscious mind to keep them in a state of anxiety and depression.

This chapter is about putting words and statements together that reverses negative trends and creates positive ones. The bottom line on our conversational statements become self-referencing by virtue of that is the way unconscious mind processes our conversational statements, if you call someone a Sod, the unconscious mind takes it "personally" and thinks you are calling yourself a Sod. So at least to some degree depending on what the conversations about, be aware of this and re-frame your understanding of conversation, as not talking to someone else but talking to yourself about yourself, because the more you understand the way unconscious mind is reading your conversations the easier it is to adapt your conversations or statements so there not working against you, this manifests reality as much as any mind's eye visualisation or hypnosis sessions, it is absolutely a part of what creates and manifests what we call reality/actuality, possibly the largest part, as our statements can alter our values and beliefs which effectively shift our reality/actuality.

When you think about it most people do not use self-hypnosis or mind's eye visualisation, so effectively the whole of their reality/actuality is formed from the values and beliefs they already have, and the conversational statements associated to them. So this is a really important thing to understand, when we talk, we are sending clear instructions to our unconscious only for the best part people are doing this without awareness, and you can't really change something if you're not aware it needs changing, you can only change things when you have the desire and intention to do so. If you were not aware of this, you need to look at what you are saying in conversation, or you won't have the motivation to change the desire or intention. As you are reading this, and I am sure you understand this so now you can create the desire and intention to change the way you talk. All the tools to do this are in this book "language patterns," model operators, but obviously it takes a little time and practice, however I am sure you can see the benefits and positive outcomes that will come from practicing this. We manifest our perceived reality almost entirely be the continuous conditional statements we make on a day-to-day basis, some statements fire of like a firework and just fizzle out, but the ones that have continuous focus put on them manifest. People's day to day linguistics are most people's biggest problem, because they talk into reality what they constantly make statements on, people cast spells for good health and money then go about their day telling everyone how ill and poor they are, it would actually be quite amusing if it wasn't for the fact, it's creating personal chaos in people's lives. It can be a bit like lifting your mood then deliberately sabotaging it by accepting and stating a personal association to poverty, anxiety, or depression.

Milton Ericson became prolific as a hypnotist partly because, he highlighted when we look at the individual word in terms of necessity, possibility, and probability, add positive or negative attributes to it, put them together in a string or paragraph and we really see where the words have power, and how these become language patterns. If you take two separate people and analyse their linguistics and look at statements they make on a daily basis, one may have statements full of negative and necessity, the other has statements of positive and probability, the one who's linguistics are positive probability will apparently be more in control of their own lives, as these statements reflect their life. The one who's statements are negative, and necessity will probably sit there for an hour reeling off how problematic their life is and apparently have less control of their own life, this is because the language patterns directly reflect the person's life in relation to perceptual filters they have. There is an absolute science to words and words do produce a physical effect. In days of old many people thought that words with power where some archaic language or mystical symbols, there is truth to that, however it is more about what our language patterns reveal about us as individuals, they are reflecting how we perceive our reality, we have the same base instincts as the rest of the animal kingdom, but what separates us from the rest of the animal kingdom is language and our ability to conceive an idea and implement it. What gives the words power are what they are associating to, where there being directed to and what they are focused on, "can't do" associates to not having the ability to, "can do" associates to having the ability to. The use of language patterns then becomes mindfulness about choosing what we say with awareness of what the words and statements are the cause of, in terms of commands being sent to unconscious mind, remember when unconscious mind accepts the command it manifest, and this happens through repetition. The words are absolutely impacting in our physical reality/actuality. If we have a big picture in our mind of what our ideal lifestyle is, this then acts as a kind of magnetic north, the words then become directional so although some things may require some kind of physical action, like thinking I'd like some egg on toast and getting up and cooking it, whether we end up on the path we want and experience having the things we want, comes down to what we talk about, we literally talk our reality into existence. So, life becomes almost like a game of word association, what you associate your life as being, will be what your being experiences! Take the story of Pandora's box, I'm just going out for a minute but while I'm out whatever you do, "don't" look in the box, now repeat that a few times over a few minutes and the person will open the box even if they don't want to because that was the command sent to unconscious mind, there have been numerous experiments that prove this is true. Whoever conceived that story new the art of linguistics, and new this was a statement to do, even though the person listening thinks it's a command not to do, with repetition not to is dropped.

The Milton Model: Hypnotic Language Patterns

Mind read: Claiming to know the thoughts or feelings of another without specifying the process by which you came to know the information. So, a claim that you know what someone else is thinking or going to do is called a mind read; generally, the opener is; I know that you, a forced mind read opens with I know that you, know that I know that you think that. Examples: you think this is hard…I know you have a picture in your mind, of the car you would like to own…I know that you want to get out of the rut…I know you're thinking about leaving…Forced mind read: I know that you know that I think you are sceptical, But I know you know you can do this. I know you know that I think you are a responsible person. Lost Performative: Value judgment: When the performer of the value judgment is left out. Examples: That's good, that's right, that's too bad, it's good when, that's better, it is important to, it's wrong to lie; one doesn't have to, today was a great day, it's good to compete, it's good to be creative, being active is good, it's good that you know that it's good that you realise that Cause and Effect: Where it is implied that one thing causes another. Implied causes include: a cause-and-effect statement, "makes the verb to make" b. If...then...c. as you; then you. be careful with cause and effect they can create negative limiting decisions, you are untidy.

Examples Note; Embedded Commands cause the Unconscious Mind to access whatever is mentioned, regardless of the structure of the rest of the sentence. A few Embedded Commands are underlined here in the cause-and-effect pattern. Can you discover more of them in other patterns? If I help you, then you'll learn this as you sit there, then you can feel, don't do that, unless you want to outcome of it, don't sit there unless you want to go into trance, don't move your foot unless you want to go deeper, If you sit in this chair, you'll go into trance, as you listen closely, you will learn faster. As you sit there you can feel more confident. Reading this sentence, you get better and better. Just your being here makes you want to learn this as you ask that question, and then you begin to understand. The bread rises in the oven because of the yeast in the dough… when you practice this you will become better at it. The more you study the more you will understand. I was distracted because of you. Complexed Equivalent's: Where two things are equated as in their meanings being equivalent. Examples: You are relaxing, so you're in trance, being here means that you will change, your question means you know it already, asking questions means you are learning, going to bed early means you will be alert, your body relaxes as you let go of each breath, you know the answer, so you are competent, regular exercise makes you a better athlete, your being in this group deepens your trance, to do means that, getting a good night's sleep means you will be able to concentrate and be more alert. To exercise regularly means you will become stronger and healthier. Buying a ticket means you can go to the concert, focusing on your ambitions means you will achieve your ambitions. Presupposition: The linguistic equivalent of assumptions; to state something prior to the outcome. You can achieve your goals. You can become wealthy from your own efforts. When you have an open mind; you can see things in a different way. When you close your eyes and focus on your breathing you will go into an altered state… when you focus on the things you want, you will get more of what you want…You are going to be more in control by practicing these language patterns. Keep writing like this and you will have this chapter finished tomorrow. Universal Quantifier: A set of words which has a. a universal generalization and b. no referential index. Statements that have no direction or model operators. Everyone knows he did that…everyone knows it's always been that way. There is always time for that. Examples: Nobody's perfect. Everything you know All the things to learn All the people, all the time Everything you have learned Every time you think of that Everything is wonderful, we are all in trance now Everything means nothing There is always tomorrow Everyone knows it to be true.

Model Operators: Words, which implies possibility, probability, necessity; with positive or negative variations, which often form our outcomes in life. You must realise that you shouldn't have done that… You must decide. What you intend to do and if it's possible for you…You don't have to do what you're supposed to, you can do what you choose to. Examples: You should care for others you should now clearly see you should not hurry into trance just, yet you shouldn't go into trance too quickly, now you should know it's OK to learn in this room you could learn this now you could write this down or not. "Also: Double bind" You could feel more and more peaceful, you must be aware. You must be getting this now at some level.

Nominalisation: Process words (including verbs), which have been frozen in time by making them into nouns. Examples: I have a great relationship You have no respect for me Our education system stinks

Communication is a problem in their marriage NLP is easy as you just trust in the process while you're in trance and allow your intuitions to help you notice new feelings as those feelings come and other feelings may go your behaviour improves so the renewed communication in your relationships means you have made many new learnings. Unspecified Verb: Where an adjective or adverb modifier does not specify the verb. Examples: I was wondering if you knew when you are feeling like you could just let go and notice how easily you begin to enjoy and as you continue breathing you may or you may not notice going deeper and you could go deeper since you really enjoy doing this and you could even continue or if you don't you may discover how much you remember about how you're improving, now and you will, of course be wondering just where this might be going so remember if you will that your being and your learning can only help you to move towards understanding just how easily you can be changing and inducing or simply trancing out aren't you?

Tag Question: A question added after a statement, designed to displace resistance. Examples: didn't I? Isn't it? Have you? Will you? Won't you? Haven't you? Aren't we? Lack of referential Index: A phrase, which does not pick out a specific portion of the listener's experience. Examples: People can It is, you see. That's the way People can learn now you've got it! You will, you know. One can easily see you know the feeling Comparative Deletion: (Unspecified Comparison): Where the comparison is made, and it is not specified as to what or whom it was made. Examples: Right or wrong. Even more relaxed it's a higher thought you will enjoy it more. You're doing better now and then; things happen but that's neither here nor there are you going deeper and deeper. Sooner or later, you will understand this is more or less the right time before or after you come out of trance. Pace Current Experience:

Where a person's verifiable external experience is described in a way, which is undeniable Examples: You hear my voice we are in this group as we sit here now. And you're sitting here as you notice each blink as you continue breathing. As you look at me like that. Double Bind: Where someone is given two choices both of which are preferable or desired separated by "an, or." Examples: Do you want to begin now, or later? As you dream, or upon awakening. Either before, or after, leaving this room when you go to bed you will either dream, or not will you begin to change now or after I said this? Would you like to quit smoking today or tomorrow? Would you like to buy the car now, or test drive it first? Would you rather do that before or after your meeting? You either will or you won't (followed by an unspecified verb) Conversational Postulate. The communication has the form of a question –a question to which the responses either a yes or a no. If I want you to do something, what else must be Present so that you will do it, and out of your awareness? It allows you to choose to respond or not and avoids authoritarianism. Examples: Can you imagine this? Can you close the door? Will you just let go now? Can you picture doing this? Can you see what I'm saying? Can you reach that level now? Would it be all right to feel this good? Do you know that you know it already?

Extended Quotes: Quotes which are extended beyond that which is normally used to displace resistance; Examples: A friend said that they had a conversation with their hypnotherapy trainer who had said that in a conversation with-their hypnosis trainer who had said that they have an uncle who talked with Milton Ericson about advanced hypnosis techniques, when they took a trip to London to meet him with two friends Bill and Ted one of them told a story about when his mother would sit down and explain to the children how their father had said. The other day, a participant in the training was telling me that her friend had a session with Milton Ericson which had removed a phobia. Selection restriction violation: A sentence that is not well formed in that only humans and animals can have feelings. Examples: My rock said. The walls have ears that nail hurt my tire: Flowers like to be picked. My car knows how to get here put the noise down in your toe, and let it listen what did your actions say to you? Ambiguity Phonological: Where two words with different meanings sound the same. i.e.: "Hear," "Here." Examples: you're, there, they're here, here, son, sun; bare bear bottoms. Utilisation: Remember to use all that happens or is said. Examples: Client: "I don't think I know." Practitioner: "That's right, you don't you know." Client: "I can't be hypnotised." Practitioner: "That's right. You can't be hypnotised "yet." "I expect everyone has heard the metaphor, "think it, say it, do it," which defines thought and Imagination manifest through words and action. The thought becomes things and experiences scenario is real. so when you look in the mirror how you describe what you think your seeing is essentially a command to unconscious mind, so if you say to yourself you look old and wrinkly, or your saying to yourself you look young and attractive regardless of what you thing you are seeing you are sending a command to unconscious mind to manifest what you say you are seeing, if you say to yourself you feel lethargic and tiered, or you feel energetic and exuberant, you are sending a direct clear command to your unconscious to manifest that statement.

The I can't do something statement even though you have never tried to, or it may take some time and practice, so you just don't, is a command to unconscious mind and will either enable you to be able to do something or disable you from doing something, it is the attitude of the person that defines whether you can or can't, will or won't, and it all comes down to the perceptions you are creating with self-talk or conversation with other people. If you think you can or you think you can't is defining your attitude toward whether you will or will not; the biggest problem I have observed over the years just listening to what other people are saying is they are spending huge amounts of their time, focusing on and telling other people what they can and can't do, what they should or should not do, society has become almost obsessed with trying to run other people's live and interfering rather than focus on their own lives and destiny. You have been blessed with an incarnation on this fantastic planet to make your own life, but most have become obsessed to the point of becoming stalkers by the amount of time and energy they put into trying to live other people's lives for them, which is just not their job, we are here to co-exist together not co-depend.

When you start to look at your own language patterns and be honest with yourself, or there's no point, how much of your time to you spend obsessing with other people and what they are or are not doing, we cannot be other people we can only be ourselves, and we do not have the right to tell another how to live their life, and you are wasting your own life and time trying to. This book is about transforming your own life, so you need to come back to you and who you are and create who you are. You will never ever have a chance of understanding other people and their behaviour until you understand yourself and your own behaviour. Many people will tell you that they know this person and that person and what their like, but that is impossible, they are just running mind read and lost performative statements and do not know themselves. So the most important job and the first job is to know yourself and quit thinking you know other people or even understand other people until you know and understand yourself.

Transforming your life to what you want it to be makes this an absolute requirement know thyself. If you cannot control your own behaviour which you will be able to do when you work through this book, then you certainly have no place whatsoever judging other peoples. So back to language patterns when you are talking try to look at what you're saying as though you were looking from the outside in, it will tell you a vast amount about yourself, does your language on reflection tell you that you are doing your best to make your own life what you want it to be, or distracted or obsessed by what other people are doing. If it is the later then you really need to come back to you who you are and who you want to be; never mind if someone is outside smoking a cannabis or running down the street naked, that is none of your business your business is you, so to be blunt start to mind your own business and then you may end up having one. Switch your obsession from what other people are doing to what you are doing become obsessed with yourself.

The list of positive human attributes (Twenty-one universal sub laws)," non-interference and grace", have the grace to leave other people's relationships and business alone, just focus on your own and leave other people to their own, over the years I have observed people systematically without compassion destroy other people's relationships and business, with or without knowing they are sabotaging their own in the process, which will return to them the hurt the pain the emotional trauma, it will return back to them. This is law of Karma or law of attraction, and it is as real as the sun in the sky, you cannot defy or deny these laws they are the fabric of Universe itself; for those who may have an attitude of disrupt and destroy what is important to another, are poisoning their own well. Does it not say in the religious books, let he who is without sin (never made a mistake) cast the first stone, does it not say be judged as you judge. Back again to language patterns, so with that said start to judge where you are in life and if it's not where you want to be use this book to change it, it is easy to spend all your time trying to change other people however it takes real courage to try to change yourself because you have to be honest and really evaluate yourself the things you would like to keep and the things you would like to change, without change things just stay the same or you spend all your time pushing against change. What I am stating here is relevant to language and model operators to pick out when people are trying to through manipulative limiting decision statement on you, knowing this does as a state in later chapter psychic self-defence. You can start to change by changing the way you think and talk, in this "action" alone you will start to change your life for the better. There is a lot in the book about changing values and beliefs, goal setting, creating a big picture but that really pales into insignificance if you are not looking at the words that come out of your mouth and how they become self-fulfilling prophecy, how these linguistic projections become what you project as your reality/actuality.

The most important thing to look at is what are your words and there direction are focussing on most, complaining or being grateful, are they showing love and compassion for other people, or hate and jealousy, because what your words are focussed on are definitely going to impact on what your life is or becomes, do your words show that you are trying to make a better life for your-self and as a consequence helping others, without intending or desiring harm on others to get there or do they show lack of compassion and just selfishly grabbing what you can without a thought about whether it is intending and desiring harm on others.

So what I am saying is make yourself, your focus, the world doesn't need any more crusaders running around telling everyone else what to do, it needs more people transforming their own lives for the better and then they can help others do the same. So start to take notice of what you're saying when in conversation and ask yourself how that reflects on me, what is that saying about who I am. People who spend all their time criticising others are only "avoiding" looking at themselves and their own shortcomings, and they project this through finding other people to criticise, we are all human and all make mistakes, the way to change for the better is acknowledge mistakes we may have made and move forward, instead of driving other people mental trying to micro-manage their lives because they haven't got the courage to look at their own. Knowing your self takes courage maybe as much as someone who is in the frontline, but the upside far outweighs by immeasurable comparison not even trying, persevere with it and you will become someone you can love, trust, and have a life that you love living, how can you expect other people to love and trust you, if you do not love and trust yourself, and you can only do that by knowing yourself, intimately. The point to this chapter is to show that words and statements are important to understand and do impact in what kind of life you will have. The way we construct our statements will always contain what are called model operators, these words the negative and positive variations direct what the statement is moving towards, when you start to change the construct or the model operator you use in conversation you start to create real change and transformation.

Model Operators

Necessity: Ought to, got to have to, its time, it's necessary, need to, Allow, Supposed to. Negative Necessity: Shouldn't, must not, ought not, got to not, don't have to, it's not time, not necessary, doesn't allow, Supposed not to. Probability: Could, dare to, Deserve, had better, Let, May, Might, Prefer, Pretend, wish, would. Improbability: Couldn't, don't dare to, don't deserve, don't let, don't prefer, don't pretend, don't wish, had better not, May not, Might not, Wouldn't. Possibility: Able to, Am, Can, choose to, Decide, Do, Intend, it is possible, Permit, Try, Will. Impossibility: Am not, Can't, doesn't permit, don't choose to, don't decide, don't intend, Impossible, Try not, Unable to, Won't l-look at the words or model operators that make up sentences that bind you to doing something out of a sense of obligation and the ones that allow you your own choice, people talk a lot using words that make them obligated, remember you don't have to do anything you are not supposed to do anything only that which you choose to, do you find you are always doing things for people and they gain and benefit from it but you don't, part of what I learned from all this over the years is' it's acceptable to put you self-first and want things for yourself ,rather than putting everyone else first and never getting any further up the ladder and achieving the things you want to, I used to have a mind-set of doing things out of obligation and because I thought I had to, now I do things because I choose to, the best way to describe this is switching from a mind-set of co-dependent to co-exist, if you find your relationships are full of people who are happy when you are doing what they want, but not happy and throwing a spanner in the works when you are doing something you want.

That's the first sign they are co-dependent, and these are not good relationships. The love you when you do what they want, but not love you when you do what you want or go against what they want screams co-dependent and for me I got rid of all those relationships from my life and run a mile if another one like that turns up knocking. The difference is co-existing relationships obviously have common ground and you do things together, also do the other things you want to do and co-exist happily together, co-dependent one who is always trying to control the other and restrict their free will to do as they choose as well. Co-dependents are masters of depending on other people but making them feel that they are dependent on them, normally one side may not have an incredibly good self-esteem and they just accept being a door mat. Co-exist is not about one being dominant and the other submissive, but the relationships are as equal partners, fairly give fairly take, whether intimate business or otherwise.

This goes way back to Buddhism philosophy, about the way we relate to everything, and how it is split in two parts co-exist or co-depend certain groups have borrowed this co-dependency from Buddhism and added their own twist to it, you don't need these groups to change that you just need to know how to which is what this book is directed toward, so look at the model operators to help you define in conversation if the relationship you are having with people screams co-depend or co-exist, it is for you to change for yourself if you choose to, it is not for others to tell you, you have to change while they go on doing the same things. Groups orientated around problems love those in their group and tell everyone else they must change to fit in with them, you don't, and you must fit with yourself that is what knowing yourself is about. If you have an addiction or there is something about yourself you want to change this book will show you how, for addictions one of the most powerful interventions I have come across is swish patterns. I would recommend either self-hypnosis or NLP interventions for addictions or go to a practitioner, either hypnotherapist or NLP, the reasons swish patterns tend to work better is because you change one preference for something that is not harmful but healthy, rather than just quit something and leaving a void open where it feels like your depriving yours-elf of something, You don't need to sit in groups for donkey's years and be told you can't have a relationship for a year that's not true. So, understanding language patterns can help you avoid co-dependent, manipulative relationships quickly before you find yourself neck deep in an abusive relationship.

The key to breaking addictions or getting out of abusive relationships is to have the desire and intention to do so, that's it but it must be your desire to not someone else's, most or a lot of the things you may want to change you can achieve with self-hypnosis and other techniques found in this book, if you do not feel confident enough to start with then seek a practitioner preferably someone who practices both, hypnosis and NLP. Most of this becomes quite intuitive when you understand the main keys like language patterns. So, you can use model operators as a key in identifying where you are by the language you use and then work at changing those patterns to create a life you can love and attract people who love you for who you are not what they can get from you. And look at the model operators if you are editing a hypnosis script or creating your own and avoid words that double as negatives like don't, because when these are repeated you may as well say do.

I came across a hypnosis script written by someone else that said I don't want to be a smoker eight times it takes a little more work but replace the negatives like don't with something else like I choose to be free from tobacco, or I prefer peanuts to cigarettes as a swish, it doesn't have to be peanuts but you get the general idea, when you have time try to jot down statements you make that contain model operators that are working against you and replace them with ones that work for you; make that contain model operators that are working against you and replace the whole point at looking at your own conversation and other peoples toward you is where is it directing you to, I go deeper into this in perception is projection, and it is also a part of psychic self-defence are people trying to tell you, you have to or must, when you don't are people trying to co-exist with you by allowing you to be yourself or trying to manipulate you and the decisions you make to favour them not you, this is also about taking control of your own destiny by recognising when people are using veiled statements to manipulate you whether it be veiled threats, guilt trips or promises of something they will never deliver on, you will recognise after a while just by talking or chatting online whether to hang around with them or run a mile.

Changing your language pattern will change your life and you will recognise when people are talking to you with a metaphorical mask on and what they say is not from their heart, after a bit you just start to intuitively feel you way, and everyone has this ability without exception you just have to practice a little, you can choose to follow people who will constantly tell you, you can't or are not able to or that is impossible, or you can choose to tell yourself you can and you are able to and it is possible, you always have the choice and anyone who tells you that you haven't is either lying to you manipulating you or both.

Until you recognise like me and everyone else that learned this, the power in language patterns then you are wide open to any manner of manipulation, and will not have the tools to change it, now you have the tools to change it. Put that together with goal setting creating your own big picture learning to recognise when you intuition is really trying to tell you something and you will have mastery, not of other people but yourself and your own destiny. Our linguistics our one of our most powerful tools in manifesting anything we really want, and we never have to desire or intend harm on others to have a fantastic life, whether you have a religion or not all religion points to not harming others; not taking what is someone else's, or not coveting other people's relationships, I don't follow a religion I believe in an infinite force/sprit that resides in everything, a vital life force which is often referred to as God/ It, it is neutral with only one bias toward procreation; I believe the three absolute universal laws are real, in fact I know they are and the wisdom of an it harm ye none do as thy will, in other words not to intend harm on others but we have free will to do as we choose. The harm ye none means if you cause harm deliberately i.e. premeditated you cause yourself harm. What is dubbed the law of attraction is stating what you send out you get back and what we say with linguistics is doing exactly that, the words you send out come back as manifested objects, relationships, experiences, it is also known as the law of personal return, in other words you do good then good will return, you cause harm then harm will return, understanding this is living with mindfulness of what you are doing as opposed to ignorance of what you are doing. So, knowing model operators is extremely useful for constructing your own hypnosis scripts and gaining a far better understanding of the use of linguistics and they are not just words they are doing something they are subjective and effective. The metaphor, "sticks and stones can break your bones, but words can never hurt you;" is simply wrong and scientifically proven to be wrong. When you look at the examples of language patterns you will see the sentences are predominantly driven by the model operators.

For example; you say you can't do that because it is impossible, and your right you can't do that because it is impossible, all the time you say that, or you could try to do that and know that you can achieve whatever you want to, if you want to, because you know don't you that were there is a will there is a way, and you know that if something is impossible then it has to also be possible, by virtue of everything is a half-truth. So you can believe the half that is possible can't you, and now you know you can do that, and it is possible don't you.

Can you see now how you can take yourself from self-doubt to self-esteem in one short paragraph? People fall well short of what they could achieve because of their own self talk and saying or thinking can't or impossible before even trying; so you see now how model operators are like yeast in a dough they are an active ingredient and they are doing something, when you watch the news or adverts which personally, I would avoid, look at the model operators they are using to send commands to you unconscious to go in a certain direction like buy their product or vote for them, It's a good idea to as conversation is also communicating with our own unconscious simultaneously and defining what we perceive or judge our reality to be, to take a good look at what you talk about the most, the direction your conversations go in, what are your conversations saying about yourself, because your conversations and self-talk for that matter are defining what you can and can't have, do you have to change the type of people you have conversations with to change the direction of your conversations these are thing that have to be taken into consideration, because things and events appear in people's lives and the majority of what is manifesting this is their conversation.

CHAPTER ELEVEN

HOW WE CHANGE OUR VALUES AND CHANGE OUR REALITY

Neurological levels of change, creating change (reality shifts) through the process of elicitation and applying re-framed versions which effectively cause shifts in physical reality. "Purpose, meaning, desire, intention, action" also define the way we change our reality or stay the same. Neurological levels of change. 1: Mission/purpose-refers to a larger system of which you are a part; "Who else". 2: Identity- How do you think of yourself/your personal identity "Who" 3: Beliefs-emotional held views. "Why" 4; Capability's-Skills, quality's, strategy's that we use. "How" 5: Behaviour-what you do and speak. "What" 6: Environment-Where you live and work, "Where" This is a bit like a hierarchy of parts list, in relation to how things change on a neurological, level take a look at each pat mission being the top one and environment being the bottom one; designing and defining your own big picture which will define who you are, ask yourself questions based on these six parts to achieving your big picture. What type of environment would fit best with what I want? What type of behaviour would fit best with achieving what I want?

What capability's, skills quality's or strategies would I need to achieve what I want? Why do I want to have, be or do what I want, avoid asking others "why" it attacks their sense of self however it is good to ask yourself why. Who am I what do I want to have be and do. With focus on self-development. It becomes like a mission to sort through the values, beliefs

Values and how to elicit them

Identify with now what do I want to identify with in the future? Who else who will I be likely to be co-exist with? Why do we make the decisions we make each day? The answer is around these three elicitations values, strategies, who we model off. Step 1: What is important to you now about? What else is important to you? What else is important to you? Step 2: Motivation strategy, can you remember a time when you were totally motivated in the Context of. Can you remember a specific time? As you remember that time, what was the last thing you felt just before you were totally motivated? Can you give the name of that feeling? Chunk up to get the value. Continue to repeat step 2 until you get repeat words. Step 3: Threshold Values Now look at the current list of values all these values being present, is there anything that could happen that could make you leave/stop? All these values being present, plus (the one just mentioned) what would have to happen in order to make you stay/start again? All these values being present, plus (the ones just mentioned) what would have to happen such that would make you leave/stop? Repeat step 3 until you get repeat words.

Creating the Values Hierarchy

Ask yourself of all of these values, which is the most important to you? And the next, and the next; Do it quickly so that you don't get confused or overwhelmed. If you get stuck say, assuming that you have (the values already chosen), is this or that more important to you; or assuming that you have (the values already chosen), if you couldn't have this but you could have that would that be, ok? Step 5: Rewrite the list according to their importance; Write in the way you normally would, phrase values Alignment: 1. Level of abstractions the Number 1 value the most abstract? Are all the other values a subset of the higher value? 2: Working up the list. Does the value support the actualisation of the next value? 3: Motivation Direction: Ask "Why is it important to you" Is the underlying motivation what you want or what they don't want? Look out for:

Negations, Comparative deletions, and Modal Operators of Necessity.4: Towards and Away Conflicts-Sequential Incongruity 5: Towards-Towards Conflicts- Simultaneous Incongruity 6: Away-Away Conflicts-Sequential Incongruity/Simultaneous Incongruity: Identify conflicts by asking "Are any of these values in conflict with each other". Values relate to our perception of an area being focused on, and an elicitation can give your insight and direction into your life, a way to see goals and have a hierarchy that supports not blocks your desired outcomes, can show ways of achieving things you may not have thought of before, and give you direction to achieving what you want, and produce coherence, toward your overall big picture.

Beliefs cluster around values, the beliefs and values make up the general or overall attitude toward the value being focused on; an elicitation starts to define and redefine who you are, this isn't an exercise that you do and get nothing at the end of it, this done properly will be a change maker, If you have ever read anything orientated around law of attraction, you would be familiar with the connection of beliefs and manifestation, this exercise gets you in touch with you beliefs and an better understanding of what they are and what they do; it goes through the whole process of thoughts, turn to thought form, then physical form. Also, after you will have a feeling associated to achieving something or doing something toward attaining the outcomes you want, which becomes a moving toward action; many people's actions concerning personal goals actually move them away from what they want because they haven't got a coherent hierarchy of value that supports their outcomes. This exercise is designed to create change on a level of thinking that impacts positively in physical reality. It affects a level of perception, and changing what's perceived, changes what's projected, these are the small steps to start with that get you to your big-picture desired outcome.

Values Hierarchy Elicitation

The first stage is to write down six values, Career, personal growth, spirituality, relationships, family, health. You can add as many other values as you like after. Next off, on each value you work on, write out around six to eight words or phrases that best represent that value for you, and its importance, The next part is to look at what level each one is on from one down to however many you have, if you have more than seven then select which ones you want to drop, then look at the order of impotence the others left have, now you have the first stage of the elicitation complete. Take a look at what it says as a table showing levels of importance, are there things there that look like a block, all the ones under the top on the hierarchy run subevent to the top one and the others underneath should flow up to the top one, so you're looking for the next stage to change the structure of the first one, so it flows coherently and represent a reflection of your highest intention toward the key value.

Now right up the second stage putting them in the new order of priority, and you have the elicitation finished and your list of hierarchy toward that value, it will also give you a better understanding of your overall attitude to that value. If someone said well this is great but why not just use mind's eye visualisation, or just gaze at a vision-board, well you can do those things, they tend to be more object orientated though, these exercises an others in the book, are more about changing the entire attitude/perspective toward what's being changed, which isn't just objective orientated in outcome, but can change the entire environment that reality's being experienced from.

Change happens on a level of thinking first, you create the mind-set that projects the overall attitude, towards something, for example, I have heard people in conversation, who are very wealthy and apparently happy, state they have money they can do what they want, this statement is more than that, it defines the whole attitude toward the value, money; and that definition becomes part of their environmental backdrop of their life. The difference between being focused on a way that's just object orientated, and a way that is attitude orientated is massive. Mind's eye and object visualising gets the object, the attitude that the object associates to only changes in as much as having the object, but the overall attitude is the same. Values` and the beliefs that cluster around them; values elicitation has a specific purpose in NLP. The framework of NLP is working with an individual to help that individual become more self-aware to understand behaviour and to find the true self, when we start to look at

HOW WE CHANGE OUR VALUES AND CHANGE OUR REALITY

our values the inevitable question arises is this my value or one that has been impressed on me by so called peers, am I independent self-directing, or dependent on outside for direction, am I a self, an independent unit or a part of a group of units, am I fully functional as an individual or dis-functional as an individual, it is a statistic that the majority of the human population don't operate as individual units, but operate as part of a group, my point to this really is finding balance of self and others, as opposed to having no real sense of self. Family, political, Religious, or other organisation, the need to fit in, which makes people far more compliant, rather than be different.

Society often stigmatises different, because it does not fit in with the group consensus, so what makes these elicitations so important for many people who choose to be coached by an NLP practitioner, or read NLP literature and attempt to coach themselves, is these elicitations maybe the first real attempt they have made to discover who they are, why they believe what they believe and where the beliefs come from, and in terms of values whether the values they have are after scrutiny their choice of values, whether they are resourceful or non-resourceful. Imagine a value as a small magnetic disc, a bit like one you would find in a CD, DVD, or hard drive of a computer, each value disc has beliefs associated to it, from a start point of someone deciding they want change in their lives, the only way change can happen in a persons perceived reality, is for a person's beliefs connected to those values to change in the first-place other manifested change in the persons reality is secondary to this.

The question to ask is, if I want such and such to change or have something you have not got yet what you would need to believe different for that to happen. With Values come beliefs, a belief is something that has a value to it, whether that belief is that something is true or not true, possible, or not possible, if living for eight hundred years is the value then the belief is whether that is possible or not, and a person's reality cannot extend outside of that belief unless the belief is changed. A value can be a concept, and the belief can be the perspective of the concept. So I created self-hypnosis session around this idea, instead of using clinical hypnosis for specific things I had a script of perspectives I wanted on Money, Health, Relationships, it actually started to work after a while I had money come to me completely unexpectedly and the way it came I don't think I would have scripted in a million years, so this is something I use regularly to keep in alignment and to direct myself to where I want to be, the reason I mention this is because it seems to me the idea of perspectives of concepts and beliefs around values are very alike if not identical. Values are often the anchor of sets of beliefs, so to change this we can either remove the value or change the beliefs around the value.

But it's not just this that is important on its own, it's a combination of this and whether the person has a moving toward or away from attitude, moving away from is focusing on what they don't want, and having beliefs that are fear based, moving toward is focusing on what they do want, and having beliefs that are free of fear. Just after I finished my Hypnotherapy course, I concluded something remarkably similar to what values elicitation is about. It became apparent to me that everything that relates to a modern-day reality manifest by virtue of the perspectives people have around three core concepts, Money, Relationships, and health, pretty much everything can be rooted back to the beliefs/perspectives of these three concepts.

So, if the beliefs /perspectives can be changed in relation to the concepts they are associated with then in turn the reality related to them will change. So, looking at values really is a great way to discover orientation and personal direction. It can also help people realise if the values and beliefs connected to them are actually the values they hold now of if they belong to, In terms of values elicitation for the self or clients, I think what maybe the biggest surprise for people is in general terms realising that the largest chunk of their decision making has come from peer pressure, which acts as a motivator to comply, even if it is against their will. So, part of the value in a values elicitation is to be able to identify if the values they hold are their own. Is what is important to someone motivated from Religion, Politics or Family? (Peer Groups) or are their own values genuinely their own? "To study a subject to gain approval of their peers is to give oneself an Achilles heel." To study a subject because it is something you have an interest in and want to master, is to be yourself and gradually generate an income from it, this is best done with an attitude of gradual progression, and building well-formed strategies toward the desired goals

HOW WE CHANGE OUR VALUES AND CHANGE OUR REALITY

Values Elicitation

This exercise is designed to create change on a level of thinking that will impact positively in physical reality. It affects a level of perception, and changing what's perceived, changes what is projected, the first stage is to write down six values, Career, personal growth, spirituality, relationships, family, health. You can add as many other values as you like after. Next off, on each value you work on, write out around 6-8 words or phrases that best represent that value for you, and its importance. The next part is to look at what level each one is on from one down to however many you have, if you have more than seven then select which ones you want to drop, then look at the order of impotence the others left have, now you have the first stage of the elicitation complete. Take a look at what it says as a table showing levels of impotence, are there things there that look like a block, all the ones under the top on the hierarchy run subevent to the top one and the others underneath should flow up to the top one, so you're looking for the next stage to change the structure of the first one so it flows coherently and represent a reflection of your highest intention toward the key value, Now wright up the second stage putting them in the new order of priority and you have the elicitation finished and your list of hierarchy toward that value, it will also give you a better understanding of your overall attitude to that value. If someone said well this is great but why not just use mind's eye visualisation, or just gaze at a vision-board, well you can do those things, they tend to be more object orientated though, these exercises an others in the book, are more about changing the entire attitude/perspective toward what's being changed, which isn't just objective orientated in outcome, but can change the entire environment that reality's being experienced from.

    Change happens on a level of thinking first, you create the mind-set that projects the overall attitude, towards something, for example I have heard people in conversation, who are very wealthy and apparently happy, state they have money they can do what they want, this statement is more than that, it defines the whole attitude toward the value, money; and that definition becomes part of their environmental backdrop of their life. The difference between being focused on a way that's just object orientated, and a way that is attitude orientated is massive. Mind's eye and object visualising gets the object, the attitude that the object associates to only changes in as much as having the object, but the overall attitude is the same. Strategy Elicitation There will be times when you want to discover the strategy another person is using, either to model it because it is good or to change it because it is not getting the results they want. Can you recall a time when you were totally absorbed/exited e.g.? Can you recall a specific time?

As you go back to that time now what was the very first thing that caused you to be totally---? Was it something you saw or the way someone looked at you? Was it something you heard or someone's tone of voice? Or was it the touch of someone or something? What was the very first thing that caused you to be totally---? After you saw, heard, felt that what was the very next thing that happened as you were totally-? Did you picture something in your mind? Say something to yourself, or have a certain feeling or emotion? What was the next thing that happened as you were totally---? After you list previous, did you know that you totally? Or, Something I have noted during my time working on strategy's is the link to a possibility or necessity level of thinking, and this impacts in our reality in ways many people don't realise with any conscious awareness, that this is going on, and what is going on is strategies are part vibrational and something done out of a necessity level of thought is going to return a different emotional vibration return, so we do things every day, brushing our teeth to making the first pot of tea of the day, some things we view as part of our routine, so cleaning teeth is necessary to keep healthy teeth, and it serves us to do so.

With NLP though we are looking for strategies that aren't serving the person and who maybe experiencing various levels of event's they see as problematic, what is often the problem is what is problematic is in relation to strategies running that almost create the problems by the vibratory level their emitting/traveling along. So where applicable strategies are changed to relate to possibility and overlay and override the old necessity programmed strategy. And part of what changes with this is the vibration of the whole strategy; hence forth the emotional value in return, will be

HOW WE CHANGE OUR VALUES AND CHANGE OUR REALITY

pleasing to the person as opposed to a negative emotional return. By virtue of understanding the thought level associated with Possibility and necessity, respectively. Gives us an understanding at least in part of the way attraction works, and why it works for everyone in the same way, also most people have not got conscious awareness of this, to the point it makes any difference to them. So through strategy elicitation we can find what part of the strategy isn't serving them. A strategy that is running from a necessity perspective response, will give a different emotional return than when a strategy that runs with a positive possibility perspective response, will bring a higher emotional return, more in line with what the person wants. So with that I pretty much got the concept, when you change a strategy from a necessity to a possibility, the return has to be different, and understanding this, gives us access to our own personal destinies. Having the conscious awareness of this really puts a whole different light on things.

The Doctor who had authored a book called "why do people make the decisions they make," and the answer was pretty much orientated around the day job, what they could do, and how intelligent there were seen as, was rooted to this, which means they are operating on a necessity wavelength, and the best part of their responses, are necessity. Which explains why the motivation strategy, states to only use possibility words not necessity ones. Other things I learned from this were, after a bit of practice I got the abbreviation method of writing the elicitations, the VIR's and AD's etc. all in my mind the actual elicitation felt quite easy, it also made me far more aware of what their saying in their reply's, in terms of representations, becoming behaviour, this really helped me understand better the 8 levels, lowest one is closer to necessity, and the highest one is closer to possibility. Implying three vibrational levels of thinking, which defines the emotional experience felt on return.

There is a statistic that less than 10% of the American population are financially independent, so that means that over 90% of the American population haven't got a strategy that will make them financially independent. So, a person that has sets of personal strategy that keeps then in a loop with no exit point are unlikely to experience positive changes because their decision-making strategy won't allow them, so individual personal strategies behave as a block in the same way that a conflicting belief in the unconscious mind will block a conscious belief for someone who isn't aware of this. This can fit in with the visualisation concept so someone who regularly takes some time to visualise what they want so when the object or objective, or opportunity that's in line with what they were visualising arrives they don't have to decide of whether to buy it buy into it or take the opportunity because it already fits into their criteria. So visualisation is a decision-making strategy the person is forming the criteria in the visualisation process.

A few years back I want to a business start-up seminar in London, it was set up by of the "Dragons Den," UK television programme for budding Entrepreneurs and there were some famous names giving talks, one of whom was Julia Myers. Now she said something that still strikes me as very profound, "the more dependent on Government a country is the bigger the Government, the less dependent a country is on Government the smaller the Government is." Now going back to less than 10% it may even be 5% of the population has financial independence, this really becomes food for thought when we are looking at the subject of strategies with NLP intervention. Julia Myers, strategy for setting up a business was a three-point statement.

"Think big, start small, and then move fast." my interpretation of that statement is this, think big; create the big picture, when you have the big picture, you start to have self-direction, Start small; come back to where you are in the here and now and work out what you can do no matter how small that is on the path to the big picture. Move fast; when you have the component parts in place and are working within your ability's and knowledge, then you can hit the ground running, and build up and expand as you go! When we look at films like the secret and meta-secret, what a lot of the presenters are doing is saying model off of me. And these are the strategy's if you want this that and the other. And there are also many books that offer the same thing, strategies, and a symptom of negative strategies are a shopaholic who habitually buys things without intention or purpose, after the purchase experience shopper's remorse. So a thing like this that someone does habitually behind the habit is the strategy built around the habit. Like with a phobia, you elicit the strategy around the phobia, and change it, thus removing the phobia, all perceived gains or losses come by strategy's, strategies are connected to values and beliefs, so one way to change a strategy is to change a core value or belief connected to that strategy.

Hierarchy of ideas, are the structure of a strategy, change the hierarchy and you change the strategy. Or create a hierarchy of ideas to formulate a strategy, Techniques of anchoring are orientated around Visual, Auditory, kinaesthetic and touch, anchoring hooks onto points of focus, by a Visual, Auditory, kinaesthetic, touch, action, the anchoring techniques have the potential to bring thigs into existence, through connecting associations together, anchoring chains together and stacks ideas, so they run as a set of associations, after the trigger of the strategy, is pulled, the strategy after anchoring will be the persons preferred choice of outcome rather than an unconscious impulse that they had no influence over before. The key component to a strategy is the overall vibration generated by the sequence in the strategy dictates what vibration it is sent out on and returns with the emotional respace equivalent so a statement of positive possibility will return a more desired emotional equivalent. Strategy building, looking at what vibrational level the strategy is on, takes a strategy that is in response to something and turns it into a strategy that has the appropriate vibration to it, and changes the anchor of the original strategy that works better for the person.

What's interesting about Human strategy's is the format by which they run, very similar if not the same as a block of say, PHP include codes, or Java Script the block codes all work as strategy's, blocks of strategy's that make up the whole script, so an individual strategy will have an open/start part, the content of the strategy, and the end/close part of the strategy. Anchoring is then sued to change a strategy, strategy's all contain a value/belief, so also strategy's to change beliefs/values would also create an update to the related strategy that has that value/belief attached to it. These processes give us the ability to hack into our own memory bank and change the memory of a value, belief, or strategy; these could be looked on as the primary source areas to create desired change. So effectively we create any positive change through changing memory association around what we ae going to change. The objectives of these processes are to re-remember associations, to the things we want to change. An exert from the psychic encyclopaedia appears to confirm this although the unconscious mind is referred to as sub-conscious, it means the same thing. Memory storage system the sub-conscious mind, which functions like a computer; when the sub-conscious mind is given instructions from the conscious mind as each new event happens, the subconscious stores the instructions in categories, into a "hold" file; when the future orders are given from the conscious mind for that programme to be activated, the computer surfaces that category material to be used in the new decision; the button to surface this material seems to be labelled "related activity" the conscious awake mind is not aware of this function; (john Lilly) "A dimension always infiltrating with the moments experience of the present moment is altered according to the individuals, Memory storage system. Value; Money negative/: moving away from beliefs, scarce and hard to get; Positive/moving towards beliefs; Money comes easily and frequently. Relationships: Argumentative and problematic Harmonious joyful and loving. Health: Negative moving away from beliefs, I'll, and depressed, Positive moving towards, full of energy and healthy.

Installing Strategies

A new strategy should work as quickly and as automatically as the old Strategy - There are four main ways to install strategies. Best results are achieved by using a combination of all four. 1: Anchoring - Strategies are a sequence of representations, so you can use anchors to chain one step to the next. As you fire the anchors, you want the client to rapidly go through the steps of the new strategy. You could use spatial anchors and literally move the client forward step by step as they go from one step of the strategy to the next. Then you can walk them through the completed strategy faster and faster. 2: Repetition-We learn fast when we see It Is In our Interest to do so and a new strategy is a powerful way of becoming more effective. But it still helps to take the client through the new strategy several times until you are certain that it will run automatically, and the client will not have to think consciously which step to do next. 3: Mental rehearsal - Future pace the client through the new strategy and have they mentally rehearsed it at least three times. 4: Metaphor-give a metaphor that takes the client through the strategy: You want the metaphor to illustrate the strategy and to be interesting so that the client associates into the story, metaphor can be the morals to the story or a statement with underlying meaning, it has surface and deeper meaning and purpose, down the rabbit hole.

Anchoring Techniques

Anchoring beliefs and the process of anchoring beliefs, when we look at a child from birth to six a child in this imprint stage is in a lower brain wave state associated to delta, hypnosis, so the child is essentially downloading all the information received through the senses and builds in those 6 years a database of information, so everyone's early belief system is formed in this way, these become the internal representations and the basis of their world view. Creating beliefs after this period which is known as the modelling period seven to fourteen happens the through repetition as the child's consciousness speed up to a beta state, full consciousness. These are the two ways beliefs are downloaded into subconscious mind, knowing this as a scientific fact gives us clear resources for creating and downloading new beliefs from conscious choice, and takes us out of the by luck or chance mentality.

This gives us the mentality of being able to create, co-create our own path through following a process or set of processes which will impact in a specific way with absolute certainty. The problem with a lot of people when it comes to changing beliefs is that they have been with them for a long time and have a lot of time energy and even money invested in those beliefs, so often people will initially resist the idea of changing beliefs because the old beliefs are still at the top of the hierarchy list for that subject with those beliefs associated to it. Again, the two ways we download new information is hypnosis and repetition, beer in mind when your comfy on your sofa watching television after about ten to twenty minutes your relaxed and in around theta state which is hypnosis and more susceptible to downloading information unchecked, obviously the advertisers are aware of this, "are you though." The process of anchoring is something we experience every day but most are unaware of it, main anchor techniques are, with practitioner touch anchors self-anchoring by stepping in and out of disks paper or visualized, and tapping which can be done by yourself or with a practitioner, Re-modelling, seeking different mentors, Steps to re-modelling.1: Identify dominant personality types, people past or present that have or are influencing you in some way, maybe from the imprint period or all of the growing up periods. (More information on dominant personality's in hypnosis chapter). 2: Identify which values, beliefs, strategies, work for you and which ones work like blocks, hex's, curses. 3: Look at previous directions past peers may have set you on, is they in line or out of sync with what you want. 4: write a list of things you actually want, start with environment then, behaviour, capabilities, beliefs/values, self/identity; Mission/ purpose; who else. 5: Who and what are influencing your values and beliefs on a daily basis, again write out a list 6: Now take your lists and split them to positive and negative, you should see where you need to balance and let go of that which keeps you focused negatively and switch to positive focus, it's the art of changing states of thought

Modelling project

My advice before you start looking at who to model off is look for people whose earnings are above that which is known as financial independence and if possible, have ten to twenty years wisdom or experience in their field financial independence is approximately £70,000 per year, even better is above that and not in the salary waged sector more about generating an income from their own efforts. A good question to ask yourself is what I would like, what skillsets can I master to do that which would give me financial independence, which is a big step toward self-sufficiency which is more co-exist than co-depend. Try to focus on more creative than competitive. Modelling is an unbelievably valuable tool in helping you master techniques and various other things by modelling from excellence. Find a person, who is excellent at something you also want to be excellent at, I can tell you one of the things required is dedication to achieve your desired outcomes, Milton Ericson said it takes in linier terms fifteen thousand hours to become a master at anything! So if being a master at something is part of your path then yes you can use self-hypnosis and visualisation to subjectively create an alignment, but you still have to roll your sleeves up and put some hours in as well.

Wealth is not just about having money, it's about having resources or product that benefits others in some way, doing something or a group of things you love to do and are interested and enthusiastic in, look for different areas to have modelling projects on, ones that represent wealth ones that represent Health, ones that represent Relationships would be a good start point as any.

And with wealth before you commit to any modelling project, try to think outside of the salary waged income think more income from your own efforts. The process of modelling from someone.1: Find someone or someone's behaviour that is worth modelling. Find a model of real excellence. 2. Find their: Beliefs and Values Strategy (Mental Syntax) Physiology, 3. Install this in yourself. Step 1: What do I want who is excellent at it how are they excellent at it how can I replicate that excellence. Step2: Elicit their beliefs, values, strategies, The Modelling Process. Key Elements in Modelling: 1: Physiology; Key is breathing, then posture. 2: Filter Patterns (Including Meta programs, Values)-Provide the emotional energy. 3: Strategies; elicit other points.1: Modelling is separating what is essential from what is idiosyncratic. 2: In modelling, you may have to chunk a large behaviour down into the Individual functions. 3.Then feedback. Where they are getting feedback from, and what the mechanisms are, and the adjustments, two ways to do modelling. 1: Imitation: A. do it then model self to see how you did it. B. Essential to all modelling is to separate what is essential from idiosyncratic the difference that is effective. C. Then consciously start dropping pieces to find what's essential. 2: Cognitive Approach: a. Analyse into components, b. Physiology c. Strategies d. Motivation e. Contrastive Analysis-separate what is essential from idiosyncratic— the difference that is effective. Then consciously start dropping pieces to find what's essential; f. Sensitivity Analysis— Determine what's critical. Start changing things to find out if they make any difference. Find out if it is effective in terms of results. Strategies.

CHAPTER TWELVE

CHUNKING UP, CHUNKING DOWN, CHUNKING ACCORSS

Chunked Up/Big picture thinking, chunked down, fine detail thinking, Chucked Across, Lateral thinking. The orientation of "Self-Motivation": In terms of gender scientifically speaking through various experiments that have been carried out in this area, males are naturally in general more chunked up/big picture, and Females are generally more chunked down/fine detail, that is generally speaking, however the bias is significant, it certainly doesn't mean that men can't chunk down and women can't chunk up, this chapter is about using both techniques to generate self-motivation and to avoid being overwhelmed. A quick tip before we get into this is if you find yourself feeling overwhelmed by things at any time, switch over so if you feel overwhelmed and your very big picture then chunk down, and if you feel overwhelmed at any time and your very fine detail then chunk up, success comes from a balance of chunking up and chunking down; you won't get success in anything if your just one or the other. A simple explanation is chunked up is, big picture, purpose, outcome; Chunked down is, fine detail, specifics, and parts; Chunked across is, counter example, lateral thinking, is there a different way of thinking or a different example of the same thing. Think of a jigsaw, the box has the completed picture printed on it, inside are all the parts to put it together, there's not necessarily a right or wrong way to put the pieces together, you can start in the middle or on the

CHUNKING UP, CHUNKING DOWN, CHUNKING ACCORSS

corners whatever way you like, in life we do or don't achieve things by virtue of thinking all big picture and no fine detail, or all fine detail and no big picture, or achieve many things by big picture and fine detail; like a jigsaw you see the big picture and then you put the parts together to have the jigsaw version of the big picture.

The way I worked with this and the way I would define this in applying it to life is, when you have thought through all the things you want your life to be, the house, the car, the relationships, come back to the here and now what your perceived reality actually is now, and decide on the smallest things you can do the smallest actions you can take that act as moving toward your big picture, it may be signing up for a course or actually sitting down and writing that book, whatever it is start from there, the lifestyle of your dreams. Or you can just sit in front of the television all day complaining about everything and everybody, it's your choice after all, you don't have to have the lifestyle of your dreams you can just, daydream never take an action and jolly well stay where you are; would you like to still be where you are now five to ten years from now, or living your dream lifestyle, if you want your dream lifestyle then yes daydreaming what that would be like and what it would include is part of it, but it will stay just a daydream unless you put a moving toward strategy in place. Initiative-taking; Possibility; Goal setting, moving toward big picture, (action toward) creative, achieving happiness, Love, compassion, hope. De-motivated; necessity moving away from big picture, or no big pictures at all, competitive, anger, fear, resentment, jealousy.

You could view chunked up as corresponding to subjective and chunked down as corresponding to objective; Motivation requires motion/action of some sort, here are some esoteric definitions that correspond to what this chapter is about. Motion the action of a body or system shifting one position to another, completely related; (esoteric) energy patterns in the Universe; common denominator between the planets and sound involving repetitive movement or cycles; caused by resonance in the Universe and it's transference; uses principle of attraction and repulsion and a result of the law of vibration." Esoteric: "within, withheld, fuzzy, not clear" pertains to inner or subjective information, as opposed to objective information; pertains to information and knowledge that can be intellectualized, but will not be accepted by the individual unless they feel comfortable and compatible with it when the belief system is ready for its incorporation; pertains to information and knowledge that is better understood by the feeling nature than the intellect.

Cannot necessarily be proven by scientific means, but its value is not discredited for this reason. Esoteric; also refers to subjects that are of etheric world intelligences, corresponds to subjective information held in each person's value and belief systems, and points to having to have a mind-set that matches the desired reality, not just having what is desired, but having the beliefs and coping system in place to support it, prior to manifesting the desire physically. Fuzzy not clear, can be turned to clear and coherent, many of the most successful happiest people in the world had no idea how they would achieve their goals, (fuzzy, not clear), they just knew they would, or desired it enough to take actions toward achieving their desired goals. Richard Bandler described NLP as" the study of the structure of subjective experience;" as an attitude of curiosity, a methodology that leaves behind it a trail of techniques. It has also been described as the modelling of excellence, essentially it is how we know what we know. So we'll start off with applying pre-suppositions subjectively, creating a cause that manifests a physical actuality, response/effect, we actually do this every day without realising it anyway, so what we are doing is swapping awareness to, we can do things subjectively that then support doing those things physically, believe it or not you do this daily in your conversations throughout the day, your life as is now in this moment is already coming from your mind over matter, and effects matters in your life. Think of being in conversation with someone, then look at all the words you are using as you are describing your perspective of your reality in the here and now and are systematically at the same time mirroring back more of the same perspective being projected in the conversation, when we're talking to other people or talking to ourselves, we are projecting our self-perspective of our actuality.

When you start to look at what you're saying, you start to see what reality you're pre-supposing, and that can be changed, which means you now have access to being able to change your own reality with pre-supposed linguistics, if you want to buy a house outright without getting a mortgage, then pre-suppose it subjectively first. You can't have something physically if you haven't already got it subjectively, our reality is what our unconscious mind holds as our beliefs and values, habits, and strategy's, what we experience in the moment is actuality, when we are talking or thinking we are doing so in the here and now moment not ten minutes before or after but in the actual moment. Opinions, preferences, Feelings, can be created subjectively.

When where in conversation with others or yourself, you give out abstract commands to the unconscious to manifest the implication of the abstracted statement, and these manifest thousands of times faster than repeating an affirmation consciously. Because that command already fits in with your values and beliefs at that time and because the statement defines your self- perspective of your reality, so the way to change realty is to change the abstracted statements being sent to unconscious mind which then run, effectively as command statements, so things for you to keep an eye on are your values, beliefs, habit's and strategy's, when you start to change these subjectively then you start to change who you are as a person and what your lifestyle is.

The thing is when unconscious gets a specific or vaguely specific command what manifests is by virtue of the principle of history repeats itself, so the command statement is repeated daily, it will repeat itself and effectively manifest; it doesn't wipe out the old belief or value as such but because it's being focussed on repeatedly as opposed to the old value or belief it then becomes top of the hierarchy and is the belief that unconscious mind will send back to conscious mind as true. Say for example someone was talking with someone else, and they are pretty much finding things to complain about, the statements they are using to describe this contain abstracted commands to the unconscious mind to repeat the perspective they just described; I'm going to go into more detail on this because when you get this, then you have a real tool to change, mind's eye visualisation that you all know about is part of this, there are other component parts though and this is a big one of those parts. So the reality being projected with linguistics is the reality being repeated, this is why so many people's lives run almost like their on a loop, and it happens through day to day conversations, and self-talk, and because it fits with current beliefs and values it runs automatically, so if you earn say 30,000 a year, and you tell yourself and others that and that is what your earning are, then earning 500,000 a year will be impossible for you because, which one is in with your current belief, so if you want to earn 500,000 a year then you have to find ways to change you beliefs and what you do to start to make that a reality.

It doesn't all just happen through mind's eye visualisation; you need to create a belief and values system that supports that; and create strategy's that support you moving toward that big picture. So you chunk up what you want that is different to what you have now, then create a subjective perspective to support bringing that into reality, there is work involved in this, there is also work involved in staying in the life, lifestyle or job you want to change, so you can work hard to stay the same or work hard to change your reality, but as you change your reality it changes from hard to easier.

Which brings me to the self-hypnosis part of the programme, the abstracted commands that run in conversation can be reciprocated in hypnosis as suggestion, which runs as a presupposition of already having, or having experienced, the way I put hypnosis scripts together is using this method, I've perfected over the years which is effectively a virtual conversation, that includes abstracted commands, the other thing with conversation and what's being projected, is there a repeated perspective of their reality.

With this self-hypnosis programme you repeat the sessions using the same presuppositions on a daily basis, effectively repeat until manifested, it will manifest because they will become the presuppositions focused on, our reality is in essence pre-supposed. Something else I discovered on the way, is that everything we focus on at any one time is orientated around three core concepts Which are Health, Wealth, Relationships, being happy or not happy is really a kinaesthetic spin off from our perspectives around these three concepts, and our day-to-day pre-suppositions all presume our state, in terms of health, wealth, relationships, which creates the outcome of having those things and experiences in the way we have them. So things to consider with pre-suppositions, vaguely specific pre-suppositions are enormously powerful because, they abstractly include the

CHUNKING UP, CHUNKING DOWN, CHUNKING ACCORSS

specifics, without defining how it is possible, just that it is possible, that's enough to at the very least start to create real change.

So to start to be self-directing you can create your big picture of the outcomes you want, possessions, lifestyle etc. and when your creating this think having, not how, from that you create the pre-suppositions of have those things, then come back to the here and now and think what thing or things can I do that will direct me toward the big picture not away from, this creates action in line with and supported by subjective pre-supposition, if you are doing things that you are genuinely interested and enthusiastic in then that acts as a kind of turbo booster, in fact I would suggest actively focusing on what you're interested in and enthusiastic about, because that is also influencing your direction/path. Imagine everyday twenty-four hours a day you can do whatever you want to, what would you fill that twenty-four-hour space with? Imagine you are stood on a barren landscape, what would you fill the landscape with? Maybe answering those questions may help you build your big picture. Another good tool when deciding your big picture is right out your values, for example if independence is a value, then look at what kind of values best support being independent, working from home may be better than working in a cooperation, if you want more independence, creating a company offers more independence than working for a company. If you're in a day job and want out of the day job what you can replace it with, what would you do instead of the day job? Many people have time on their hands and their board stupid, so you don't want to be bored, you want to be doing things you enjoy and that in some way benefit or add value to others as well as yourself.

So when people say to you stop dreaming or that's a pipe dream come back to reality, reality is only reality for as long as you accept it being that way and it can be changed, scientists didn't put a rover on mars by accepting it would be impossible they did it by finding a way to do it by using their imagination and making it possible and actual. You will not manifest a dream if you can't imagine it being possible first, and you will not manifest a dream if you don't dream it first, dream in this instance means using your imagination, projecting into the future of what you want your future to be. If I had not have used my imagination and dreamed what I wanted my future to be I would still be a chef in a care home, I would not have become a hypnotherapist, NLP master or coach and I would not have authored this book!

Even if you only do a little bit each day or each week toward your dream with gradual progression and then doing a bit more and a bit more you will get there; but you won't if you don't even try. You can buy a bottle of hair dye, to change the colour of your hair; but your hair colour won't change if you don't apply the dye to the hair. Accept that you won't make millions just by reading this book; you have to apply what its saying, you won't make millions just by visualisation or vision boards alone, you won't make million in a month, but that doesn't mean you won't make millions; that comes by following a path to your big picture. But I can assure you when you create good self-hypnosis scripts for yourself, look at what the words are actually doing and what direction there taking you in and visualise, your life will become your big picture, yes you have to chunk down from time to time and do the mundane nitty gritty for a bit, but now you can do it knowing that you are in the process of transforming your life to what "you" want. When you have concluded what you're going for, you can use things like vision boards, the best way to use them is to have pictures that create a visual representation of what you want so you have a visual association to the type o house for example, then leave the vision board and focus on the pre-supposition of "having" or in the process of becoming, in self-hypnosis not the how's or what the process will be, just in the process of becoming, or having, trust unconscious mind to do the rest: it's very smart. Just focus on the vision board for long enough each day that you can close your eyes and visually recall the image at will, you don't have to stare at it for weeks on end. We are in effect creating internal representations and associations, internal representations project as behaviour and behaviour is in part defined by your representation of daily life, and the way you react or respond to them; The point is what we associate to the most, is what we experience the most of.

When you start to insert chosen representations then this is effectively what's called a reality shift, which can happen for one when a new belief replaces an old belief then reality shifts in accordance with the change in belief, for example if you believed that something was not possible then you decide it is possible these cause reality shifts in allowing something in that was first believed not possible, the change in belief then opens up to it being possible often inspired ideas come when this happens, reality is shifting all the time for most people though it is un-noticed because nothing significant is changing in what their perspective of what their reality is, reality shifts are generally only noticed if a significant good change occurs, in general these happen when we change a perspective, belief or value.

Hypnosis is a tool/resource that is the initial action for creating reality shits, If you spend any time studying the way unconscious mind learns it's through repetition, you didn't get on a bike and pedal off on the first attempt, it took repetition before it became habitual, the same goes for installing pre-supposition's, which are also known as in NLP, as mind hacks, similar to adding blocks of computer code to a programme which in some way changes the way the software runs, so what you are doing in effect with this pre-supposition work is updating the hard drive which is the unconscious, so that the programme which is your reality is in some way changed. If all that makes scene, then you as good as there in terms of having some understanding of what makes things manifest, although there are still a few component parts to add on as we go through this programme, basically we know as manifestation is caused and it's caused by amongst other things linguistics, audio, which is part of NLP, visual, audio, kinaesthetic, kinaesthetic being the emotional return, elated, happy, etc.

We have as I see it visual mind's eye and audio mind's eye, I prefer audio because it can create the images and if you do a little vision board work then you have the visual memory anyway, the other plus side of doing this through self-hypnosis is it's easier day by day to keep the focus on what's being repeated without drifting off track of the visualisations intention, purpose and outcome. It can be hard to keep a mind's eye visually exactly the same each time, it can be done it takes practice and disciple though. Hypnosis is in a lot of ways like meditation; its purpose primarily is to enter an altered state of consciousness, or absorption to the point of an altered state being experienced. There is a reason for this which is to reduce conscious (critical mind) obstructing the suggestions, having enough time in a meditate state to let go of the daily grind, is generally enough to be relaxed and open to suggestion, which is the point of an induction in hypnosis to reach that state, where the critical mind has checked out so to speak, we then have a conscious type of sleep. when we are properly asleep, we are in the unconscious realm, so this is also representative of being in the unconscious realm, or at least communicating with it in a language it understands and will process as we expect and want it to, which is as a command statement which becomes habituated to loop continually, unless changed again in some way.

The way we have manifested before getting an understanding of what causes manifestation, this was probably largely from outside influences rather than self-influences, there is a reason why company's spend millions on advertising, especially television adverts, they can portray visual, audio, and kinaesthetic, it generates familiarity to the product making it more likely that you would buy that one over a lesser known brand, when the pre-supposition's are repeated they create also familiarity with what's being supposed making it more likely that will manifest over any other because the focus has been habitually held or a period every day, in doing this we are drawing in not pushing away, many things people do and say are actually pushing away what they want not drawing it in, they behave/act in a way that is chasing the money, which pushes it further away! There's a metaphor that sums this up; if the horse makes a bolt for it if you chase it will run further away if you leave it, be it will come back on its own accord.

Create a mind-set of drawing in not pushing away; this also takes a bit of patience, it's well worth it though; this also comes up in NLP moving toward or away from which is also connected to the reptile minds, fight or flight, reptile mind moves toward pleasure and away from pain, when you master understanding that, it really does open doors, an example of this is, how many people do you know that go on diets and end up back at square one, look at the phrase they use lose or loss of weight. So why they are consciously with all their will which makes it even harder they try to lose weight, reptile mind however is moving away from loss, if the phrase they use was gain a slimmer body, then life and the diet would be easier and more likely to succeed. The way something is worded can just in the wording be the deciding factor of success or failure; linguistics is the most powerful and pervasive tool we have, and when we understand it gives us the key to our own destiny, our destiny is then controlled for the best part by the inside/self-opinion, not the outside opinion. We become more self-validating rather than more dependent of outside opinion of us, outside opinion only has a say if we accept it, if someone says I like your black T-shirt, and you have a white one on, you're not going to be bothered by their opinion because you know the T-shirts white. So you don't accept what they say, outside opinion can be very useful, for the large part though it is not, and it is not relevant to your life or who you are.

If your modelling from someone or being mentored by someone their opinion will be very useful, it's the difference between choosing what's relevant to you, rather than just accept what isn't relevant or being directed in a way that is not you choice to go with, you start to see if you're not influencing yourself then something, or someone else is, you only have to study social science a bit to see that, the structured system is designed to keep you where you are, it's up to the individual to educate themselves in ways to get out of that system of thinking, it's probably not going to be taught in the school curriculum any time soon, so if you don't like what your being taught or were taught, then self-education is the way forward.

Which is what this book is about, "self-actualisation", only let your life be influenced by what you want it to be influenced by, by doing that you automatically repel what you don't want it to be influenced by; the opposite of what you draw in is what you repel or keep out, most people are operating in a way that keeps out what they do want, and draws in what they don't want, when I say most I mean probably 90% of the Human population, they do everything outwardly inward, instead of inwardly outward. They focus almost entirely on physical objectives and get bogged down in small detail, with no conscious awareness of non-physical, "subjective imagination work" being a causation of what their trying to get. Hypnosis, pre-suppositions are imagination work and are an action of conscious awareness, toward the intended outcome or desire moving toward/drawing in, also looking at your intentions and actions and assessing if there a match or mismatch, as I go through the book I'll get a bit deeper into NLP, mismatch is often something people neglect to consider, it is in part about the thought level a person is predominantly on, it's also about intention and action, thoughts in line or out of line with, you want to live in the country for example, you have always lived in a big city so strait off is your mind-set in alignment with living in the country the answer is no, so you work on ways to bring your mind-set in line with living in the country, then you have the mind-set that will support the outcome of living in the country, you could start with a list, of what you think living in the country would be like, find mentors people that live in the country, what would you do differently when you live in the country, this also builds a coping system for living in the country, this also builds a coping system for living in the country as well as ideas for pre-suppositions of living in the country.

The hypnosis sessions with pre-suppositions are designed, generate a mind-set of having, if you listen to any millionaire mentors, they pretty much all say if you want to be rich then you have to have the mind-set first of being rich, reading or listening to people who are already wealthy gives you an idea of what mind-set a millionaire actually has, most people have a mind-set of get a mortgage to own a house, a millionaire would probably have a mind-set of buy a house outright with their debit card, I you really want wealth then study wealthy people, use their biography's as mentors, understanding what's going on with mind-set is an important part of being able to manifest desires, in NLP this is known as modelling, when we're growing up from seven to fourteen, it is known as the modelling period, when we seek out role models/mentors, heroes. Mind-set, what is it?

A Culmination of perspectives on all areas of your life, on the way you relate to specific areas of your life, it contains beliefs that may support or limit you, beliefs can be changed at an unconscious level, what causes your realty is what your mind-set says your reality is, your realty is a projection of what you believe and value, your perspective of what your life is to you, these can be changed, so if your reading this and stuck in a rut, it can all be changed, the first course of action is your own mind-set, to take ownership of your destiny you have to first take ownership of your destiny. What your mid-set is at any one time is what your life experiences are manifesting from, if you were like most others fed negative opinions of money, then you probably haven't got much and will be unlikely to get any more than you have up until now, and it's almost entirely down to mind-set. what is held in mind-set is what is supporting your reality, if it's not in your reality then you have not got the mind-set supporting it, anchoring it into your daily life; and because the thing you don't want are in your daily life, that's why they don't wants, come up more often than not, because the mind-set supports them.

The way to change this is to overlay these unwanted perspectives with new ones; the old one's state having what is unwanted; the new one's state having what is wanted. You may have a belief that money is hard to come by, you literally switch it to, money comes easily and with lest effort, just that one thing starts to change your mind-set on money, some people would just repeat this consciously as an affirmation, they do it consciously, so conscious critical mind will challenge it, in hypnosis the conscious mind is held in temporary suspension, then the suggestions get strait through to the unconscious, faster, there are less filters for it to pass through. To briefly explain this, from when where children we are constantly open to suggestion, at that age though most of the suggestion gets through,, so we end up with a pile of beliefs which have been installed in us, and which may or may not benefit us, the suggestions most of us got about money and many other things become like blocks to having those things, I someone has a belief that money is in some way bad, and only bad people have money, the unconscious mind will do things to ensure you have little or no money because it's protecting you from money which is bad, right?

I am going through this in this way so that rather than just say do this and say that, you can understand the reasoning and processes that are going on between conscious and unconscious mind, in some ways this is like sitting at a blank canvas and creating your model of the world from you chosen perspective, one thing to remember is that everything we believe comes from suggestion, a child see's it's parents arguing over money, this suggests to the child that money causes arguments and makes them sad, we are getting suggestions constantly, visually and through audio listening, so if all we believe comes from suggestions, we can then unbelieve something and replace it with suggestion, with a something else. With pre-suppositions in hypnosis we can change these core beliefs around the three core concepts, when you think that we our shaping our lives each day by what we talk about to others, then it stands to reason we can shape our lives also by what we talk about daily in hypnosis, so my suggestion is to use self-hypnosis daily, the same as some people meditate daily only this form of meditation changes the mind-set, by changing beliefs, values and perspectives being projected.

And in knowing and doing this we are no longer left open and helpless against being stupefied by outside influence and suggestion, which has up to now for most of you the way most of your reality has been shaped from, so when you look at what reality is, well, it's generated by suggestion, suggestions from internal representations, which impacts positively or negatively on our behaviour, the suggestions were going to create with pre-supposing, change the internal representations of our reality, and change our realty in accordance with the representations. Limiting beliefs, the beliefs you don't know you have are holding most people back, statements and metaphors that we are told from a young age, repeated so they become beliefs that influence us often against what we are trying to will in, the reality we have; outside observations of who we are, have overridden our self-belief of who we are, and are self-beliefs become the outside beliefs.

We are then effectively running like a programmed robot, being programmed from the outside, you can however do that same programming for yourself on yourself and stop being like robots. Robot actually means slave, and we are, slaves to our mind-set we cannot do what the mind-set says we cannot so we have to start adding a few can do's to the equation , as I said earlier manifestation isn't just about mind's eye visualisation, there are other components and what the mind-set is, is what you need to think about before you think about what you're going to manifest your life as, like attracts like, like mindedness, this is about making your mind-set liken to your desires and goals the mind-set is the support network of physical experiences, how many of you knew you had a support network that's invisible, and part of who you are as a person, the inner self! When you work with the inside you change the outside, form the environment you live into the cloths you wear, so you have twenty-four hours of space a day to play with, the simple question is what are you going to fill it with? Out with the old in with the new, somewhere along the line most of humanity lost track of how to effectively communicate instructions to the unconscious part of our mind, there is communication going on but for the most part is being blissfully unchecked, our body is like a car with our mind driving it, imagine buying a brand new Rolls Royce and someone else gets in without you consent and starts driving it, you'd be pissed off wouldn't you, that's probably where most people are at, someone else is driving their Rolls, though wonder most people, look pissed off most of the time.

Changing mind-set, self-hypnosis induction induces the optimum state you want to be in, which is being open to suggestion, remember being open to suggestions when we were young when our critical mind wasn't fully developed, is where most of your reality is being driven from at this point, so the object of self-hypnosis is to be like a child soaking up the suggestions without critical mind being involved, in terms of inductions which I'll start going go into a bit deeper, rapid or progressive inductions work perfectly as recordings you can play back each day, Imaging your mind set like a library, crammed with books and all those books hold perspectives of your life, which are formed by statements that imply pre-supposition's of having or not having, (positive-negative possibility's,) problem is unconscious mind doesn't process negatives, unconscious minds highest intention is only positive outcomes for the self, although that may not be apparent for most people when they look at where they are in life; statements of complaining about how bad things are, actually end up being a pre-supposition that the complaint is a preference, a desired outcome, which is generally speaking is the way most people are manifesting their reality/destiny.

The idea that we are literally talking our physical reality in may come as a bit of a surprise, even shock to some, that is the way it is though, if it still doesn't make sense or seems a bit foggy it will become clear by the time you reach the end of the book, there's really no need for a magic wand, you just need a better understanding of linguistics and the way your silent partner (unconscious mind) is processing those linguistics; this is essentially why hypnosis and NLP work, the pure definition of manifestation is Suggestion; this is why politicians use propaganda and advertisers spend billions of pounds on adverts, when people read newspapers or watch television they generally become absorbed in what their reading or watching, they are effectively in a state known as being open to suggestion when you watch television or are reading papers indoors, your generally on the sofa in a relaxed state and this leaves the viewer wide open to the pre-suppositions being suggested.

Very few people are actively creating their own pre-suppositions internally in comparison to the amount of outside pre-suppositions they are being bombarded with every day, which are effectively like being under a constant "psychic attack." Most people's beliefs and values are being moulded from outside, so it's really time to take control of your destiny and create beliefs and values from the inside which over-ride outside opinion by focusing on your own opinion, and really having a good look at what your own opinions, beliefs and values actually are, and whether they belong to you or belong to someone else. These are dominant personalities you may not even know you have they may be beliefs, values installed by parents, teachers, friends, (peer pressure) which you have been conditioned to comply to, that may or may not benefit you, obviously some of the things do benefit you and some don't, negative beliefs of money, i.e. People who have money are bad, or the love of money is the root of all evil, these beliefs will keep you poor forever, there are of course bad people out there not all people who have money are bad though, far from it, most have worked as hard as anyone else to build a business to make money, there are two types of making money, the ones who rip people off, take from others without adding value to their lives, and ones who make their money by adding value to people's lives, this book is about adding value to your-self and others who purchase the service or product their paying for.

If you have ever read Wallace Wattle's, The Science of Getting Rich he defines this very well and I would suggest reading it, it's a little dated well worth the read though, apparently this book inspired Rhonda Byrne to produce the secret, the only problem with the film is everything presented is true, but it doesn't go in depth enough in telling you how to apply it, it does do a good job of directing people to look at what the law of attraction actually is and implies that the more you study and research this subject the more you will find, it faced some criticism because of people's expectations, most thought that after viewing it they would be millionaires within a month, it's not quite that simple and there are a fair few component parts to get, before the pieces in the puzzle all fit together, so why I put this programme together is because I'm a certified Hypnotherapist and NLP Master practitioner. I know all the component parts and the way I present this to you is so you can become a millionaire or have amazing relationships and good health, by following a structured how to, rather than just being told that it is possible to but I would advise not having an expectation that you will have all this in a month but with gradual progression some patience and being prepared to do some work on yourself.

You most certainly can and will attain those things you desire most, remember a lot of limiting beliefs you may have that are acting as blocks have been there a long time they can be switched to the beliefs you want to have, it will take probably more than a month though, you can visualise having something, however if the beliefs don't match up/align then it's little more than a day dream, your paradigms have to match up, I came across a comment made by Bob Proctor, he said he had a lot of correspondence from people who said they had followed what was said in the Secret and nothing happened, his answer was the same, it's because your paradigms/belief system doesn't yet support the outcomes they are trying to achieve.

The Law of Attraction is the description of the complete cycle of thought to manifestation through Cause and Effect, So this strategy starts out with re-setting paradigms/belief systems, and creating a mind-set that is supportive not disruptive; using self-hypnosis is probably without doubt the best place to start from, alongside a good understanding of Universal principles/Laws; whether you are religious or atheist you need to understand the implications of these principles, otherwise it's going to be like trying to get the bulls eye with a dart with a blindfold on. The first law of Mentalism ;Mind is Universe equals Universe is mind "which is an absolute", means everything in the Universe has some form of intelligence, i.e. a stone can't talk but it knows what it is; Its atoms contain information which means it has, no matter how small a degree of knowledge, we live in an atomic electro-magnetic, holographic Universe, which produces the effect of like attracts like; An act object or event begins with a mental impression of suggestion in the mind, impregnated with Emotions until exteriorised. Pre-suppositions are anchored to this law. Objective: Chunked down finer detail. In general, most people tend to be Object/Objective orientated with a scarcity mind-set, so focused on finer detail they "can't see the woods for the trees."

A good general description in terms of their motivation, is a mortgage that has to be paid, by the day job, but when the day job stops the money stops, is pretty much where most people are at. Most people aren't conditioned to think about creating a passive income, they just chase the active income which for the best part leaves people on a kind of treadmill; chasing active ways to get money with almost no subjective connection just entirely asleep of in beta state of consciousness. Effectively chasing the money away as quick as they get it, they are in a perpetual state of moving towards don't wants and away from do want's; this is the more severe end of objective scarcity mind-set, which makes it harder to have self-direction and self-motivation. Triggers and sub-modalities: Emotion, Repressed emotion, Integrated parts.

The Key to life (June Bletzer) To "balance" with emotional stress every day, whether the stress is good or bad: 1. To have the correct attitude toward each experience that life presents, resolving any unpleasant experience as it happens; to handle all personal emotions (pleasant or unpleasant) comfortably, intelligently, and satisfactorily in accord with one's belief system to put each undesirable, subordinate or traumatic experience in its proper perspective, integrating it into the whole, as opposed to putting it to one side without attitudinally resolving it; unresolved emotions aren't put " aside" as supposed but rather they go inside the body to turn up later as a disease or chaotic life situation: It is just as important not to repress experiences that are painful, as it is not to dwell on the activity with resentment, jealousy, condemnation or pity: "Esoteric Principle of attitude." nothing in the world can hurt a person, no death of a loved one, no accident, no environmental catastrophe, no loss of job or marriage; it is only the attitude one takes toward the experiences that hurts the person. 2 Attitudinal healing-to help one understand the reason for life and change in attitude toward the emotional aspects of life to alter one's body chemistry; this gives the body cells an opportunity to normalise and heal themselves; one's attitude towards ones-self, lifestyle and sickness has a great influence on one's state of health; the more informed one is regarding attitude and how to balance with them, the more normal state of health one manifests. Emotion; influenced by values and beliefs. The kinaesthetic plus or minus that accompanies thoughts, intentions actions, responses, or reactions: this is the way things mirror back, or personal returns.

The Mind over Matter Key

Mind over matter-1: Metaphysical doctrine; Human beings live in a mental world and everything in it is made and held together by their thoughts and emotions; Humans co-create life forms, inanimate objects, atmospheric conditions, their bodies and the earth proper, the invisible electrical impulses that emanate endlessly from their heads direct the course of the cosmic atoms; these impulses are influenced by peoples daytime thinking, speaking, reading, Inner dialogue and their dreams and sleep thinking, bringing about a three dimensional manifestation; he or she can deliberately co-create whatever one desires to manifest by using, "Visualisations, affirmations, hypnotherapy, NLP, and disciplined thinking." Swish patterns: Acceptance, avoidance, In the beginning of the evolution of Human mind we have what has been dubbed a reptile mind, Which in survival mode is where the instinctual fight or flight comes from, out of survival mode we are at acceptance or avoidance, being orientated toward acceptance or avoidance, an example of this is, take a man who has all he desires, health, wealth, fantastic relationships, they are clearly more orientated towards accepting their life because it contains all they desire, as opposed to a man who has nothing no ambition, no big picture nothing, they're going to be more orientated towards avoiding the reality as they see their reality as being. So, our motivations and consequent actions are influenced directly through which way your orientated, which effectively means the more you, can create being in a state of acceptance over avoidance then your well on the way to self-mastery and creating your own destiny, consciously with awareness.

We are either in Survival mode, thrive mode or a degree in between, in NLP these are known as levels of thinking which range from one to eight, the vast majority of the population are operating from one to four, the percentage gets smaller the higher up you go; I will go in depth on the levels of thinking later, these levels of thought are driving the emotional state and emotional state is present in everything good or bad, so if it's part of everything that makes up our life then it's worth taking a look at. Our emotional state is a by-product of the outcomes being caused in our reality, happy or sad are defined by what outcomes we are responding to at any one time, how much of what you do on a daily basis is motivated by avoidance? How much of how you perceive your life to be now would you accept and keep? and how much of it would you rather change to something else? If you want to change a large part of how your life is you have to focus on things you want to accept in place of things you're trying to avoid, the point of this is you get what you focus on most, and more importantly the way the unconscious mind is processing what your focused on, things you do that are motivated by avoidance are more often than not sending the unconscious mind a message that, that's what you want more of, then you get stuck in a loop of having mostly what you don't prefer and little of what you do prefer; part of understanding who we are as individuals and knowing the self, is to look at what we avoid and why, and what we accept and why. A lot of avoidance comes from, fear of doing something different, and fear of outside opinion of it; the fear of doing something different is triggered by it not being familiar, the fear of outside opinion is triggered by, it may or may not be accepting, however if you accept it, then does outside opinion even matter; and if it does why?

Doing something different may be viewed as a risk, quite often though it's not actually a risk it's just different, we quite often find ourselves avoiding doing what we want because what we want is different from what we have now, our mind sorts for what's familiar, so our mind even thinks different is risky, so you have to re-frame different as familiar; so it doesn't get chucked out as to risky, so to get different accepted by unconscious mind as familiar. You can use affirmations or self-hypnosis, repeating the suggestions makes them familiar, it creates a paradox that what is familiar is true, but this other truth could also be true, so the mind starts to sort for which one is true and the one that's focused on the most or longest will be the true one, and manifest.

This is how you start to re-programme your mind to accept what you want and decline what you do not want, and it comes back again to suggestion. Suggesting what you want to be true for you, as already being true for you, in a way that unconscious mind will accept, this is mind over matter, pretty much in it's pure form, so if you didn't know you were using mind over matter already, you do now. Sub-modality's are specifics contained in a generalisation, when I was studying hypnotherapy, the style of suggestion scrips was designed for specific objectives or object, now that side of hypnosis works, there is another form of hypnosis that where working with here that has its difference in the scrips of suggestion, one being specific and object orientated and this being more vaguely specific and more general, however the vaguely specific statements contain the specifics. So the two key elements here are mind-set and the content of our conversations, most of our conversations are automated perceptions of where our mind-set's at, most of our linguistic responses are an automated reaction to a conversational statement that cements the reactionary statement as a perception of their reality, so you see when you use self-hypnosis for changing the mind-set, and practice overlaying conversational statements that reflect the perception you want that these are the actions that cause a noticeable reality shift, that will take you from rags to riches when applied with mindfulness.

"like attracts like," with manifestations Like mind-set like reality; like conversational pieces-like reality. Milton Ericson a famous Hypnotherapist showed with what's known as the Milton model that word groupings, like necessity, probability, possibility; and the negative and positive sides of these words, the words are causing an action, the way the words are woven into statements are directing the statements, if you look at one person who talks a lot of necessity statement and one who talks a lot of possibility statement you'd be able to see the difference it's making between the two peoples reality's, words conversation are causing physical outcomes in unconscious reality and conscious actuality.

Affirmations and power statements

The concept of mind-set being for each individual, their own individual God/Goddess, creating and changing meaning and purpose, identity, Beliefs and values; Self-identity/association; How you see yourself and how others see you; Identity is occupation, associations or organisations someone belongs to, a person's Intelligence in general is measured by what their occupation and income are, although there are IQ tests to measure intelligence people have biases and will view a road sweeper as being less intelligent than a solicitor, although he will certainly earn less the=an the solicitor does it mean in real terms he is less intelligent or just less resourceful, or less ambitious, lower self-esteem there are other things in the equation not just someone's perceived intelligence. "A man who study's because it's something they have a deep interest and enthusiasm in has a path. And the man who study's to look good in the eyes of his peers has an Achilles heel" Again how someone sees themselves will influence what their motivations are, whether their resourceful or not; are they motivated by the belief that life is fated, it's hard and a struggle, or life is a joy and there in control of their own destiny, each perspective creates a different type of motivation that directs them in a different direction; one will be motivated by necessity the other will be motivated by possibility. "To study a subject to gain approval of their peers is to give oneself an Achilles heel. To study a subject because it is something they have an interest in and want to master is to be oneself." When you are directing yourself through what you study and moving towards your own big picture not someone else's,

The chunked up and chunked down of a personal big picture is, chunked up is the abilities and skills to take one forward as a self-made professional or businessperson, that which is moving toward doing what you're interested in and generating an income from it, which effectively

CHUNKING UP, CHUNKING DOWN, CHUNKING ACCORSS

at some point takes you out of the salary waged day job mind-set, to independent, self-sufficient, self-directing. Chunked down is all the stuff that comes under personal lifestyle, the type of House, car, etc.

CHAPTER THIRTEEN
PERCEPTION IS PROJECTION

Like perception creates like Projection, Controls and re-rights Genes; "History repeats itself", by sameness opposite or degrees in between; this effectively means that what you project/experience is your perception repeating itself, "limiting belief" is a negative self-perspective you may not even be aware you have, and will act like a block towards your desired goals, insults or undermining your ability's by someone else is a way they can form, they damage self-esteem and hinder a person's true potential, if you were constantly told you were stupid, clumsy or any other negative like that "especially as a child", then you will have that as a limiting belief logged in your unconscious mind, and your behaviour will reflect that belief. An example of cause and effect limiting beliefs are self-sabotaging (the victim), bad things happen to me, I always attract the wrong type people, I am not worthy of, I always get it wrong, which can be changed by reversing the belief to a positive one, and applying it through self- hypnosis or affirmations, this will change a victim outcome, to a self- assured and good one, when you find yourself saying or thinking a limiting belief, write down a positive counter belief and repeat until manifested, it really is as simple as that, to change a limiting belief to an empowering one. You can use self-hypnosis or affirmations repeat the affirmation that's positive several times after you find yourself stating a negative one. The reason this works is because all the limiting beliefs we have come from repeated statements, so we have to re-repeat positive counter ones. Desire, intention, action, form our outcomes, go into things without expectation of the outcome, be hopeful of the desired outcome but try to drop expectation, especially negative ones and just allow thing to flow and unfold; you can have a preferred outcome your hopeful of, and although it's not easy to start with, and takes practice things become more free flowing if you do it this way. Try to get out of the habit of expecting a certain outcome, you will be happy when the good outcomes come, and not feel let down if they don't or it takes longer than you had hoped, to leave it in the hands of the Universe and just trust Universe will deliver.

Parents biggest flaw with children younger or older is they put far too much expectation on the child performing well or whatever it is, the child does the best they can, they didn't let the parent down the parent put too much expectation into the equation and the parent felt let down, as I have stated previously children have so much pressure put on them by parent's, teacher's and society in general, that you have youngsters hitting burn out and even committing suicide because of this unreasonable expectations built around them, the pressure on them is simply too much. Happiness, health, wealth and great relationships come from; "The vision to see what you want and the ambition to achieve it; often you will hear people say oh that person is just like their Mother or Father because we mimic behaviour, but that does not mean we have to mimic other people's negative behaviour forever, we can change our behaviour by changing our perspectives of ourselves our environment and our way of life by applying new perspectives, focusing more on what we really want instead of what others want for us.

Wallace Wattle said it is not for us to want for other people but only to want for ourselves, the perspectives then mirror back as real because they become a belief and our reality is a jigsaw puzzle of beliefs around values that make up what we perceive our life to be. Someone with no money or ill health will constantly see this as a problem and stay focused on the problem, they continuously project and perceive a loop of not having money or being ill; so the effect of these perceived causes is the effect of what they see as the reality of their life, instead of focusing on a perceived problem ask yourself what is the problem not, then write down the answers you then start to find the solutions to the problem, think solutions instead of problems. People who are constantly critical of others are expressing a sub-conscious criticism of themselves they essentially become trapped unknowingly in a loop of self-criticism even self-hatred, and project that onto others they are effectively wearing a mask to hide their own insecurities of themselves

Take the control freak their projection of trying to control others and make other people fit in with their conditioning, it shows they have little control over their own destiny and that is the way they project it, so they try to control others to avoid focusing on themselves, it's easier to criticise another than to look at your own shortcomings. This is the basis of relationships, healthy, happy, co-existing or destructive abusive relationships; the point to this is that our self-esteem, the way we perceive and value or not value ourselves is rooted in this, the way we are treated growing up as children, and further on as adults has a massive impact on the rest of our lives, and the way we end up treating others, the way we accepted being treated is then the way we treat others, some change, many or most others continue this pattern of abuse or being abused throughout their life. Because other people did not value us, we accept that and do not value ourselves. So again it comes down to reversing the negative and start valuing yourself and not accepting being treated badly and staying in those type of relationships, (interaction causes the observation) stop interacting with abusive people and what you observe changes. Did you find yourself being constantly criticised while you were crowing up or constantly encouraged and praised, if you were constantly criticised, I'll bet you are now a pretty judgemental and critical person, even if someone has done well do you look to find fault or nit-pick? if so then it comes from this and even if you don't remember much of your childhood, it's a good signifier that you had very critical role models.

And so the loop continues this is part of personality traits as well if you look at them and find your very judgemental it reflects back to your upbringing, and is part of what you perceive and continue to project, so to change parts of your personality you have to take a look at the root cause, and change it from the root upward, or the people you attract in your lives will stay the same because of what you accept or decline in terms of the way you are treated. This will also give you a big clue as to the structure of your values and beliefs, and the more work you do o this the more positive changes you will be able to make. You can change the way you see yourself and the spinoff will be you will attract different people who see you as you see yourself.

We project a reaction or response to what we perceive our reality to be, that reaction/response is in direct alignment to whether our thought process is positive or negative and the balance in-between reaction and response is reflective of the way we see ourselves our reality is made literally by this loop of "perceive and project." Dropping old personality traits that come from other people, which could be a metaphor that may have come from a relation like "money doesn't grow on trees, " which if you have never had much money is part of the reason why you have never had much money, these kind of perceptions of are self will remain hidden away until you start to look for them and change them, a positive metaphor I use is "my ability to communicate with language is far greater than the value of money" this puts you above the value of money not underneath it, and is self-empowering. For me perception and projection are something that when we have knowledge of it and start to apply it, we become able to break the loop of a mundane life full of misery, with a perception of a life of doing things we love to do, that is the Magic that creates the change.

Perception is a perspective of what we see, hear, touch, and taste, and smell our physical senses, what we project is a response or reaction of what we are perceiving; our perspective is our point of view, opinion of something. one person may have a perception that sprouts are delicious while another may have a perception that sprouts both look and taste horrible, personal preferences influence our response of what we perceive. The way we perceive ourselves and other people comes from preferences which define the choices we make, one person may view another person as bad because of a difference in religious or cultural beliefs, and see them as bad, the truth is a religious belief doesn't automatically make someone a bad person, there is good and bad trough all religion and culture, but if someone has a bad experience with someone of a specific religion there perception may be that all people in that religion are bad, so on this point we really need to be more discerning rather than out and out prejudice and be aware there is good and bad in all. A person may see another person as ugly, while another may see the beauty in the person, a person may perceive someone who is skinny as weak, only to find out they may be skinny, but they have a far stronger will than the one who sees them as weak; an opinion or preference becomes the projection, also people project a persona, some may project a persona that is an accurate or close relation to the person then are another may project a persona of themselves that is a very inaccurate reflection of who they are, the idea of masks that masks the real person behind the projection.

When we pre-suppose or pre-judge something it comes from a complex set of beliefs held in sub-conscious mind as truth, sub-conscious mind only holds perceived truth which is what makes up our beliefs and belief system, so we tend to have pre-conceived perspectives of an array of different things that only change through experiences or consciously changing paradigms/beliefs already held in sub-conscious mind. Our perception is often focused on an effect of something, rather than perceiving a cause, and our perception of the effect is in general hooked up to an emotion or elemental, an example of an elemental is Love, Happiness, Joy, a negative elemental is anger, hate, jealousy; so these elementals are hooked on to our thoughts and actions toward the effect, and what defines whether something returns back as a positive or negative manifestation are the elementals we are attributing to what we perceive.

In fact, when we react or respond to an effect, we pre-perceive by suggesting what we are pre-supposing into reality this is why people who have predominately negative reactions/responses experience more negative events, and people who react/respond in a positive manner experience more positive events, through responsibility "ability to respond." Whereas a more measured approach reduces the negative fuel to the fire and may even be replaced with elementals like compassion, forgiveness, empathy. So cultivating an attitude of measured response instead of instant reaction can greatly reduce or neutralise negative return, though it does take practice to be mindful, the other side of the coin is reacting without thinking first to something; very positive in an exited way will draw more positive return through the sheer joy or happiness they are expressing from what their perceiving. Why do people make the decisions they make, was actually the tittle of a book that won a Nobel peace prize, the book originally about social science/human behaviour, a science book actually got the prize under the category of economics, the reason for this was the advertisers, banks, and other organisation that study human behaviour for economic purposes where all over this information that the author had discovered like a rash, the answer "why do people make the decisions they make" was concluded as being for the best part their day/salary waged job; peoples orientations and the way they see themselves and others, and the way others see them is down to the day job. So let's look at this a bit deeper in terms of perception is projection, how intelligent someone is, is assessed by the type of job they have, someone with a menial cleaner or factory job will be viewed as less intelligent than someone who has a management position, someone on a low wage is more likely to have a negative view of money and experience life as hard and a struggle, were someone who has plenty of money and a job they love to do will have a more positive view of money and may view work as easy and effortless.

Very often children at school will be pigeon holed into work categories of what job types they will be suited to by view of the establishment, because of what their parents job and wage is, teachers would often view kids from council estates as being less likely to be successful and have a good job than kids that come from a private housing estate, this view and pigeon holing is still very much alive and well in schools today, judging intelligence by the day job also becomes a firm belief that their intelligence is less or more by their status in the workplace; which is why it is so difficult for many people to attain wealth because they perceive their intelligence level through their parents job or their own job as being where their station in life is.

We gain further insight into the conditioning machine and the way people can have negative personal perspectives of themselves and believe they are less intelligent and less worthy than others who may have come from a more affluent background. So conditioned "Mr average" has a personal perception of what size house they can have by their annual wage, and how much they can get on a mortgage how much they can borrow for cars and holidays, and for the rest of their lives debt is part of their lifestyle! when the job stops the money stops. This is probably most people's story, there is always the threat of losing what they have because they don't actually own the house for many, many years, and they live with a perpetual fear of losing it all, the banks of course love this because of the interest they make and the constant flow and demand for loans and mortgages, it's a well-known fact that banks do not particularly like investing in business because there is a loss risk, in the UK ninety percent of businesses fail in the first year! However mortgages are guaranteed.

So the banks play along with the conditioning that keeps people in jobs where they are dependent on loans. The day job also keeps people bound to one town and restricts the amount of time they have to themselves people in low waged jobs will often have to work very long hours sixty plus in some cases just to cover bills rent or mortgage, so they feel trapped cannot see a way out of it and resign themselves to their fate, so they perceive their life as hard, and a struggle and that loop often plays out that way for the whole of their lives. This perception of themselves and their lives will obviously be a factor with their behaviour and their decisions. What is the solution?

To question what we believe and look at where the beliefs originated from. To build a strategy and apply visualisation techniques alongside physical action, like study to build a business, these are the key factors to breaking the conditioned loop and creating a strong self-esteem which is essential for success; what we perceive as our reality/lifestyle is viewing the projection of what we perceive our reality/lifestyle to be, in other words when we change our perception of our reality/lifestyle we change what we are projecting our reality/lifestyle to be, then we shift from one reality to another through shifting our self-projection and self-perception. The other important factor when working on ourselves or with clients is to chunk up perceive the big overall picture of what is wanted, then to chunk down and work on the strategy which can include visualisation. Other people are doing the best they can with the tools they have whether their life changes for the better or not depends on how open they are to new learnings or whether they stick rigidly with what they already believe; if something is explained in a way that makes sense they may be likely to be open minded to it however many may just stay closed minded and when we see they are that closed minded then it becomes binding someone to your will if you continue to try to convince them, when someone is openly closed off then we just have to let go. Are we set at cause. Causing our own reality consciously with awareness or set at effect, reacting to our reality, Probably at a guess eighty percent of people have a default setting of effect and what they do not realise about this is when they try to effect other people, they create a cause that effects them, because the effect of the cause goes back to them; they mistakenly believe that if they direct a negative intention or action it goes outward to the person.

(one dimensional), it may cause another person a negative experience however the negative experience will loop back to them often with more intensity if the other person was harmed in some way, negative behaviour in other words reflects on the person behaving negatively not the person they direct it to. I did have a fairly clearly defined big picture of what I wanted several years ago and now most of the jigsaw pieces are in place, I started creating the big picture living abroad, being able to work from home with my own business gaining financial independence, then I focused on ways to make this possible, study was involved it was trial and error for a time but I stuck with it, when I started to use self-hypnosis and understood the right and wrong way to word scripts, it became an unfolding path,.

I changed the way I perceive myself my abilities and life trough hypnotic script, visualising, and mindfulness. We can change almost all we perceive our life to be and help others that are open to this to do the same, by changing what we project we change what we perceive, "like attracts like," Interaction causes the observation, Hypnosis scripts, affirmations are interactions that change what we observe our life to be. The projection is like to the perception. That which has similarity will be in sympathy with or compatible with that of like nature, working both subjectively and objectively. No one escapes this principle in this physical plane or in the etheric world. Negative and inferior thoughts bring about undesirable and subordinate manifestations. "Self-fulfilling prophecies," what you perceive you receive, if you say to yourself this is going to be impossible or this will be really easy these become "self-fulfilling prophecies," the way we interact with ourselves through self-talk in general, or musing out load to ourselves, these are the same as interacting in conversation with others, Interaction causes the observation. "Perception is projection" in relationships, if you take your overall attitude/internal representations then you have your perception, which you can also define as pre-suppositions or interactions, your actuality is a projection of that perception pre-supposition is interaction, so if "like attracts like", "attitude attracts like attitude"; you may think you define an intimate relationship by the way you see them physically, in truth that's the book cover the whole attraction must have happened on a deeper attitudinal level first, internal representations, values, beliefs and strategies, are essentially your attitude. So any work you need to do on relationships, health and wealth must come from a change or shift of attitude that corresponds to relationships. When more you cultivate an attitude of "know thyself know thy craft."

CHAPTER FOURTEEN

QUANTUM PHYSICS AND ESOTERIC SCIENCE

Quantum Physics, Mechanics, Entanglement; The Way It Corresponds to Esoteric Science, Hypnosis and NLP, in relation to Human reality and Evolution. Quantum physics or the plural "Quanta," is the framework of understanding and describing nature. Quantum by definition is the smallest amount, i.e. a particle. Quantum physics in relation to our reality states that a particle when observed will behave differently, so what we interact with or think we perceive is causing an effect, the original findings of the split light experiment was that the observation caused the wave to collapse into particle, now it has become obvious that the interaction cased the observation. This is highly significant in relation to NLP and Hypnosis, as whom and what we interact with causes what we observe our reality to be, which in turn interacts with what makes us what we are which is thought, electric pulse, thought form (crystallised thought), subconscious, superconscious (non-physical) consciousness (physical). Electrons, protons, atoms, particles, are effectively the physical building blocks of our reality, and Universe. Thoughts, Emotions, Intelligence, create our reality, quantum physics attempts to explain the way all these things work and relate to each other what nature and its purpose is. Esoteric explanation of light waves is, "a harmonious vibration of etheric matter that projects through space in perfect rhythmic waves, strikes a surface and homogeneous are through into sympathetic vibrations with the incoming current; a form of manifestation of cosmic law, visible or invisible dependent on the great central sun, or light source." This means that we can change what we observe in terms of our reality, rich or poor healthy or ill by changing our thinking/verbal reaction towards it. There was a recent experiment by a group of GP's who wanted to know if someone went to them for diagnosis of an illness, whether after they were told the diagnosis if the illness became worse far more rapidly after being told; when they did have an illness they had been tested for, the result was that after being tested and told they had an illness and had tested positive immediately after the speed and decline in the patients' health increased far more rapidly, two factors to this are they trust the GP's word without question, so it becomes a belief instantly, and the interaction with the GP, which opens up the question if we feel ill and interact with others that we feel ill are we causing the illness to get worse by interacting with others and stating that we feel ill in the first place, according to the GP's experiment the answer has to be yes.

Can we stay fit and healthy forever and even live far longer than is expected just by self-interaction that we are healthy and can live far longer than is expected, our expectations are also "self-fulfilling prophecies", we are talking on a scientific level of chain reactions, for every action there is a reaction, so when we start to look at questions like what is reality, surely it's a chain reaction of interaction and observation in that order, we are talking proven science here not wishful thinking. " Universe is mind and mind is Universe," and when something is observed it is the effect of some kind of interaction, it is not possible to observe something without interaction being somehow involved. what this would mean in terms of NLP, is thought directs our destiny and as we are surrounded by and made up of particles, atoms, then it is us who influence our lives by the way we direct thought and whether the thoughts we direct are attached with a positive or negative vibration.

Without realisation most people are accepting from others and describing themselves and their lives in a very negative way and this general presupposition becomes what they will draw/attract into their future here and now's, they have little hope of changing very much in their lives and will stay on a perpetual loop/treadmill and their life continues on a default setting of their own making, until they realise this and change it. When we look at energy waves when our thinking is positive in orientation then any negative energy waves being directed at us will be cancelled out by virtue of science findings that an affirmative thought is hundreds of times more powerful than a negative one, that which has a higher vibration can and does supress that with a lower vibration, so our reality really is what we associate to in correspondence to what we interact with and to Esoteric Law of matter helps explain this.

"All matter is composed of atoms vibrating at different frequency's made by the constant repulsion and attraction of electrons and protons trying to balance, the repulsion and attraction is activated by the human mind and emotions and keeps on until atoms of the same number of electrons aggregate together forming the various rates of vibration or matter." (Jean Chardin) "Matter is conscious energy; mind and matter are one, poles of continuum. Matter is the Human mind in action; there is no substance except conscious energy." Law of polarity also sheds more light on this (excuse the pun) "A state of repulsion and attraction and balancing of negative (female) and positive (male) energies of primordial essence, necessary to make the thousands of vibrational frequencies in the entire cosmos under the direction of mind activity. The way a construct reacts to an electric or magnetic field manifesting two opposite tendencies, positive and negative, everything can be split into two complete opposing principles, and each contrasting principle will contain the potential of the opposing principle." So what is mind activity, well it's thought, and the outcome of the thought is defined by interaction it's being directed toward with continuous focus, what we associate to continuously we attract what we dissociate from we repel, which is the basis of the NLP principle of moving toward moving away from.

There was an experiment conducted by a scientist with ice cubes and discovered incredibly that the ice cube with no emotion focused on it showed no pattern under the microscope, however when he directed specific emotions at separate ice cubes; Love, Anger, joy, different patterns formed in the ice cubes similar to a snowflake but all individually different. In Quantum physics reality is three dimensional, but when you put altered states of conscious into the equation it becomes four dimensional, with quantum entanglement being proved as real in nature, this also means effectively that we live in a four-dimensional reality not a three dimensional one, as I said earlier in the book about dreams when you come out of a nightmare or good dream how real was that dream, real enough to say "thank God it was only a nightmare."

However in that altered dream state it is very real, in Beta state and in linier thinking reality is three dimensional in reality altered states of consciousness are the fourth dimension, powerful enough to switch someone from feeling pain to not feeling pain just by putting a person in a specific hypnotic state, people have been having operations for a long time in the east using this method without any anaesthetists chloroform. So, with the new ideas and discoveries in quantum mechanics and entanglement, things are becoming remarkably interesting. we can no longer just accept mathematical linier equations to explain Universe and nature without including "conscious mind" which is left out of mainstream quantum physics: Quantum physics has achieved a lot of things (like getting Rovers on Mars) and explained a lot of things, it's only problem is you cannot quantify that which is not quantifiable, which is conscious mind "universe is mind and mind is universe" you cannot, not have this in the equation. On an individual and collective level in general humanity's biggest drawback is assumption that something is impossible without looking at the "possibility of it being possible," so the idea of three-or four-dimensional reality is also reflected in the greatest mysteries, the pyramid you can make a pyramid with three triangle sides or four, is this reflecting reality as being viewed and lived with a perception of three or four dimensions to it. This is the difference between modern mainstream medicine and holistic healing and reality shifting through hypnosis and NLP, mainstream medicine is three-dimensional object objective orientated, hypnosis and NLP are four dimensional subjective as well as objective.

Which is the difference between mainstream science and esoteric science, mainstream science is three dimensions orientated and esoteric science is four dimensional orientated. First dimension: A line moving straight unto itself has one dimension, length; if the strait line or simple basic vibration moves in its own direction it remains only a basic vibration; motion only is all that exists and motion only in the same dimension of which the basic vibration exists, e.g. a leaf growing, sense of light, elementary movement through space was in one direction only, linier measurement. Second dimension: Matter that has length only and is able to move backward, forward and sideward; when a line moves in any direction not in its own length, it generates an is giving it two dimensions, the length and width; found when a line or direction can be taken at an angle to the first flat plane or strait line; two different lines of force; two opposing currents meet, intersect and fuse; this gives an interaction of fusion, attraction repulsion and cohesion to resist, i.e. touch gives second dimension; as one contacts the surface, he or she fuses and has a sensation of what kind of surface he or she is feeling. Third dimension: Depth the additional feature by which a solid object is distinguished from a second dimensional object; has depth along with length and width; an "area" that moves out of its plane, becomes a solid, and has three dimensions (a solid remains just a solid wherever you place it); third dimension line has lines, area and solids; it can move backward and forward and now up and down; it takes three numbers measured in three mutually perpendicular directions to determine and mark out any particular point from the total of points.

Dimension of time determined by the human nerves system; third dimensions are affected by the law of gravity and affected by the motion of rotation; the Earth plane and all its inhabitants are considered third dimensional. Fourth dimension: 1: The part of the etheric world that is filled with thought forms from the Earth entities: a plane in which the actual life forces play and reach there concrete forms, both influential and causative, 2: the cause of growth the link between mind (ultimate mind) and matter (fifth and third planes): radiates motion and life energy through mankind, 3: a single motion in all directions, simultaneously, formless with continuous radiator movement: 4: A plane of successive existence, being three dimensional in space as is also each successive instant of time; 5: (AMORC)" nothing more or less than the rate of electronic vibrations"; electricity, telephone communication, radio waves, x-ray, and ultraviolet ray; 6: Mundane substances which cannot be measured or weighed, has the power of movement; 7: relates to the astral plane and its functions and peculiarity.

A lot of hypnotherapists ask their clients at the end of a session how long they thought the session had taken, and most of their clients replied they thought the session was much shorter than the actual time it took, signifying the presence of time distortion; implying being in another non-physical dimension as well as this one. Which is saying there is a 4th dimension to our 3-dimensional world that is four-dimensional. If the time dimension in a lucid state is perceived as different to the time dimension in a hypnotic state, then a different time dimension, is involved; the dimension could be called extra-terrestrial; action that happens outside the earth; the earth being one boundary. Everything that exists as physical dimension, must also exist as non-physical dimension," Law of corresponding opposites." So nothing can exist on a physical dimension, and not exist in a non-physical dimension; so we create our physical dimension, through the non-physical dimension. And that is what visualizing is about, putting a structure in the non-physical, and adding form to it through repeating the script, until it has enough form to manifest in the physical; so for example if someone is constantly giving thought to something they don't want, it gives form to what they focus their don't wants on and they push it through into happening because structure and form were added to them through constantly thinking about them, so through a simple shift and focusing on what we do want constantly, we give that structure and form to that and that pushes through into our reality instead of the don't wants. When we understand the supple, we manifest in the physical. It has put some of the final pieces to the puzzle together for me and helped me come to understand that when we follow a habituated way of communicating on a subtle level then we receive on a physical level; it explained to me the whole concept of self-healing or manifesting a so-called dream life. Living the dream!

The Seven Planes of Existence

First plane of third dimensional matter (physical plane). Created by the soul mind as a means for it to express itself and grow in a manner that only third dimensional matter afford; matter held together by thought energy, (conscious mind and unconscious mind activity); the earth and all the material things on it. Second plane of existence, (Astral plane); a level of awareness in the etheric world having its own principles, inhabitants, and purpose for existence; the second body of earth vibrating faster than earth, or earth's etheric double, this plane interpenetrates earth to the core and extends out from the earth surrounding it. Free from the law of gravity; recognised as the fourth dimension; considered a halfway house either entirely mundane or entirely ethereal but a mixture of the two Third plane of existence: a level of consciousness consisting of "thought" where most negative thinking has been eliminated by astral and physical existences; a faster vibrational frequency than earth, interpenetrating it and extending out from it; composed of the seven divisions of matter; solid, liquid, gas, ether, super ether, sub-atomic, energy, and atomic ether; houses the mental bodies; has two distinct levels of function; upper half is the region of abstract thought, where plans and ideas are designed into blueprints for earth life, called the causal plane; lower half is the region where the abstract thoughts, begin to become concrete ideas weaving into manifestation; referred to as the mental plane, a level where the forces of will find expression. Forth plane of existence:

A level of consciousness recognised for its wisdom, with the emphasis of constructive thought, and the full development of the imagination facility, here constructive imagination is taught because the etheric atoms of the froth plane use the thought of the fourth plane; ones consciousness develops universal love and humanitarianism which motivates the plane below where the earth blueprints are drawn. Fifth plane of existence: A level of consciousness in the etheric world of self-realisation, Universal "will", wherein the monad reaches close to perfection; monad loses all thought of self and finds the purpose of becoming one with totality; total Love is for the soul purpose of progression of the Universal seed; group souls function on this plane working as a unit, to maintain balance in the solar systems; this group consciousness is involved in motivating earthlings to desire and do that which is for their highest good in the overall plan.

Sixth plane of existence: home to the monads; a level of consciousness wherein the monad begins and ends the necessity for using a soul mind as its vehicle for the evolutionary cycle; the vibrational frequency that triggers off the involution of the monad and gives it the potential to envelope itself in a soul mind, implants a demand for an evolution back to this plane. Seventh plane of existence: A level of controversial concepts highest conceivable spiritual attainment that each soul mind will eventually be a part of; indescribable in language and beyond human comprehension; unknown perfectness; happiness beyond ones strongest imagination, which is recognisable, understandable and appreciated, because one has experienced all the opposite of this happiness; controversial concepts regarding the time when the soul mind slips into this consciousness; one keeps his or her individuality; one losses his or her individuality into the total consciousness; totality in its entirety, God consciousness. As Einstein Said! "If will, where to come into conflict with imagination, will, would always lose." This is because imagination exists in the fourth dimension and cannot be overridden by just physical will. Paradoxes: except for that which comes under universal absolutes.

Everything is but a half truth, until a different truth on the same theme is presented that could also be true, this creates a paradox. For all intent and purpose this actually becomes scientific validation of what I just stated, we talk our reality in, our linguistics reflect our thought level, our thought level reflects our behaviour and outcomes, so you see, if someone continually complains about hating their job, never having enough money, that's where they're going to stay, by virtue of the linguistics assuming that is the way it is, which acts as self-observation. if their conversation constantly reflects being bored, then that's where their stay until they change their linguistics and level of thought, you must change the linguistics first of the way you are observing yourself, and to some degree ignore outside opinion of you if it does not reflect the way you want to see yourself. You see now how there's no such thing as luck or chance it's all been pre-self-observed and pre-assumed.

What if it goes wrong is pre-anticipating it going wrong, then observing it going wrong, if you listen to anyone coaching law of attraction when they say keep telling yourself you're fit, wealthy, happy, and you are pre-assuming, and that is what you will observe, which shows you that the self-hypnosis sessions you'll be creating for yourself are pre-assuming what you will be observing, by utilising imagination and suggestion. The Faraday chamber experiment: an experiment was conducted by Cambridge University utilizing a lead shielded and airtight Faraday chamber to conduct a particle experiment. In theory, if the internal chamber was pumped down to a vacuum environment such as in space and the temperature reduced to absolute zero (-460F), all particles should stop vibrating and there should be no energy present in the chamber. What was discovered with their instrumentation is that the chamber contained an enormous amount of energy according to their experiment, so much of it, that if it were possible to fill the inside glass bulb of a 100-watt light, there would be sufficient energy to bring the Earth's oceans to a boiling point. The Faraday experiment concluded the existence of dark energy. WMAP findings; On June 30, 2001, a deep space probe named the Wilkinson Microwave Anisotropy Probe WMAP was launched from Cape Canaveral Air Force Base aboard a Delta II rocket.

The purpose of the WMAP probe was to accomplish deep space research utilizing X-Ray Cameras to map the composition of The Universe. Two years later the results were examined and are accurate to within 4% according to WMAP scientists. Their findings are as follows: Dark Energy: (73%) An extremely tenuous invisible energy that pervades all of universal space and is the cause of space itself; it is an unexplainable baffling mystery to science. Universe responds to energy because it is 73% dark energy, could this also be what is referred to as pure energy, as scientists originally thought that energy could not vibrate at absolute zero, yet it does. This may be baffling to mainstream science, but esoteric science already knows this as vital life force that permeates the whole of universe. Dark Matter: (23%) "The invisible powerful grip that keeps galaxies from flying apart as they rotate and generates the gravitational force to keep them in a cluster formation as they travel through space "If there were no dark matter the whole of our galaxy and all the others would simple fly apart.

Dark matter Is part of the space in solid objects, dark matter acting as the blueprint of that we perceive as physical matter, could dark matter also be what is known as though form. Physical Matter: (4%) "The familiar particle or material world that we see with our eyes, as we live, move, and have our being within it." The Great Physical Plane" is one of several planes of existence, which contain sublevels in each plane, our physical plane of existence is one of these planes. The WMAP experiment separates Dark energy, dark matter, and physical matter; however, the three are infused together and cannot be separated, they work in fusion or entanglement with each other with the exception maybe of black holes. Well physical reality only makes up 4% of universe the other 96% is invisible reality, everything that exists in physical reality starts off and comes from invisible reality, with though it becomes denser and manifests in the physical realm. The relevance of these findings of WMAP and Faraday connect together when we apply words to the equation, the power lies in the Universe itself but when well-structured linguistics are applied with understanding of what the words are the causation of this can be like having the metaphorical magic wand or the keys of personal destiny, because interaction defines the observation which effects the particle then so do the words these both act as directional forces of energy that produce the effect of the intention. The uncertainty principle- (Albert Einstein, Werner Heisenberg) "any realistic description of the universe must describe it in all possible states at the same instant of time, e.g., a person would be alive dead and unborn simultaneously." This points to the same as Esotericism, all things are possible, however it's the possibilities they tune into or impossibility they tune into that really define what is and isn't possible for them at that time, so in essence Quantum physics has validated through its own discoveries what the Esoteric definitions in this book are describing; as real, actual.

CHAPTER FIFTEEN

THE WAY HOLOGRAPHIC THOUGHT DEFINES OUR ACTUALITY

Holograph-oneness of all things, i.e. The all (universe) a unified living whole unit having no beginning or ending, constantly printing its likeness in all sizes shapes and forms of all living material; everything is a small piece of the whole, containing the same information and life as a whole, only reduced in size, shape, texture, and speed. Definition of a holographic universe is a hologram contains all the information of everything that exists and every conceivable variable by degree of that, which exists; universe is a fusion of separates that are separate only by virtue of varying by degree. Everything that exists in universe exists, it cannot not exist because it exists, every possibility exists whether believed by Humans or not, we as Humans will always exist by the same virtue there is no death only a continuum, past, present and future are already known about, they are not entirely separate but fused together, we have only to believe that which is seen as impossible to be possible , to make it become possible in physical reality, because that possibility already exists we just have to tune into that frequency. Our reality can be whatever we choose because every possibility already exists; impossible is just a resistance to that which is already possible. Law of personification-Anything can be a person. Anything that has a real existence, such as an object, a skill, an event, has characteristics and a "Personality" of its own and should be treated as though it were alive. This uses the theory that mankind makes the world and everything on it with their minds; therefore, everything else is an existence of humanity and embodies like qualities. Any phenomena are considered to be an "alive" entity, e.g. hurricanes are named after a person, cars are named patted and talked to, (Herbie) the car in the "Walt Disney" film. To go even deeper into this we need to look at what separates humanity into the ones that can manifest a life they will, and those who can't! this is the dividing line without question this is what separates us, the one's whose lives are taken up by approval seeking, people pleasing, adhering to the demands and opinions of so called peers, everything in their lives becomes about what other people are demanding from them every day; the best part of all their daily thoughts weather they realise it or not, are given over to other people opinion's and demands of them.

Their vibrational frequencies are a lot lower because of all the usual emotion's that their life is creating for them, fear, guilt resentment, anger, I don't need to go on do I; and their lives continue on this toward spiral because of what they are focused on, they are focused on everyone and everything except themselves they look for love from others but don't offer any love to themselves they are just focused on how well their doing as people pleasers, that is the trap of the ego when you drop the ego and judgemental options, and accept or realise that the universe will give us all that we require, the only approval you need is from yourself, Those that operate on a level of universal confidence have become in harmony with the universe, not pushing against it.

Those of us that set out on the journey as seekers of understanding that there is more to life than we were being told came to understand universal laws, on a deeper level than just quoting them to look smart, people who have stumbled if you like on this understanding of this knowledge probably came from a background interest in Quantum physics, science or from an interest of the psychic, no one went from not getting this to fully understanding it overnight. For the most of us it was a journey in acquiring the knowledge and most importantly understanding this knowledge on a deeper level; the real understanding of this for me unfolded over

THE WAY HOLOGRAPHIC THOUGHT DEFINES OUR ACTUALITY

several years some through reading and re-searching and a fair bit from intuitive thought, and when we accept that knowledge truly can come from intuition, then that is a real revelation; those eureka moments when you understand something that you didn't understand five minutes before, that's intuitive thought and I can definitely vouch for the fact that it exists. That there is a super-consciousness that holds all information "past, present, future.

" So how can the future already be known about; quite simply because everyone is sending out telegrams to the universe all the time about what we are intending to draw in, so everything that comes into our perceived circumstance has already bean pre-ordered, therefore already known about, because the future to a point has already bean visualized and drawn into existence, and part of how we visualize is with our feelings/emotion. An example of things people has achieved using reality shifting techniques; "Improved vision" seeing clearly without glasses when in the past you could not, new teeth coming through, affecting weather, reverse aging. Money flowing in consistently when in the past it was always lack of money. Traffic lights staying green until you go through them. Getting the specific parking space when a parking lot is full, appreciating everything naturally from your heart; Experiencing desires manifesting more quickly and effortlessly, if you think these things are impossible then for you, they will be impossible, if you think they are possible then for you they will be possible. What would you like to be possible that you think now is impossible, because "anything is possible." There's so much more we can expand on this list; the important thing is experiencing any or all these things yourself so that it builds your universal/divine infinite confidence.

No matter how much work and practicing it takes with focused intention, it's always worth it all." What all this points too really, is that, that we cannot perceive or imagine is just something we haven't thought about yet, does not mean that because we haven't imagined it yet that it does not exist or is not possible. So in effect we had become pretty much from birth conditioned and separated from our sub-conscious, so much of our lives if not all of it was manifesting from outside suggestion and we became to switched off to challenge it, so we ended up with run of the mill lives that were built up on what we were told to expect, so our lives became a re-run of what we were being told to expect, remember the subconscious generally does not interfere, we have to communicate our intentions to it before it can help us and manifest what we choose, so if we do not remember or learn how to communicate with our sub-conscious then we cannot manifest that which we desire.

People have been told to expect a job that pays an annual wage and not really expect money to come from any other source, that's what their told to expect they accept it as their fate and guess what they get, what they expected. That is the curse of conditioning, we are lead to believe we can achieve far less than our true potential, receive money in far less ways than we actually can, so once we break free of the conditioned norm then, we can condition our own lives, tailor make our life to suit ourselves; this is the "law of free will" restricted people are restricted by being conditioned to always question "how" something will come about remember, "how" is part of the process but only part; the rest is the unconsciousness job, so all that is left now is our own individual selves and our unconscious, and the knowledge that the universe will grant us all that we ask for. Some of the clues come in dreams or the nature of dreams, if you have ever had a good or bad dream and wake up feeling good or in a cold sweat you will know how real that dream was when you were in a dream state, I know you can all relate to that, so if the dream state feels so real is it reality? Well surely if it feels reel it is real, the dream is in the mind, (dreams are the realm of unconscious metaphor and imagery) as stated before, how many times have you woken up from a nightmare and thought thank God it's only a nightmare, it was real when you were in it though, or woken up from a dream which was bliss and just want to go back to sleep and enter into that dream again, so reality must be in the mind, unconscious mind.

So we lead into the realm of mind over matter, many, many people have stories of visualising every day and the visualisation manifesting exactly the same as the manifestation, so reality is all in the mind, what we experience and call reality for most people is the projection of what's in the mind, remember the universal principal Universe is mind. Mind is universe; our whole existence is a holographic representation of what's

THE WAY HOLOGRAPHIC THOUGHT DEFINES OUR ACTUALITY

in our mind, it cannot, not be any other, how can it? Everything in our little physical worlds are as real as our dream feels, so we can change our physical world through a process of kind of dreaming it, visualising it or scripting it because mind over matter is cause and effect, which is real isn't?

Now if you have had, or are having problems with people interfering in your life or causing you disruption or grievance, although it may be tempting to take revenge on the them in the form of retribution never do it, because whatever they have done to you "Will" be done to them, only focus on what you want anything negative in your life will then fall away like autumn leaves falling off a tree, "success is the best revenge" if you focus on an enemy you will attract more enemy's if you ignore them then they cease to exist in your existence, this has been proven over and over by a great deal of people, your scripts are what you are generating to come into your life as quick as the universe can manifest it, there are lots of story's, true ones about of people who were being abused in one way or another who started taking the whole reality shifting seriously and created their scripts with the content being entirely on what they did want in their lives, then after a few weeks, sometimes months, all the people who were abusing them literally left them totally alone or disappeared from their presence with no influence over them again, the key word here is "focus" this is worth taking notice of, if you have people who are completely incompatible to you then the universe will not allow their existence in your life and believe me the universe is bigger than they are, no matter how big they think they are.

And remember unconscious mind takes things personally so if they say you're a sod, unconscious mind processes it as they are a sod it reflects on them not you. Once you start running positive self-suggestion in hypnosis or affirmations your vibrational frequency will change to a much higher one and those on a lower vibrational frequency will not be able to get near you this is Universal fact. Only focus your scripts on end results of what you want to experience trust me if you feel someone owes you or they should pay for what they have put you through the Universe will deal with it and the fact is they have already started the process of receiving their negative intentions and actions against them so if anything, pity them. Because once you have your communication with the sub-conscious back then and you are creating your life then others can no longer compete with your decisions and freewill, because you are creating not competing. When you switch this round those who were competing with what you worked for or what was important to you will quite literally fall flat on their faces, so never push against these type of people or join organizations or groups that push against them and focus on them all the time, just do your scripts, and trust the Universe.

The holographic self-defines that every possible reality a person can conceive for themselves already exists, within the hologram, if the mind can conceive it then it already exists, so when we presuppose with conditional statements, we tune into and manifest that reality we tune in to by law of vibration. An example would be, I am incredibly happy and grateful for my life, has a different vibration attached to it than my life is rubbish, and everything goes wrong, these statements of acceptance attract in physicality more of what's being accepted. Let's take a scenario that there are over eight billion people on this planet, now although you can't physically see all eight billion people you know they exist on this planet as you do, now imagine that all those eight billion people are you, and each person is living out a reality that relates to past choices you made or didn't make, now when I was reading on Astral projection, a good few years ago the concept of astral planes was introduced to me, which equates to the same thing, that although you can't physically see all these other reality's that are you playing out from the most positive to the most negative and all the varying degrees in-between they are there in invisible holographic form, so the point is we are not creating our own reality, but merely tuning in to a reality that is already a probability, it's the reality we focus on having that becomes the highest probability and slips into our physical here and now, so quite often an action doesn't have to be hard and a struggle as most people assume but merely choosing a reality that you would prefer.

Like tuning in an old transistor radio, you focus on the bar as you turn the knob to tune in to the transmission you prefer, and if there is interference in the transmission you fine tune it out so you have clarity. So I have read and herd people who work in different subject areas that say the same

THE WAY HOLOGRAPHIC THOUGHT DEFINES OUR ACTUALITY

thing; your life/reality is what you focus on most, because what you focus on is tuning you in to a reality you prefer that is your choice; at least that is how your unconscious mind interprets it, even if it is not actually what you prefer it's what you focussed on so that is what you get; if the reality that manifests/projects back is something you don't want then you tuned into the wrong station, this is what is meant by moving toward or moving away from, drawing in or pushing away.

What we focus on from outside can also have a massive influence if not checked, it's a combination of self-talk, and external influence. Also expectation if you have a lot of negative stuff going on in your life then you tend to expect more negative things because that is the cycle of thinking you have adopted, limiting beliefs like if it wasn't for bad luck, I would not have any at all, or whatever I do goes wrong, these become habituated cycles of thinking, and you automatically expect the negative stuff to happen. You can get out of the negative cycle of thinking by dropping automatic expectation and exchange it for hope, be hopeful that any negative trend will pass, and things will improve this breaks the automated cycle, try to go into each day consciously without expectation of good or bad things happening, be hopeful you will have a great day, or things will go well for you, it shifts the messages you send to your unconscious mind. If you encounter any negative comments or criticisms during your day, say to yourself "other people's opinions are none of my business," it shifts your thinking from accepting negative views of you, to declining negative views of you, because if it's none of your business then their comments belong to them not you; that statement essentially sends the criticism back to them rather than taking it on board yourself. Remember the nature of a holographic universe is that every possibility exists; it's the same in our day-to-day reality every possibility of our reality exists both good and bad reality is choice not a forgone conclusion without choice what we think about and what we say, what outside influences we have our, own choice.

Wealth or poverty, illness, or robust health, co-existing or co-dependent, relationships are a choice and changing these things is an absolute science; the information you allow into your subconscious is effectively programming the hologram of your reality, so be more consciously aware of what you're accepting what you choose to interact with in terms of self-talk and outside influences. we are creating and choosing our own life to a degree what we see that physically comes in is the choice of what we are tuned into in terms of what we project and pre-suppose our life to be, the reality we want already exists and it's no effort to the Universe to shift a non-physical reality in as our perceived physical reality. People who spend most of their time worrying about their health or finances or thinking negative what ifs, things that could go wrong are in the "action" of worrying about it, choosing that as their preferred reality because that is what they are focussed on and tuning into.

I am sure that every NLP coach has had clients that are so absorbed in the "action" of worrying about a perceived problem that that it escalates at breakneck speed because they are inadvertently choosing that as part of their preferred reality, they are doing it consciously without conscious awareness they are doing it. When a person is sick but focuses on being healthy, they create a paradox in their belief system which has the power to heal the sickness. When a person is poor but focuses on wealth, they create a paradox in their belief system that has the power to give them wealth. In terms of this being an "absolute science" I have included some esoteric definitions below Reality; "esoteric definition" 1: an awareness of life that is different for each person; "individual concept "and ones inhabitant, constructed by the mind of the individual; "that which is real to the subconscious mind or psychic mind regardless of actuality"; 2: feeling of being on a plane of existence where ones conscious puts one; 4: (living organisms) the entity's individual concept of itself and its inhabitant, constructed by instinct depending on the state of "Evolution" at the time of perception; 5: (inert objects) "Conscious of Being "within all things; the intelligence in the cells making an awareness for that object. (State of Evolution) "Esoteric.

" 1: a timeline of consciousness that puts each thing, living and non-living, into an awareness of reality of its own as it progresses from one existence to another, fulfil the potential within the seed of the "Universe" of which it is a part." Hologram Brain Theory"; 2: (referring to humans) a degree or step in the process of "Soul Mind" unfoldment; each step makes its own rules and functions to benefit that level to perfect itself;

THE WAY HOLOGRAPHIC THOUGHT DEFINES OUR ACTUALITY

each step is measured by the amount of "Wisdom" one has acquired through experiences of activity, emotions and thoughts, from ones various incarnations on earth; the correct reaction to these experiences make changes in the electric vibrational frequency of the body giving each individual a different conductivity of electricity in the body; conductivity changes according to the "quality" of correctly learned experiences, regardless of the "number" of incarnations; the soul mind acts like a "voltage regulator" for the amount of "Cosmic Electricity" utilised in the body. Everyone is bombarded with the same amount of cosmic electricity the amount the body uses is according to the soul mind evolution; the more cosmic energy utilised, the more refined the body and lifestyle one has; the rate of the vibration of each individual (stage of evolution) will be the key to what happens to one as the earth purifies itself. To define reality is to say it "corresponds" to the past and future as it exists in unconscious mind.

Our here and now things we are experiencing in our touch and feel moments" here and now" conscious awareness is actuality "not" reality, reality is defined by our values and beliefs and also by our reactions and responses to experiences in the here and now, which keep the same unconscious reality or changes it thereby changing our here and now actuality, conscious awareness of this takes us from somewhat deluded and self-deluding to self-actualised, the realisation that what we do in the here and now moment is not real but " actual".

This effectively implies that the persons perceived reality at any one time has its opposite and varying degrees running on "astral planes" simultaneously or at least the possibility of every other possibility, which to some degree at least makes the concept of impossible a "limiting belief", we are not so much creating our reality but choosing the "actuality" we experience by a cycle of perception is projection or interaction/observation defining unconscious reality and conscious actuality, our experiences what we have and do not have come from this cycle. The key must then be the connection of conscious, unconscious, and superconscious minds and the electro-magnetic fields we exist within, tuning in is done through a series of electronic pulses from the brain that produce a thought and the vibratory rate that is attached to the thought which becomes emotion. so the tuning in aspect would be vibratory and that's how we manifest, as when a thought is produced it must then contain a vibratory rate which associates to it, the memory's we have and emotion attached to it must then be stored as a Gestalt including the emotional vibration, what is known as our Aura an electromagnetic field of the person which radiates from within the body and outside the body, is possibly where memory and emotion are stored, as well as in the body in the nerves system , at least at this point that is where we think they are stored.

When negative unresolved issues are stored they vibrate/spin at a rate that can degenerate the body, cause illness and depression, repressed negative emotions definitely lead to illness and the degeneration of the body; so when we use techniques to separate the emotion from the event like timeline work, we move towards having an Aura that has a more positive vibration and allows the body to operate effectively as an organism that can constantly regenerate to perpetual perfect health, and extend a person's life beyond anything previously known or recorded. Science now suggests that between two, to several years we have a brand-new body but whether the body looks or feels the same or different is down to what we focus our thoughts on, imagine what we have the potential to achieve through understanding this and having control of what unconscious mind stores as beliefs.

The line then between positive thought and emotion, and negative ones is a frequency, above that frequency is positive below that frequency is negative, a line between these two types of thinking, the principle of association is a connection to what is being associated to," tuning in" or disassociating from, "tuning out", so a problem stops being a problem when a way is found to disassociate from the problem, if the perceived problem is not having something they want to have, providing what they want isn't going to negatively impact on others, then they find a way to associate themselves to what they want, so with understanding life becomes like a game of association and disassociation; when techniques are used in conjunction with this principle such as timeline work, self-suggestion etc. Then you start to achieve mastery of personal destiny, both timeline and suggestion are reframe tools, as suggested in a previous chapter on the twenty-one Universal sub-laws or human characteristics when you aspire to the positive ones i.e. hope as opposed to a negative counterpart then this changes the way you vibrate and a body vibrating more positively is going to be far above one that vibrates more negatively. The way we perceive actuality is through our senses

However we only perceive through our senses a three-dimensional actuality when actuality the reality of actuality is four dimensional that is multidimensional/holographic. We don't necessarily get the full picture of actuality with just our physical senses, so it could be said that what we cannot sense physically, we can sense with imagination and intuition, which are essentially non-physical senses because that which is non-physical is invisible although we can't see it or point to its exact location, we can perceive its existence. The work of quantum physicists has helped us understand that we can't see dark energy, but we know it exists, and even if there are still many questions unanswered about the nature Universe. The fact that we can perceive and conceive the existence of something means it has to exist or we would not be able to perceive or conceive of something not in existence. A lot of scientific experiments and their findings may go over many people's heads, but what the finding of quantum physics proves and points to is we are all connected, empty space is not necessarily empty, there is a vital life force (a tenuous substance) that moves through everything in existence, everything is in some way energy, when we move past the dogmas of religion the laws of Man, the outside and self-imposed restrictions, we find everything in our lives we complain about can be changed to being happy about, we can achieve anything we want, what we have not got we can have, the only real rule to all of this is we only have control over one life, and that's "our own", we have not got the right to tell another what they can, or cannot do, for they have free will to do as they choose, however, know it or not they will endure or enjoy the consequences of their actions.

However scientific we are or are not, the relation to quantum physics and NLP is that the words we state as our life conditions become the actuality we perceive, if a person spends ten years telling himself and others, they are poor, they will spend ten years being poor; if a person spends ten years telling their self and others, they are wealthy, they will spend ten years being wealthy. What we are stating we perceive "will be" what we will be receiving, and I know this with absolute certainty through my own personal evolution on the path that is my life. The holographic self-defines that every reality a person can conceive for themselves already exists, within the hologram, if the mind can conceive it then it already exists, so when we presuppose with conditional statements, we tune into and manifest that actuality; we tune in by law of vibration and manifest and actualise through Law of suggestion.

What this describes is holographic universe and everything that exists in universe is holographic, as in every perspective exists simultaneously. Everything exists in the here and now; past or future is just a story, so if we want to change our life, we only have to change the story. This leads to all sorts of paradoxes, like the particles being in two places at once, or appearing to be separate but are connected, we know now that the interaction causes the observation, as opposed to what was previously believed to be observation caused the outcome. Although all of this can seem complicated and confusing to some, it simplifies actuality as reflecting in physicality the unconscious perspective individuals choose to perceive, by virtue of what their unconscious mind hold as true belief is a choice. Only some think they have no choice in what they perceive which if they have no understanding of how to change beliefs, is true, however if they understand how to change beliefs then it is not true. Some realise and are aware that they can choose what they wish to receive, and their physicality will reflect their choice

An example being someone who chooses to find things to constantly complain about will find their reality constantly throughs up things for them to complain about without realising that it is happening by virtue of their own choice and would probably find something in this statement to complain about! Is your glass half empty or half full, (it's whatever half you focus on it being,) you either complain about the empty half or are grateful for the half you have; whichever one it is attracting more of the same. What gives something value? The desire to have it, that which gets us something of value, the intention and action toward the intention; Words with power; words are a thought animated, either verbally or symbolically with letters words are like an egg yolk in cooking used to bind the ingredients together. Our words can, and do crystallise thought and bring it into physical being, the problem for most people is they fire off words all day long and essentially take absolutely no notice of what their "actually saying", and that words as statements that are repeat are actually forming their reality and actuality, fortunately for us we realise this but you have to feel pity for those who don't, or who cast off the idea that reality works in this way, a brief example.

I read a statement on an online forum where a person was describing a craft he enjoyed doing, making pendants etc, now a craft you enjoy doing puts you in the highest level on the mood table of interest and enthusiasm, but here is the problem, he then stated that it takes his mind off his anxiety and depression, written as "my" anxiety and depression, so on the one hand he is doing his craft, but then cancelling out the real benefits by focusing and associating to his anxiety and depression. Think about the concept of a spell for a moment and the idea of casting a spell, in real terms what is a spell, a spell is a group of letters which make up a word, then extend out into a string or statement, so we are casting spells all day long, and they manifest. That kind of statement works on more than one level, it states having in the here and now acceptance, it states that it is a part of him, thus creating potentially a permanent attachment to the condition that is being associate with, I couldn't define a statement of moving away from any better if I tried it just sums up the power in self- talk, hence the conditional statement. This unfortunately is extremely common with people with illness they continually accept it and associate to it, if they find techniques to dissociate from it the illness would disappear because there is no association and interaction with it. We manifest our perceived reality, actuality almost entirely be the continuous "conditional statements" we make on a day-to-day basis, some statements fire of like a firework and just fizzle out however the ones that have continuous focus put on them manifest and become actualised.

Peoples day to day linguistics, are most people's biggest problem because they talk into unconscious reality what they constantly make statements about; they are stating what they associate or dissociate to, people cast "spells" from books of spells, for good health and money, then go about their day telling everyone how ill and skint they are. It would be quite amusing if it weren't for the fact, it's creating personal chaos in people's lives. That which lifts their mood then on the other hand they are accepting and stating a personal association to anxiety and depression by stating it, this could change just by remembering to say I feel happy and motivated instead. Milton Ericson became prolific as a hypnotist because he understood correspondence and connectivity and the way model operators direct the string or sentence, he clearly understood the physics of linguistics and the way a string of words, suggestions actually can effect reality and behaviour; Quanta defines the smallest part so can and cannot are the smallest part of statements or paragraphs; smallest part in linguistics is the individual letter, symbol or word when we look at the individual word in terms of necessity, possibility, and probability, add positive or negative attributes to it, put them together in a string or paragraph and we really see where the words have power.

If you take two separate people and analyse their linguistics and look at statements they make on a daily basis, one has statements full of negative and necessity, the other has statements of positive and possibility, the one who's linguistics are positive possibility, will be experiencing a better life than the one who's statements are negative necessity, who will sit there for an hour reeling of how problematic their life is. So I added the part about Quantum Physics because there is an absolute science to words, and words do produce a physical effect! In days of old many people thought that words with power where some archaic language or mystical symbols, which they can be (however are you going to cast a spell in an archaic language when you don't know what the words mean) but in real day to day terms, the conditional statements are going into unconscious and being logged as beliefs which then actualise. What gives the word power is what is associated to.

Cannot do associates to not having the ability to, can do associates to having the ability to, So quantum mechanics and entanglement does an amazing job of helping us understand the nature of the universe we exist in even if only a part of Universe can be quantified, it shows us that everything physical starts life as non-physical,(pure thought) but in terms of what causes some people to have fantastic lives even if they started in poverty, and others to just have lives that feel like a constant nightmare, is quite literally down to the use and construct of their use of language.

THE WAY HOLOGRAPHIC THOUGHT DEFINES OUR ACTUALITY

Mindfulness then really is about choosing what we say with awareness of what the words and statements are the cause of, and awareness that the words are absolutely impacting in physical actuality by being logged in unconscious reality. If we have a big picture in our mind of what our ideal reality is, this then acts as a kind of magnet, the words then become directional so although some things may require some kind of physical action "moving toward" like thinking I'd like to wright a book then actually writing it, whether we end up on the path we want and experience having the thing we want comes down to what we talk about most, we literally talk our reality into existence. So life becomes almost like a game of word association, what you associate your life to as being, will be what your experience!

Take the story of Pandoras box, I'm just going out for a minute but while I'm out whatever you do, "don't" open the box, now whoever conceived that story new the art of linguistics, and new this was a statement to do, even though the person listening thinks it's a statement not to do. Darren Brown showed this to be true in one of his tricks of the mind programmes, he had a student in a room with a cat in a box and the box had a wire running from the box to a red button, Darren Brown said to the student, do you like cats, she replied I love cats, Darren then told her that if she pressed the red button it would electrocute and kill the cat, so in the space of several minuets Darren while chatting to her repeated a statement that I will go out of the room soon, when I do don't press the red button he repeated the statement, Darren left the room, and with about ten seconds left on the clock the student just pressed the red button, but had no idea why, she didn't want to she just did, this is the power of words that are directional and processed differently by unconscious mind unconscious does not process negatives! directional and are processed differently by unconscious mind, unconscious.

Do, don't, can, can't, be careful with these words and understand what they are saying to your unconscious they are immensely powerful. We live in a society now where people take in information and talk twenty to the dozen without thinking for a second where the words they are listening to, or speaking are directing them to. Linguistics equals unconsciously perceived reality; I may not be a quantum physicist, but I know

I have got that equation right. As I stated before that although you cannot physically see all these other realities that are playing out from the most positive to the most negative and all the varying from polar opposites to degrees in-between they are there in invisible holographic form, so the point is we are not just creating our own reality, but tuning in to a reality, actuality we choose what we prefer through beliefs and what we focus on the most, what we focus on the most becomes like the turning the button on a radio, this is another way of saying that every possibility in our incarnation exists already and those possibilities, are how eight billon as a linier number choose their reality, by focusing on having, which then becomes the highest probability and slips into our physical here and now. So we have all read and herd people who work in different subject areas that say the same thing; your life is what you focus on most, Think, says, does, in spellcasting, Desire, Intention, Focus; because what you focus on is tuning you into a reality you prefer that is your choice, if the reality that manifests is something you do not want then your tuned into the wrong station.

This is what is meant by moving toward or moving away from, drawing in or pushing away. When you constantly say do not want, consciously thinking you're moving away from what you do not want in-fact the opposite happens, you move toward it, with dimensions i.e. four-dimensional reality it works in an unexpected way, instead of following a linier one, two, three, four, it works like this one, two, four, three, it comes from fourth dimension into the physical third dimension.

When you have something, you have it and the how's do not get focused on, just the having. How is the realm of the unconscious mind. How is like expectation, take the expectation out and just allow things to unfold to the outcome you desire; if you cannot visually see images like a visualisation, it makes no difference, as long as it's perceived, unconscious mind will sort out the visuals, which is down to the way people process information some are very visual and have no problem visualising and some are not. However it makes absolutely no difference it comes down to "perceiving." Perspective is everything, subjective thinking is the realm of imagination, and we can manifest using these subjective tools, it's a different way to what most people are used to but different gets

THE WAY HOLOGRAPHIC THOUGHT DEFINES OUR ACTUALITY

different so if your tied of constant sameness then this is the direction to follow. So to get some direction into the equation that moves you toward what you do want and away from what you do not, focus on creating a big picture of what you would like to be doing or having, keep it in context though, for example if part of what you want requires a degree or formal qualification that takes more than a year to achieve then consider that as being part of a four-year big picture, the point of the big picture is not to focus on amounts of money as such though, write out what financial abundance is for you. Focus more on experiencing the outcome without considering how it would be possible only that it is possible, you can create it like a vision board which defines the type of things you want, but if you are just gazing at it and that is it, then it is not really going to do anything. It is however something you can use it in a way that inspires writing out pre-suppositions of having, vastly more powerful than just gazing at an album of photos, it's the pre-supposition of having already acquired what you desire most; scripting them out in the right way and repeating until they manifest, and they will when you follow the right way to do it. and often it's the small parts that are just as important as the big parts.

For example understanding the way a structured sentence works by virtue of the way it's interpreted by unconscious mind, what the small model operators are doing to the structure of the sentence, i.e. if the model operators when repeated translate as positive or negative, an example is do not, repeated with instruction becomes an instruction to unconscious to do, as opposed to not do. The timeline most associated with moving forward is intime, the one most associated with the past is through time. The difference in timeline can be defined into more creative, or more competitive.

CHAPTER SIXTEEN
TIMELINES EXPLAINED

The concept of timeline is well known amongst hypnotherapists, NLP practitioners, Shaman are but a few who understand the concept of timeline, it is a therapy in itself and does not just stop there, it can be used for regression with "qualified practitioners", or other forms of timeline are, in-time, through time and between time, these relate to the way we perceive past and future. In-time is when a person perceives past and future as out in front of them, through time is when a person perceives their future as out in front and their past as behind them, between time is when this shifts from one of these, back to the other; someone maybe in-time during the week at work and be through time at the weekend when their off, as an example of between time. Timeline therapy is used for an array of things such as PTSD's, phobias, this therapy releases repressed emotions. Conversation is self-hypnosis; we are always in a hypnotic state, Gamma, Beta, Alpha, Theta, and Delta. All these states are hypnotic states, however high beta state appears to be disruptive, and the point of induction is to come out of high beta state, periodically. The history of timeline is not just in NLP but has its roots in Shaman culture this has been used for probably thousands of years, it is a skill, and you must be a qualified practitioner to apply timeline therapy, what I have put in here you can apply for yourself and gain a deeper understanding of what timeline therapy is. If you are affected by trauma of phobias, etc. seek a consultation with a therapist, although there is still much you can do by yourself. In this chapter we will cover what I have dubbed timeline future stepping. Future pacing, which is the process of scripting short paragraphs, like a page for each day in a diary except instead of writing the day's events in as they happened but as you want them to happen future pace each one each day twenty-four hours ahead. Let's look at our speech patterns we talk in the here and now moment always, we are not in a past or future moment but the present here and now; so we talk mostly either in what "has" happened past, and what we would like to happen future, were talking all this in present tense because were present in the moment talking either past or future which Darren Brown said the past and future are stories; so in conversation we are essentially storyboarding.

It is a bit like a progressive relaxation induction in hypnosis, the only difference is in hypnosis a session is twenty minutes to about hour max in general but from when we get up to when we go to bed, we are storyboarding essential in a hypnotic induction. Somewhere in that storyboarding unconscious mind is receiving accepting and applying command, which may come in the form of metaphor, presupposition and strings that run as a command statement to unconscious mind. So, what if we consciously construct ways to talk that would be talking experiences we have not had yet as tough we have had them in in conversation would it cause a so-called reality shift? My answer is yes it would, the concept of quantum jumping is by definition that we are moving through multi dimensions seamlessly by virtue of what we are choosing with or without conscious awareness.

The components of quantum jumps are the energy transfer of an electron within an atom, containing knowledge that will come through physically, this can be knowledge transmitted in conversation of reflections. When we talk, we tend to talk and converse in a way that portrays a reflection, a note to ad on this is it would be a good idea in constructing your reflections is to have anchored statements that actually represent positive events or outcomes that you are already experiencing, does not matter how small or big, it generates a correspondence of already have experienced the emotional equivalents and the dangers of repressed emotions are; Anger: Heart attack, Heightened Cholesterol; Sadness: weakened Immune System, depression; fear: excessive stress, post-traumatic stress disorder, Phobias. Guilt: Lowered healing energy; Inner conflict, cancer; the interesting point of this is the correspondence of fear, anger, guilt, etc. are opposites in nature to the sub-laws or positive human characteristics, wellbeing is not just about a balanced diet, and exercise, and it is also about this "emotions" and the way emotions are a side effect of which side of the sub-laws you are directing yourself to the most! How the timeline works; you have the "here and now, future, this incarnation past, the womb/conception, past incarnations."

Which brings us to the gestalt memory, a memory is not stored in one place like a folder but split like pixels stored in a multitude of different compartments, which include corresponding emotions; are stored somewhere, when we recall a memory all the associated gestalts associated with the memory collect together to form the memory picture, which brings about the framing and re-framing concept. Timeline stores memories in relation to time and not in relation to time, it is the way we define past, present, future; this unconscious process is also known as the Akashic records, which are constantly being bombarded with requests from conscious mind, it's stored as not in relationship to time and when recalled are in relation to time, the memories played out will be recalled as their world view and self-perception in relation to observation. This process can be used for changing feeling states, so you feel a little under the weather, thing back to a time when you felt totally free and elated, hold that thought and focus, as you do this you draw in the feeling state associated with that, it feels good doesn't it, that's how quick you can change feeling states.

Using a memory as a gestalt trigger to draw all the associations to that memory, and the same things happens when we recall unpleasant memories, we recall the feeling state associated with it. If anyone has problems recalling a time when they felt free and happy then I would suggest switching to through time and then try. Before going into this in-time through time traits, bear in mind "cause an effect" different timeline different direction; effectively causing different outcomes, by virtue of what people are and are not associated to. Associated to or not associated to causing and effect in relation to that which is being focused on most. What we are associated to and dissociated from various subjects or objectives throughout the day, a person's overall daily missions or tasks and whether they are achieved comes down to the level of focus, so if

TIMELINES EXPLAINED

someone is working on three or four small things to achieve during the week, they're not really multitasking and probably achieve the outcome because they focused on a small amount of things, and are not scattering their energies so far and wide and give themselves multiple tasks which are unrealistic to achieve in the time given, this sort of aligns to the idea of say starting to build a big picture but you set a timeline of a year which for most is unrealistic.

However when you build a big picture with a timeline of four years it becomes easier and more realistic in terms of any actions required to achieve the overall big picture. For example, you may end up doing a course that takes two years before your big picture really starts to become real, something that would not be achievable in a year. You can set your own time schedule to motivate yourself, however, allow for circumstances or your ideas to possibly change, the thing with setting your targets are it's all right if it takes longer than you thought, because you're doing it for yourself toward your own big picture. So really, the more focus you put in building your own big picture, the more likely you will be to be more "perceiver" biased at least eventually, without changing the timeline deliberately, the point is you can change the timeline and it can be extremely beneficial, because this timeline can be associated to the personality traits of Judger/Perceiver, take a good look at the traits on each one, no one is one hundred percent either one so decide what aspects of each one fit with whatever tasks you have to achieve your big picture, can you appreciate how life transformational applying this can be, just on its own put together with all the other parts in the book and life transformation becomes "possible" whereas before it may have seemed impossible. once you start to put things in perspective with "subjective and objective" parts being applied as opposed to just objective then this starts to take a different path. People will more often than not, "overestimate what they can achieve in a year, and underestimate what they can achieve in four years."

Take this to heart it's an "excellent framework" to work with; this tends to reflect in business start-ups as well, the majority who fail in the first year fail because they overestimated their income in the first year and underestimated their outgoings, and that's the way most businesses fail -

in the first year. It also reflects their attempt to achieve too much in the first year as opposed to a more balanced four years. If you are using subjective and objective when if before you only used objective, then it may well all manifest a lot sooner, somethings may just literally manifest unexpectedly or you may get an inspired idea of an action to take that's pretty much the way it all unfolds, and this is all part of the description of "Law of Attraction, desire, intention and action" but different actions to the ones that were keeping you on a metaphorical treadmill; Judger is the chunked down opposite of the chunked up perceiver, but when we do projects for ourselves we have to chunk up and chunk down by ourselves or to chunked up or down means the project doesn't get done, so we have to find balance between the two an pressures whatever timeline after knowing this we choose to keep as an overall bias.

Knowing this means we have that "choice" which when you ponder it for a while is "self-empowering" and adds to having control of our "own personal destiny." And in appreciating ourselves and what causes our behaviour, and why we do the things we do, in turn makes it easier to appreciate others, and their behaviour and actions; It means if you have trouble relaxing you can switch to in-time and may find it easier to relax without the past being out in front all the time, if you have trouble motivating yourself or fine detail work you can switch to through-time and that could help chunking down jobs or tasks.

For people who have had problems with depression and that which is generally associated with apathy then switching timeline so it's permanent or for a long enough period to move on from the past maybe, especially if it means moving away from relationships that maybe or represent constant conflict. There are often many reasons for conflict in relationships, if you look at how many of your circle of friends or associates are on the same timeline or not, if not and your happy with your timeline and what you're doing then find ways to draw in more people of the same timeline and less that are opposite. The whole point to any of this is to have harmonious relationships not conflicting ones, at least as far as is possible, everything we experience, focus on, laugh about moan about, everything we think do and say is done in the here and now moment, time essentially only exists in the here and now moment, when we think of the past, present, future we do it all in here and now moments; we can be so in the past the we never experience the here and now or so far dreaming of a dream life but taking no action that they never really experience the here and now.

Timeline and relationships: high bias Judgers and high bias perceivers can balance or clash, Judgers will tend to be more competitive whereas perceivers will tend to be more creative, so a judger will want to win or be first, and a- Perceiver will just want to get the project done; Timeline and the workplace: Judgers will see perceivers as slackers; perceivers will see judgers as aloof or jobsworths. Through-time: associated personality types (Myers Briggs) Judger; time is money, will work to rigid deadlines, more likely to cut corners, focus more on the time it takes to get the desired outcome, more likely to be analytical in terms of hypnosis; Can change to non-analytical through changing TimeLine. Positive: Through-time attributes; If all time is in front then the past is easily accessible as a reference, store memories in a dissociated way. Being dissociated from bad memories; are good at diary management; Orderly, planned existence. Negative: Through-time attributes; find it hard to let go or relax, as the past is always out in front of them, associate far more with that which is proved to increase illness.

In-Time: associated personality types (Myers Briggs) Perceiver: the enjoyment is in the doing as much as the getting there, deadlines less important, more likely to be non- analytical in terms of hypnosis, can change to analytical by changing timeline. Less likely to cut corners; focus more on the desired outcome than the time it takes. Positive in-time attributes; can stay focused in chaotic situations, find it easy to return to positive a state. Negative In-Time attributes; may lose track of time, assessing timelines can be done in several ways, one way is to look at the Judger perceiver traits, and if when you find the highest bias then you are in that timeline at least most of the time. So high Judger traits are more through time and perceiver are more through time. Changing/eliciting Timeline; Once you have assessed your timeline, you have control basically of your "direction" if you choose to apply this and decide for yourself what would be the best balance of timelines for what you want to achieve, I have put in too change timeline interventions, the first is for the self and the second one if you have friends who are interested in this can be done with two people, 1: You identify the timeline you wish to move into. 2: You shift your vibrational state to match the timeline. 3: You lock in the vibrational state, so it does not waver. 5: You take an action that is an expression of the new timeline.

5: Anchor. Elicit your Timeline. Clean up the past negative emotions (especially Anger, Sadness, Fear, Hurt, Guilt), limiting decisions. "Here are the consequences of shifting your Timeline. Is it ok with your unconscious mind to make this shift, allow it to remain, and to be comfortable? Rotate the Timeline. "Now just float up above the Timeline, right up above now, and as soon as you like reach out and grab each end of your Timeline and rotate it so that it is in the new direction (location), and when you have done that. Re-associated to now; good, now just float down into the present, and notice that your Timeline is organised in the new way." Lock the Timeline into place: Do you know the sound that Tupperware makes when it seals? Just like that, lock it in place." Test: "As you think of it, will it be all right for your unconscious mind to leave your Timeline this way, and for you to be comfortable? Future Pace: Is there any reason in the future why you wouldn't be totally comfortable with this organisation of your Timeline?

The difference of highest bias toward through-time or-in-time is; for through time having their lifestyle organised for them, for In-time organising themselves is a preference, and actions that become working out of the salary waged day job, and making most of their decisions orientated around the day job, to generating an income independently with own service, product or both, requires being far more through natural progression of doing, In-time orientated, which is far more the timeline direction of, Shaman, Entrepreneurs, and individual thinking and doing in general, so in part it is about developing different personality traits from old to new. All this brings you in line with your own big picture, and develop the abilities to be like an entrepreneur, and be able to depend on yourself far more than in the past. You can switch timelines in an instant, however, to keep let's say in-time bias then ask yourself what are the things you want to do that are more effective with in-time bias, so to start with look at what in-time is so, it's perceiver, so look at the traits for perceiver, then

TIMELINES EXPLAINED

piece together something you think will fit with what you want and move toward that you have to be living the timeline in terms of what your associating to that associates to in-time, to a large degree where perception is projection is concerned, the difference in timeline bias does make it seem like in-time are projecting their actuality off of on side of the mirror, and through time are projecting off of the other side of the same mirror, and pacing things with a more gradual progression attitude as opposed to rush, rush, attitude, also helps with coping with the transitions that occur in the process of change. Too fast and you will get overwhelmed, for example when I was studying, I did not go for the work all day and study after work, I used to chunk up and chunk down so I wasn't overwhelmed, so I would work six months, study six months and rotate it like that., which meant pacing things out and not rushing. So It's not all just mind's eye visualisation, however a combination of understanding principles and techniques and applying them, as you go along stuff just starts to make more sense and things start to slot into place and synchronise not just happen by chance. It's not about trying to achieve one hundred percent in-time or through-time all the time however it is about balance between were you are to start with and where you want to be, which means looking at the traits that fit where you want to be and creating ways to fit in with those traits Rath than just fit in with other people

CHAPTER SEVENTEEN

HYPNOTIC SUGGESTION AND THE THREE CORE CONCEPTS

Wealth, Health and Relationships, Self-referencing and self-fulfilling prophecies. Now for the part that pulls everything together "self- hypnosis", it the first part covers clinical self-hypnosis which is specific, to get started on this find a resource like hypnotic world.com or many other hypnosis sites that sell scripts online most are very affordable, hypnotic world has over a thousand scripts that cover all the mainstream clinical hypnosis stuff, and I would advise using the ones appropriate for you, the reason this chapter is further down in the chapter list is so you get the whole linguistics first, so you can edit the scripts to tailor them for yourself. Use the induction, deepeners, and suggestion scripts as templates, it's a good way to learn how to script for yourself and feel free to edit any part, that is after all what templates are for, get familiar with working with these first and remember if you find any words that unconscious mind will drop because they are negative simply edit the script accordingly, refer to the model operators table if you get stuck with which are negative or positive model operators, remember these are directional in the stringed sentences of suggestion. The second part is about the three core concepts, and a bespoke suggestion script I call cluster scripts, which are in essence metaphorical and vaguely specific which is very powerful. I have also included a progressive relaxation induction and deepener which is a deep hypnotic state induction specifically written for cluster suggestion scrips; unlike clinical hypnosis scripts which are generally two to six sessions depending what they are for, the cluster scripts are done in a medium to deep hypnotic state, you repeat daily until manifestation; remember what I said earlier about reality being the realm of the unconscious and actuality being the realm of consciousness, suggestion scripts will change the unconscious reality and consequently change you actuality, that's the way it works and it absolutely works. When in hypnosis we can re-write the imprint period by virtue that the imprint period is around birth to six years old, this means the conscious mind is not developed, when the conscious mind develops in the modelling period the suggestions does not go straight to unconscious mind, because the critical conscious mind blocks most of what gets trough to unconscious mind, however when in hypnosis it mimics the imprint period because, the conscious mind is essentially on pause, while in hypnotic state. Part two is more about ambiguous statements as suggestions, in other words vaguely specific, vague but contains the specifics in the vagueness.

What exactly is Hypnosis? It is an altered state of consciousness known as a hypnotic state, not trance; a hypnotic state is reached on various levels from light, medium, to profound somnambulism, these states are defined and separate by virtue of the speed of brainwave frequency's, so our beta awake conscious state has the fastest brainwave frequency's, the next is Alpha which is slower light hypnosis, the next is theta which is slower, which is medium, the next is Delta the slowest which is deep hypnotic state, the cusps, Alpha/Theta are light to medium, Theta/Delta are medium to deep. Most if not all clinical hypnosis, which are your quit smoking, weight loss are done in light or light to medium hypnotic state.

Theta and Delta states replicate the brainwave frequencies of a child, Delta is birth to too years old, Theta is too to six years old, and these states are used to change beliefs created in the imprint period, of birth to six years old. As we close our eyes within a few seconds we go into hypnotical state where the body starts to relax and we drift into an altered state, the difference between a hypnotic state and trance is hypnosis is with eyes closed trance can be attained with eyes open. A hypnotic state is a natural state we go through these levels of Beta to Delta every time we go to sleep, which is why James Braid coined the term hypnosis, Hypnos is Greek for sleep. If anyone has any anxiety about going into hypnosis either self or with a practitioner, be reassured you can bring yourself out of a hypnotic trance instantly whenever you like, you are still in control; how it works is if you can imagine a veil between conscious and unconscious mind, in Beta state the veil separates conscious and unconscious, in light hypnotic state the veil is opened enough for suggestions to get through, in medium to deeper state the veil opens to the point of no conscious interference, in lighter states the conscious is partially suspended enough to be in a more heightened state to allow suggestions in, in other words open to suggestion, which is why most clinical hypnosis only requires a light state to medium state..

Technically you can be in a hypnotic state with eyes open, this happens in relation to levels of absorption, so for example when studying, reading a book, watching television, reading a newspaper, we become open to suggestibility by virtue of absorption, which is why there are so many adverts on television in newspapers and magazines, the advertisers know that there is a high percentage of the suggestions in there adverts getting into your unconscious, because they know there is a very good change when you see the advert you are absorbed enough through what you are reading or watching for you to be open to suggestion effectively, in a light to medium hypnotic state. So that in a nutshell is what hypnosis is, being open to suggestion without conscious critical mind blocking the suggestion; the other aspect of this is repetition, unconscious mind accepts suggestion and learns through repetition, so suggestion and repetition is what makes hypnosis work, also the desire to want the change that hypnosis is being used for is very important, you have to have the desire to change whether it be changing a belief or habit, if the desire isn't really there then it's not likely to work, you can go to a hypnotist or hypnotise yourself, you can intend it as in I want to stop biting my fingernails you can intend it, but if the desire to stop biting your nails isn't there i.e. you're doing it because someone else wants you to, it's unlikely to work, you have to want the change "yourself", for yourself. There are three types of induction into a hypnotic state, first is instant which is literally instant, not what you're going to be using for self- hypnosis, is generally used by stage hypnotists I'm not generally a fan of this because it doesn't send the right message about hypnosis, as a practitioner I would only use instant inductions if I have tried several other ways with analytical suggestion, there are legitimate reasons practitioners would use this but it's not necessary in general, the next type is rapid induction which is getting a person or yourself in a hypnotic state in four minutes or under four minutes if your new to self-hypnosis. I wouldn't start with rapid induction, wait until you have been in hypnosis a few times first, the third stage is progressive which is around fifteen to twenty minutes, which is ideal to start with; if you only wish to achieve a light state, then rapid inductions fine, the deeper you want to go then the more progressive the induction, rapid is just an induction when you add deepeners then it becomes more progressive.

So, type one is instant, type two is rapid, type three is progressive. Archetypes, a good deal of negative self-opinion if not all is held in the subconscious, there for a projection of ourselves, rooting from past dominant personality's, present day dominant personality's, unresolved issues, so how do we change our projections from negative to positive, by cultivating "positive" self-perception building self-esteem. A few of years ago when I was studying my hypnosis diploma, I had an apparently intuitive idea to create hypnosis sessions for myself based around what I view as "three core concepts" which covers everything everyone has a wish or desire about, or a negative perspective of; these are. "Health, Wealth, Relationships"; What I did then was to script the perspective, perceptions that I wanted to have and in self-hypnosis project what I wanted to experience as part of my day-to-day life, the idea is that after a period of time they would become habituated thoughts and override negative beliefs or perceptions I had as perspective on a range of things cantered around the three core concepts; after a period of time when at the time living in a noisy environment which often made meditating or concentrating difficult what unfolded showed up as personal prof that this actually works, we can override what may be considered our lot in life and genetic behaviour by creating and installing in our mind-set the perspectives we wish to view our life as for real. The hypnotic sandwich, I want to-I can do-I will do, I am able to do. This is called a hypnotic sandwich used in clinical hypnosis generally in the first session to define desire, intention, the will to achieve the outcome and the ability to achieve the outcome, so for anxiety it would run like this, I want to be free of anxiety, I can be free from anxiety. I will be free from anxiety, I am able to be free from anxiety, for quitting smoking.

I want to be free from smoking tobacco, I am I can be free from smoking tobacco, I will be free from smoking tobacco, I am able to be free from smoking tobacco; for weight loss, I want to lose weight, I can lose weight, I will lose weight, I am able to lose weight; you get the general idea, never use statement like I don't want to be anxious, or I don't want to be a smoker, or I don't want to be overweight, avoid statements like I want to be a non-smoker, non is a negative, used statements like being free from. You can put this sandwich with anything to do with changing and breaking habits, a tip I picked up from NLP is include something that you wouldn't have done before you quit the habit in other words swish the negative habit to a positive preference, i.e. I used to smoke tobacco, or I used to be overweight but now I exercise regularly, or I eat healthy food.

You can use I or you," I" is an affirmation "you" is a post hypnotic, and generally viewed as more effective even for self-hypnosis, leave days and dates out, avoid using anything that could restrict the sub-conscious from manifesting, remember 'how' is the sub-consciousness job, and it does it better than you so leave out how it could manifest, just that it will. Be open to experimenting try different inductions, analytical is viewed to work for all, so try some of them try non-analytical see which feels better for you, try some scrips with "I am," and some with "you are" note any differences, soon enough you will find the ones that you prefer that will work best for you. When you record scripts do so in your normal voice as soft and relaxing, encouraging, it is not necessary adopt a repetitious monotone voice as the old hypnosis books might tell you. Pace out the suggestions with brief pauses, not to fast or slow, just an even pace. Rapid inductions which are four minutes and under, if you already meditate regularly this may suit you, the next is progressive relaxation induction, which is around fifteen to twenty minutes, you can have a ten minute induction and add a five or ten minuet deepener, the two types of induction are analytical and non-analytical, analytical inductions give the conscious mind a job to do i.e. count down from one hundred, or instruct yourself in hypnosis to repeat a tongue twister so your conscious mind is busy on that non-analytical are relaxation scripts i.e. walking in a forest, along a tropical beach or in a beautiful garden. If you're not much into writing your own there are some good resource websites that have pre-written inductions and deepeners, for under £10 a month you can download ten scripts a day.

Hypnotic world.com is one of these recourse sites, you can use the scripts as they are or edit them to suit yourself and use them as templates. I am not putting to many induction or suggestion scripts in the book, as using these recourses which have over a thousand scrips of varying kind will give you a better idea of the broad range of clinical hypnosis scripts and will be good practice editing them for your own requirements and preferences. Before you get into it all with proper suggestion scripts some pointers, start with small things first and build a history of success, i.e. don't go for the biggest problem or addiction first, just start with things you see as from one to ten one being the smallest and build up. Another good resource is Virtual DJ-pro it's free or you can have premium if you want, there are two or four deck skins on it which is ideal for mixing induction, deepener, suggestion script, and background music, it works like a four-track recorder.

I record narrated scripts on voice record on windows then upload them onto Virtual DJ-pro, it's not difficult to use and will give you top quality MP3's for you to play back. It's a good idea to always keep the idea of mind-set in mind, like a magnet we can attract or repel, but people who don't understand this or refuse to accept it often draw into their lives the opposite of what they really desire, they push away what they want, and draw in what they do not want because they are focused on the opposite of what they want, most of the time people in general never write out a list of what they really want from life, because there too busy focusing on all the stuff they don't want (an addiction or being skint all the time) so they stay addicted and skint all the time because this is cause and effect;

this one switch in mind-set changes the whole cause and effect that repeats as your daily experience.

So if you haven't already done this, take your time and write out what you really want for yourself and what you want your lifestyle to be, do you want a job you enjoy that you could do from home, do you want to travel the world, do you want to have a big house. We can categorise our daily live in 7 aspects; 1: Experience's.2: Projects.3: Family.4: Relationships.5: Lifestyle. 6: Home and home life. 7: Interest's and Hobbies. So, when you write in a part of each aspect in our scripts, then we are drawing in positive changes in each area of our life. How do we manifest things and experiences, we do it by making a desire or goal a habitual thought, a habitual thought then becomes a belief which is then the flux of manifestation, the general consensus is that it takes around twenty-one to thirty days to make something habitual, (this is for clinical hypnosis), cluster scripts repeat until manifestation. If we expand on this in view of how we are constructing our scripts, and you are writing the scripts to run daily covering the seven aspects of our lives then everything in the script will become a habituated thought which in turn becomes a belief of set of beliefs and manifests with absolute certainty. The time frame if you look at the scientific research is that thoughts become habitual after around twenty-one days the esoteric idea of cycles suggests around twenty-eight days if you are changing a deep-rooted belief about something then it can possibly be around sixty-six days.

my suggestion for the scripts is to keep each aspect in until it has manifested, then edit it out of the script and add a new one to manifest. It may be a good idea to keep a separate" journal" on this and note how long each new belief took to manifest; when you think about it weather it's an object or an achievement it's the belief in it that creates the manifestation and this is what these scripts do, is turn your thoughts into things and events in your life. My opinion on this is that manifestation can occur anywhere from three minutes, three days, three weeks, three months, it depends entirely on how deep rooted the value or belief around a value is that you're changing, and to some degree whether you're using the affirmation." I" or post hypnotic" you," (me superconscious, myself, is unconscious; I is conscious) the best way to describe this is that unconscious mind has learned the old belief you want to change, and you are unlearning the old belief and re-learning the new one, the transitional process is a paradox. It starts with the old belief being held as true, then you start to repeat the new belief, the paradox is this belief is true, but this new belief could also be true, this is how we change beliefs.

The key to this is to persevere, many beliefs especially around money (not having any) are deep rooted very often from the imprint period, so just be patient and repeat until manifested, it can be frustrating, but if the belief is not in line with the desired outcome you won't get the outcome, it really is as simple as that, using self-hypnosis techniques gives you the unique opportunity to re-write at least some of the beliefs imposed on you in that imprint period, how far you go with this and how much you change is entirely you own choice. Wallace Wattle picked up on this, his book "The Science of Getting Rich," caught the Imagination of a great many people, Wattle definitely got the whole thing about "vital life force," as a substance that permeates and flows through everything in the multi-dimensional Universe, and can change molecular structure, a big claim, and true. Most definitely true; if we look at all the successes in hypnosis, the stuff you may not have heard about, not just quitting habit stuff but reversing terminal illness, but also shows as Bruce Lipton points out, the medicine can cure an illness by changing the genes" and so can belief," in fact the belief is often more powerful than the medicine. It implies there is a Vital life fore, (which has been technically proven by quantum entanglement being proved as real in nature) that it actually is, generally viewed as an invisible fluid substance.

Wallace Wattles book inspired countless people including Rhonda Byrne, and Bob Proctor, from The Secret also pick up on this, Both Rhonda and the people involved in her project however fall slightly short of telling the whole story. They tend to stick with repeated affirmations, and emphasis is on positive thinking and putting love into what you do, gratitude is mentioned and is important part of everything, which is true and to be fair the is only so much you can put in a film that's just over an hour long, hypnosis is not mentioned directly, yet at least two of the participants of the secret are certified hypnotherapists, they skirt around the idea of script writing but still no mention of hypnosis or hypnotic programmes, that said the whole film is pretty chunked up which is fine then you have to chunk down and add the finer detail one thing they got absolutely right is never join groups orientated around problems. Fear of hypnosis, how do you take the fear out of hypnosis if you do not mention it? It is in effect like saying there is something to be fearful of, the main fear of hypnosis comes from stage hypnosis which implies the hypnotist can control you, to some degree that is true if someone was that way inclined they could, but the other side of the coin is you can pull yourself out of hypnosis anytime you like and stage hypnosis doesn't really reflect therapeutic hypnosis so it has had a stigma attached to it, which is not valid in terms of the type of hypnosis we are talking about here, one of the main reasons.

I have put this book together is everything in the book is designed so you can do it all yourself or at least for the best part. I believe many people would be far more comfortable with the idea of hypnotising themselves as opposed to going to a practitioner, although if you have a serious phobia or post-traumatic stress disorders I would recommend seeing a hypnotherapist of an NLP practitioner, because the type of interventions used in NLP for this are extremely effective and really need a practitioner and the person, for things like timeline, and integration of parts or even blow out interventions which I have left out of this book because you really need to be a practitioner to do those type of interventions. I first came to realise there was more to life than what we are conditioned to believe in my teens, I was good at Art and used to go in a small bookshop in my hometown, to buy books on art and fantasy art, they had an occult and self-help section.

One day I was drawn to a book called The Encyclopaedic Psychic Dictionary-by June G Bletzer. Buying this book proved to be a defining point in my life, it included all the Universal Laws and some, the book was a revelation to me and was the start of a path I now still follow, I can remember meditating for hours on this entry. Law of, "Like Attracts Like," this is the full commentary of what it said. Atoms will colonize because of their similarity, and thereby form various levels of matter. That which has similarity will be in sympathy or compatible with that like nature, working both subjectively and objectively," birds of a feather flock together," No one escapes the principle in this plane or in the "Etheric World." Negative and inferior thoughts bring about undesirable thoughts and manifestations. Positive outlook on life brings about happiness and beneficial manifestations. This works throughout all types of "Psychism and Mediumship." One should start with a neutral mind in order to perceive correct psychic information. (Robert E Massy) "Nonsense begets nonsense," junk gives out junk and brings back junk." June Bletzer, as far as I'm concerned produced one of the single most important books ever published. I still refer to this book regularly to this day, unfortunately when I was just getting into what the book was saying it was lost in transit, I tried to purchase it again but had apparently gone out of print, it would be twenty years until I found and brought a replacement copy.

Where do we go with this information? Focused thoughts manifest as day to day occurrences, and can be changed with hypnotherapy/'self-hypnosis', with a big stigma that still surrounds hypnosis, self-hypnosis self-suggestion' is more likely to become the most attractive way of creating positive change in one's life for a large number of people, however those who try 'self-hypnosis' and realize it actually work's may well decide to employ 'hypnotherapists' for further self-help or as a life coach, it really depend on how far each person does or doesn't want to go with this. Everyone is different so there is no hard and fast rule when it comes down to what fits with each individual at wherever there at when they start exploring all of this. A premeditated instruction to the unconsciousness to manifest into waking reality the object, objective, accomplishment, desire, sort after by the individual, acceptance of information by the subconscious brings about a kind of chain reaction whereby the corresponding opposite to suggestion is manifestation, it is however part of the same whole. Like a question and answer are corresponding opposites, the end result of a question is an answer so end result of a hypnotic script, suggestion, is manifestation.

The suggestion causes the manifestation, "the law of 'push and pull'". So taken literary "anything is possible"; however we can have anything, but not everything, it comes down to "focus" and what we are focusing on, if we constantly focus on negative end results, then the results will be 'negative, if we 'focus' on results that are 'positive' and beneficial to the self then we receive positive' results, and also how toward positive "human attributes" we cultivate or aspire to the twenty one universal sub laws, (which represents the nature of spirit, vital life force) is also a big influence in our personal returns. Therefore hypnosis and moreover the focal pinots of hypnosis, should always focus on the positive attributes of subject, the positive attribute of Illness is health and wellbeing, So on entering into practicing self-hypnosis, you have the key to being and becoming your true self, as opposed to a cloned conditioned version of the self. The belief systems you find yourself stuck with may not have been in your control back when they were being developed but they are in your control now, it's not your fault if you have a stack of negative beliefs but it is your responsibility to change them, no matter how fair or unfair that may seem that's just how it is.

Everybody wants to be 'happy, healthy and wealthy', yet the vast majority of the global population of eight Billion people and counting, believe their life is already fated predestined and they have no way of changing it, (which is a conditioned belief) there is a common belief that those who are born in 'wealthy family's' stay 'wealthy', those who are born in 'poverty' or in lower income family's stay in 'poverty' or low income, which is what social science will tell you however it's only a belief which can be changed, it can absolutely be changed.

we have original paradigms that are set this way and we can re-set, reframe them and the best tool for doing this apart from a better understanding of linguistics and the directional power of words, is through self- hypnosis this is the key to the door so to speak. Paradigms are variables not absolutes; are preconceived beliefs that "can" be changed. for instance many people say out loud or to themselves what they "don't" want pretty much all day long, everyday, which is focused thought so consequently keep receiving what they don't want, because this is what they are constantly "focused" on, they say they do not want to be poor this is the quickest and easiest way to ensure they stay poor, the solution is very simple switch over, the easiest way to do that is start talking about the positive things you do have, talk about what you do want, elevate yourself above do not want, we say do not want in a multitude of different ways, i.e. complaining about the smallest things all the time, self-hypnosis will be boosted even more if you become far more consciously aware of what you're saying and what direction what your saying is taking you. So we end up with two definite ways to manifest our desires.

1: Hypnosis either by the self or by a hypnotherapist; 2: what we focus the rest of our day to day thoughts on, every day, we apparently have over sixty five thousand thoughts a day, so the trick if you like is to focus a positive set of attributes onto as many thoughts and statements as possible each day, if this seems a little overwhelming then remember what I showed you in the chunked up chunked down chapter, when the chunked down is getting a bit much. chunk up for a while and follow that process of chunk up, chunk down. These two processes of manifestation seem to have somehow been separated on how their viewed, which in effect means what you manifest is from your own choice or outside making the choices for you, the same with hypnosis, in as much as people may use hypnosis to get specific objects or objectives, but not use it in a more subjective vaguely specific "ambiguous" way "do both" when both are applied together then we start to find whole areas of our lives actually playing out as we desired, a successful hypnosis session does manifest the end result desired, and so do chains of thought held over a period of time that could be said to be a cycle; and that's the way everything in universe works by cycles, the cycles of the seasons, what goes around comes around, the body regenerating to perfect health or staying ill all happens cyclically.

The period between thought being impressed on the unconsciousness and manifested end result is cyclic, thoughts become forms, which become things and experiences. So a spin off role for a hypnotherapist is one also of a life coach if incorporating these two processes to manifestation, the use of self-suggestion quotes stating intent as done and focusing on the benefits of the end result can really boost, and be used separate from hypnosis, effectively what I am doing with this book is showing you how to be your own hypnotherapist and life coach at least for the best part. In essence what we are doing is finding and learning processes of communicating with the unconsciousness, and accessing and changing what are known in esoteric circles as our Akashic records, whereby any old unwanted ways of thinking and doing things, and associations to things are changed to what we desired rather than manifestations that come from following blindly conditioned ways of thinking, and conditioned expectations, expectation can be one of the most limiting things you have, in a scene of always expecting the worst instead of being hopeful of the best outcome.

The key word here is focus if we focus negatively on what we expect to receive, and then surely what we receive will be negative. So what we expect to receive is as important to focus on as what we want to receive. Our entire lives up to this point have played out in accordance with what we were focused on, it's easy to get caught up in a debate but for that period of time you give your thoughts and emotions on what you're debating you are attracting the results of your reaction to the debate. Expectation: is a strong belief that something will happen or be the case, synonymous the presupposition, presumption, assumption. Hopeful is feeling or inspiring optimism about a future event, a person likely or hoping to succeed; Although this seems a bit like word play meanings are important, although expectation and hopeful are to some degree opposite in meaning, if you start of hopeful then this can lead into expecting but with a positive spin to it, so if in reading this book you have never used any of the techniques or self- hypnosis, be hopeful that it will work then as you beliefs change you can expect it to work.

This works by virtue of "history of success" you start off hopeful get some success no matter how small it becomes history of success, then you have the knowledge it will work, like anything think big, start small, and build from that. When I say for example with cluster scrips repeat until manifestation then be hopeful it will work, the thing is when I say repeat until manifestation I mean repeat until manifestation if after one or two months nothings really happened the just be patient, it will as I have said some of the beliefs you will be changing are very deep rooted so it may take a while before the new belief gets to the top of that belief hierarchy, make the commitment beforehand to stick with it, and you will transform your life; this process is a bit like planting a seed, then the simple root sprouts, and then the plant grow it's kind of along that same principle. However if you keep saying nothing's happening, well that becomes a self-fulfilling prophecy, so stay hopeful stay the course and you

HYPNOTIC SUGGESTION AND THE THREE CORE CONCEPTS

will get the outcomes you desire. However if you give up after a month and say it hasn't worked, it was working you just gave up, so be committed; a forty-five-minute session every day isn't a lot of time and will change and transform your life, script the vaguely specifics, and let unconscious mind script the how's. In the context of hypnosis, and changing beliefs, for example if you have been working on changing your beliefs around wealth, to more positive ones than before, should you expect to become wealthy, well yes when the expectation is in alignment with the belief, then you should expect to become wealthy, because they are the new beliefs, that said it probably not probable or though not impossible that you will just hit the jackpot on the lottery, it is more likely that a synchronisation of events and taking some form of action will generate the wealth, unfortunately there is no hard and fast timeline, of a set of accepted beliefs of being wealthy will manifest, and in general the most successful people became successful because they were doing something that in some way benefited others, or was something people liked, so the best advice I have whether you at school or out doing a day job is to master a craft or do something you already know how to do that you really love doing that you can Generate an income with it. The key to success is to be creative, not focus on what everyone else is doing or not doing for that matter.

All the people I used as positive mentors in recent years can all profess their subject very well, none gained wealth from winning the lottery and thinking that way is a competitive way of thinking, the more creative and less competitive your thinking becomes then the sooner you will elevate yourself, as you run scrips every day, and bring yourself more in alignment with wealth you may well get an intuitive idea, to do something that will lead to something that give you a breakthrough, I have experienced this often, if you don't know how you're going to succeed that doesn't matter just know that you will, trust the process and it will work everything in universe is systematic and runs in cycles, so follow the process of running the cluster scripts every day and things will change but remember it will not just all fall in your lap. You will have to act here and there, you will just be in a much stronger position to know what action to take, and as I have mentioned throughout the book look at what your linguistics when you talk in general are describing yourself and your life. As this will give you invaluable clues as in what to change, when you start to see a negative pattern in your description of yourself and your life in what you are saying, you can start to overlay it and put yourself on a path that you would prefer rather than one you have been stuck with, and like riding a bike just practice until you find the balance. "Like attracts like" a positive accepted suggestion, will attract a positive outcome, connected to what the intention in the suggestion is.

CHAPTER EIGHTEEN

THE PRINCIPLES OF HYPNOSIS AND DEFINING YOUR TRUE SELF-PATH

Desire and intention in a script are key; the nature of a hypnosis script is the same as computer code like HTML, or, PHP essentially strings of instructions/commands, unconscious mind needs clear commands from you, you have been sending clear commands up until now you just didn't know how to construct and send the commands that give you the desired outcome not the undesired outcome. For most people they're not doing much with them, because their actions and reactions to day to day events have been conditioned, after a fair bit of experimenting and research it has become increasingly apparent to me that the vast amount of conditioning is designed to herd us away from the idea and belief, that we have absolute free will to make our choices and change our lives in ways we are told would be impossible, however it is possible, if you think possible then somewhere along the line it has to become possible, that is what the whole law of attraction thing states, if you think it is possible then you attract it being possible and via-versa. For the time being let's focus on what free will is and what conditioning has done to stifle our free will. And the methods used to do this. Let's look at some key areas of conditioning that directly oppose our free will. We are conditioned to be Prejudice! Of sexuality, colour, physical appearance, and beliefs that are not in line with our own; even the most natural nudity/nudism. All these are in direct opposition and designed to restrict and impose on our individual "free will". we are constantly bombarded with all the things we can't do so start to focus on all the things you can do, keep it within the context of not intending hard and you won't go far wrong, you may still get the odd upset or diversion but that's just part of the path and our life path is about learning, and we make mistakes and learn from them it's all part of the path. At the end of the day as they say we are all spirit in physical for and we all have the right to a free willed life on this incredible planet.

The conundrum of this is, we have free will of choice as our birth right, a gift from the infinite spirit that resides in all things, so when we live by the guidance of "an it harm ye none do as thy will", which is effectively reiterated by the Chinese proverb of " to poison the well of another person is to poison their own", then manmade law and the though shalt not's, appear to run as an instruction to the unconscious "to do", not, not to do, and when something is made taboo it effectively makes people want to do it more because of this misunderstanding in linguistics and the way unconscious mind processes an instruction from conscious mind or outside stimuli; my point is that it seems to me that the more laws there are saying don't do the more unconscious mind is processing the don't do as "do". So when writing hypnosis scrips and listening to other people be aware of how unconscious mind is processing the words as commands, it's particularly important. You want your scripts to give you the desired outcome not and undesired outcome because you didn't take notice of the way unconscious mind processes information, it's not like it speaks a different language it just doesn't process negatives, it may do in singular terms, lets sat don't plug that in with wet hands, but when the same instruction is given with don'ts, or cant's then it will process the negative as a positive, it's very important to remember this.

Then with some time and practice you find yourselves naturally attracting the type of relationships and circumstances that are right for you and the people we are drawn to and who are drawn to us, we become more self-reliant and Independent. Our freedom of expression is part of who we are, we are conditioned to be "prejudiced" this is in direct conflict to our "freedom of expression", there are massive stigmas put on a whole range of things that represent freedom of expression; "Sexuality" is probably one of the most heavily stigmatized acts of free will and expression, the whole free love movement of the sixties was a wakeup call, that people have an individual right to express their sexuality and feel good about nudity, but still this day it is stigmatized. We are conditioned to suppress sexual feelings, feel "guilty anxious or fearful"; these are negative repressed emotions which are not exactly healthy, repressed emotions unresolved issue are a big problem for people and there is a good deal of evidence now to suggest it is the cause of a good deal of illness, because it causes inner conflict, "freewill" has for the best part been replaced with conditions will, people do what's expected of them without question rather that saying hey, actually I don't want to do that I would prefer to do something else instead.

The reason I have put this in the hypnosis chapter is because it is important, it's important to understand that we do have free will over our own choices, I'm not saying refuse to do things just for the sake of it I'm saying do you every question what you have been asked or told what to do, or do you just follow blindly even though effectively it's against your will, Esther Hicks made a brilliant comment right at the end of the Secret after the credits had gone up, "you do not have to do what you're supposed to, you only have to do that which you choose to" and it's true. When we act or respond from what are known as the twenty-one universal sub-laws which are also known as positive elementals or positive attributes, the more inline you can bring yourself to these positive human attributes, the more positive the outcomes. If you want to understand more about releasing negative supressed/emotions I would suggest arranging an initial consultation, with an NLP practitioner, as NLP timeline is the intervention for this, I have put a fair bit in the book that is NLP however timeline requires a "qualified practitioner" I wouldn't recommend trying to do it on your own which is why I have omitted timeline interventions from the book as you do have to be qualified at master level to apply this, and it does take two people the practitioner and the client.

What I have put in the book is everything I have come across that a person can apply for themselves in their own time and space. What I would say about timeline interventions though is miracles have literally happened through timeline interventions, it's a very ancient intervention that originates from Shamans; and please do not try these interventions unless you are qualified; that would also include not practice hypnosis on other people just from reading this book you do have to be qualified to do this with other people, just to re-iterate I am qualified at master level and have put many, many years study research and work into it, this book is designed to be work on yourself not on other people! Self-healing a subject which for most seems impossible, it is possible! Which brings us back to the "dynamics" of hypnosis self-suggestion and scripts; disease, poverty, war, and all the other unpleasant things you can think of happen because the larger portion of the population are focusing on them, the focus is held in place by newspapers television news, television programming and computer games, these are the main offenders of peddling negative propaganda, In short, we need to ignore this completely! When we focus on the negative, we attract the negative into our lives.

Like our sub consciousness we either accept or decline information, like computer Boolean script, true or false, there is no room for middle ground on this as soon as the "what if's" come into play we put up a negative block on our progress. Be aware of what you are focusing on, if not at all times, then as often as possible this is especially important in creating the lives that we want to live, "Create not compete", as Wallace Wattle said in the science of getting rich is very true.

As "Bob Proctor" of the Secret said, Tiger woods was untouchable as a golfer because he focused on perfecting and creating his own game, he was not competing, it comes down to focusing on being the best that you can be, at what you do. When you compete an element of jealousy is likely to creep in especially if you lose, jealousy is a negative elemental; so we are now focused on replacing negative elemental's with positive ones, erase, replace. Distort generalise and delete, Erase replace is the principle behind changing our paradigms; when we change our paradigms, we can change what our lives become. Our minds are seemingly split, into consciousness, unconsciousness, and receives information from the super consciousness, these are also referred to as left and right hemispheres of the brain, the left apparently controlling the right side of the body and the right hemisphere control's the left side of the body, the spine being like a super conscious conveying information. Also the way vital life force travels out of the body through the solar plexus. How events in our everyday lives evolve, through the connection of these three elements, information being received through the senses and then being processed for manifestation, into the events in our lives right through to habits and preferred taste, and a programming tool for this is suggestion, and the "law of suggestion" is the principle behind hypnosis. All Human civilizations have been built from suggestion; So with this knowledge and practice we can in effect write out our own lives, to play out in actuality like a film at the pictures.to the point of being able to change our so-called genes; So just what we can achieve using hypnosis and other forms of self-suggestion? Possibility and infinite outcomes, anything, however not everything it seems "if the mind can conceive the idea of something then it already exists". vision boards for example, the idea that the picture is the object or thing, and that one is already in possession of it has been claimed for many years, by substantial numbers of people to be true, what they put on their boards did materialize. Recognition: In writing scripts recognition should be given to the positive attributes and characteristics of the opposite negatives the script is designed to reframe or replace; Similar in nature, mind and computers, relationships between conscious, subconscious, super-conscious.

Computer memory, information online, the screen the instruction manifests on. The mind is an immensely powerful thing; it has the blueprint to perfection. Keywords scripts serendipitous events and what they are; what we think and what we feel become our life experience, "attraction" we can change and turn things around for ourselves with Suggestion, when these two laws are put together it creates manifestation; Suggestion creates the attraction and repulsion, when we attract something, we also repel it's corresponding opposite, suggestion creates the manifestation. Surrendering is to give up what you do want and bend to what someone else wants you to do which is not your will; everything we experience is a reality in our perception of our present life experience if everything were an illusion it would not be called reality shifting, it would be called illusionary shifting.

Illusions are a misdirection which creates the sense of illusion; we need to be careful and aware of what we accept as true, and often two or more main principles with self-hypnosis and hypnosis in general. If you want diplomas in hypnosis or NLP you have to go through all the clinical hypnosis and NLP stuff, it is a "lot" of work these things are not a game, but if you just want to transform your life then having a good induction and deepener that works for you is key, then follow these basic principles, follow the style of the suggestion script of vaguely specific, which means just getting your head into the idea of abstracts, and how the object or objectives you want are written in a predominantly vaguely specific, it can contain specific but if you put a specific location for example where you think you want to live like a town, it can restrict the outcomes maybe there is somewhere much better suited to you that your unconscious can see but you cannot, unconscious is like the mountain peak it can see over the whole mountain range, conscious mind is like the river that flows through the mountain range.

Ambiguous statements, are very powerful, the effect of the script is holding the desire and intention you then have to apply the action, the most effective way to do that is in hypnosis sprits and repeating it daily once a day, or a few times each week keeps the focus on the desire and intention which then overrides any previous stuff that may have been blocking it previously, in other words repeat the script and it will manifest, you just have to preserver and be a little patient, and just let it unfold. You can skip the first part of hypnosis chapter if you like and just focus on the deep hypnosis induction and start repeating the ambiguous, (vaguely specific), metaphorical or command statements as soon as you have put them together and literally just play it back every day or at least four times a week. If you're just interested in transforming your own life, then cluster scripts in a deep hypnotic state is really the way forward. Look at these types of scripts a bit, have you ever got a tablet prescription from a doctor and been told it takes a couple of weeks before the tablets kick in, well view this type of self-hypnosis as the same, and just keep going with them.

Forming scripts

I will explain how to write your hypnosis scripts, and in what context to write them. I will explain to you the whole visualization procedure and why it's not all about just closing your eyes and seeing the pictures. I will also explain how to communicate with you unconscious effectively on a daily basis; it is all just about following a set of procedures. Three really summed up effectively by these word's "Think Says Does" you will see as we go on why these word's sum it up perfectly. The three procedures are creating scripts and directing attitude toward an idea or concept. Self-Hypnosis (repeated daily until manifestation occurs) it is thought however that hypnosis and scripts delivered in a deep trance such as somnambulistic or coma states require less repetitions because conscious mind is completely suspended, creating real life experiences, It is this simple, what you will be doing is writing a dress rehearsal of your experience, in that context, but you will be writing as though it is already manifest, when you read it back it reads as a diary of days, and future events, "as though they have already been lived".

When you hear someone say they visualized something into their lives this is the same thing only you're visualizing your day and future, not just one thing. There are guidelines that when followed will ensure that all turns out well basically, the guidelines are mostly to do with how you formulate the scripts, If you were reflecting on the events of you day the day before you would start at how the day started and continue from there until you get to the last events of the day this is exactly how you write the scripts in that context so when you read it back it reads in past tense. Your job then is to communicate this script to your unconsciousness during a hypnotic trance.

This part of the process takes around forty-five minutes to complete, (if in somnambulism, then time distorts so you can have fifteen minutes of suggestion if you like) you are doing it for yourself so play with it and find ways that fit best for you, you can use the commonly known method of narrating your script onto a relaxing music background and playing it back on headphones, make sure any background music will take you from start to finish of the hypnotic session while just playing it back. Another method is to write the script out and read it back, out load. Then the unconsciousness comes into its own, it say's OK you can programme your daily experiences if you like, but when you don't "I will," and as you now know if you just leave it to your pre-programmed unconscious, it will script your day-to-day experiences by your reactions and conversation. So the first thing you need to realise is you have to script your day-to-day life experiences like this, every day, and you will live the life you want to live on a day-to-day basis, your unconscious is if you like, a caretaker of your life while you are not-instructing it to manifest anything differently.

So you need to make writing your script's habitual, to make something habitual like this would mean repeating this every day for around twenty-one days after this you will be writing them with seemingly no effort; the other habit you must do every day is a self-hypnosis session; When you put these together the "do it" aspect comes in, you will be doing what you're scripting. So in affect what you will be doing is creating your own space time continuum, that will play out as your life experiences; so the script actually does become the dress rehearsal. Scientists have had bio feedback equipment connected to athletes and it showed up that visualisation is like a dress rehearsal they asked athletes to visualise running a race and all the muscles that would be involved in that event fired up, this was called voluntary motor rehearsal my procedure's follow exactly the same principle if you go there in the mind, you will go there in the body. If you look at television season films they run an episode at a time, this is exactly how you will script you're lives, as day to day episodes. So now you go from just accepting lives running out on default, to setting the defaults you're self. You have now put you're self in the picture that is your life, you have painted you're self into your life which is your masterpiece.

You now Direct and have "star role" in your life, not anyone else who has popped themselves in your existence by default; in order to move out of your present perceived circumstances you have to think "meta" above and beyond, and you create the above and beyond when, you are following this formula. The "meta" then becomes your present perceived circumstance, so now I guess you're saying to yourselves one hour day I will happily spend five to six hours a day doing this if it turns my life round to what I want, and I would say, exactly! A note about this is after a while if you are through time, you will naturally become more in-time. With practice thought it shouldn't take much more than 1 hour a day. One of the first steps you could take in this is maybe thinking who you would like your life to be thirty days from now this is a good start point and starts the visualisation process, then write the outline of it backwards to the here and now.

Then you are setting your objectives and end results, to be manifested.so look at how you would like your life to be playing out thirty days ahead keep it believable to you and build up experiences and wealth, through gradual progression not trying to get it "all done" in thirty days. Also beer in mind there is a time buffer so it may take sixty or ninety or more days, before initial results start showing, so you're not likely to see instant results in seven days but keep it up daily and the time buffer will be dependent on a few things like what beliefs and values have to change to be in line with the outcome you desire, the continuous process of scripting your life is very worthwhile, and beneficial to you. In Terms of timelines in real terms different things, objectives have different variables so there is no one set timeline from script to manifestation, you just follow the process of applying suggestion. So the meaning of life, is the meaning and purpose you give to it by what you script in. A reminder on inductions and deepeners, you put these in the front of the hypnosis session it is designed to put you in a hypnotic trance known as heightened suggestibility; there are two types of inductions and deepeners, Analytical which is around twenty percent of the population and non-analytical about eighty percent of the population, the first thing you need to know about this is analytical will hypnotise one hundred percent, non-analytical will only hypnotise around eighty percent .I will go more in depth on this later. Understanding self-hypnosis is also vitally important, and extremely rewarding, the process involves narrowing the conscious in effect putting it in suspended animation, while helpful suggestions are past directly to the unconsciousness, without the conscious censoring it, so to speak, your unconscious then files the suggestions in the appropriate place, and manifestation occurs. You do not need to think of how it will manifest, that's the unconsciousness job, and it does it precisely, stating you won the lottery and things like that are just pointless.

So what we are dealing with here is "Meta daydreaming" Bringing the above and beyond daydream into waking feeling touching actuality. Ever woke up from a dream and it felt so, reel, well the scripts you will be writing will feel, so, real, and then be real. So if you were at the bottom of a mountain, you wouldn't try to jump to the top in one leap, try and bear this in mind when writing your scripts, you want to build up a continuous flow rather than erratic jumping here there and everywhere style, if you see what I mean.

You then just continue to continue from there and write in your script quick note on relationships, you should only write in the "types" of relationships and people you would like to draw into your life not specific persons, but type of person. This is especially important, you are writing your life script not anyone else's so keep the focus on you, unconscious will take care of matching you with like mind. You could play with different concepts and ideas with self-hypnosis, as we are talking a most of our life in each day in conversation how about trying a daily self-conversation script, start by writing scripts in the morning and then doing a self-hypnosis session at the end of the day, you would relive a day's events at the end of the day so doing it like this keeps it feeling natural; and is possibly an easier way to fit it into your day. I have dubbed this timeline future stepping you can also use a reflection style script. See future timeline stepping. One note about the self-hypnosis session you should make sure it's at a time when you won't be disrupted. "Finding time from distractions to focus on yourself" distraction do exactly that, distract you form your goals and intentions, so you would want to claim as much of the day to focus on "you," as you can do, this is also an important part in the grand scheme of things. To make it easy to navigate the script you could split it in three segments awake to lunch, lunch to early evening, early evening until bed. I am sure you get the general idea of this, what happens now is you are now "creating" you. Your own life existence, you are no longer "competing" this is also an important thing to understand. You are creating your own day to day experiences or will be when you're doing this on a day-to-day basis, the reason I say this is we generally look on our life unfolding on a day-to-day basis.

So it just makes it common sense to do this on a daily basis rather than just using clinical hypnosis to change one specific thing at a time; Paradigms change because the belief has changed. The difference between traditional hypnosis scripts and this formula is hypnotherapy scripts tend to focus on a specific area or thing in your life, whereas this formula is fluid, like a set of television episodes with more than one area or thing included. So it comes down to accepting attractions, and declining or repelling distractions, the more of the day-to-day thoughts you put into focusing on what you want to attract the quicker the whole manifestation process is, so if you were to practice using a prop like writing your daily script and what you're going to write in for tomorrow or next week. You then bring you're focus back onto the here and now you and away from the distractions this may take a little practice but the benefits to oneself are impressive.

Then your life becomes a loop of what you love to do as opposed to being a loop of unfocused reactions to distractions, so your job basically is to create lots of positive distractions that repel negative distractions from your life by creating ones you wanted. (a house, a car). Personal characteristics, attract like characteristics, this is the base of how and we attract on a vibrational frequency, how we draw relationships into our lives by matching characteristics hedonistic people will draw hedonistic type people, non-smokers with an interest in politics, will draw non-smokers with an interest in politics, however you should not attempt to convert others on different paths ways of doing things to fit in with you, when you know that would be against their free will, you cannot have your own free will when your steeling other people, may sound hard however you would not want the negative personal returns of converting others against their will; focus on fitting in with yourself! When a person wants to change his or Her habit or interest in say, politics to say painting, then that person's circle of friends and circumstances would change to. If someone is going round in circles in their life it is because they are only focused on their present circumstance and normally complaining about it, they may have dreams they want to achieve but they never get them because of how they judge their so-called situation, what they really want stays out of reach because they are in effect on a treadmill.

One way to start achieving what you want is to cut out as much negative input in your life as realistically as you can, you could stopping watching the news all the time, and buying newspapers all the time, this has become an institutionalised habit amongst most people it is very negative in its orientation and thus traps people into a negative frame of mind and distracts the mind from focusing on more positive outcomes. People keep doing the same job year in year out, but they are not doing what they love, or just using a job for a while to help set themselves up to be able to start doing what they love. They are just stuck like being on a merry go round but not so merry, to stop going round in circles you must get off what it is you are going round and round on, like the wheel of fortune you can stay on the wheel, going round and round, or get off at your chosen path.

The so-called work ethic can benefit people, but your work ethic should be about doing something you love and enjoy doing. This creates positive emotion which in turn create more positive circumstances, bringing your future goals and desires into the present-day experience Looking ahead at where you want to be and what you wish to have in life, is what I would call working with a life script path; then breaking the goals down into daily, or repeat until manifest cluster scripts to achieve your desire. Hypnosis plays an important role here this becomes the final part of the puzzle, it becomes the flux that creates the manifestation; this can be broken down into component parts, writing out hypnosis scripts describing how you're life is and describe what manifestations of improvements in your life are, this is important to write 'in there here and now' as though already experienced, the importance of that becomes apparent when you are applying it to your daily self-hypnosis session. Vision boards and affirmation reminders are a powerful tool that will help you write affirmations in the daily scripts, and the images on the vision board show the object and you view it as already yours, which will feel easy once the scripts that are associated with the boards are accepted by the unconsciousness. Anyone who has experienced a full hypnosis session will probably remember the feeling that the scripts are taking them somewhere!

The feeling that you are experiencing the events of the script in the here and now, hypnosis applied in this way, the scripts are moving you to your future most people can't see into the future, but we can all draw the future into our present day reality: when this is put into practice self-hypnosis on a daily basis this takes us way above and beyond as hypnotic scripts for one thing are subjective manifesting the objective, desired outcome, it becomes our own responsibility, designing our lifestyle and life as we choose to live it with free will: the alternative is a conditioned, reactionary loop of events being played out seemingly by chance, in a way that feels like you have no control over your destiny, our "health, wealth or relationships". Now for a lot of people the biggest obstacle to overcome is distractions, so the first thing to do is work out a way to get as much of the day for you as you can, to focus on yourself and your scripts: and in freeing up time for yourself you are also making space for your new lifestyle to manifest. If you have a very hectic daily routine, then making the time to focus on goals and scripts is important this now becomes one of your daily habits but is important to spend time before hand working on the theme of the path your scripting into your experience.

After doing this for around twenty one days this process becomes habitual like cleaning your teeth each day, or something you just do regularly it only takes a little effort and you do it automatically, in each daily script put in things that you already have in your life that are good and make you feel good, and write in the tense of gratitude/appreciation; the twenty one day cycle which is said to be a time frame to work off to build up good habits, is what is being referred to as a time buffer, this is because unconscious mind learns through repetition, then locks it in. I would define this as when the unconsciousness accepts receiving information in this way, then manifestation with conscious self-awareness begins. After some time, your life will start to become more of a reflection of what you're scripting as opposed to a life that's in relation to responding, as opposed to reacting which creates a more measured approach and putting things into proper perspective instead of overreacting.

There are groups that are designed for problems that conditioned people in the opposite way to free will and are to my mind in effect can become like a destructive brainwashing cult, to my mind swish patterns and self-hypnosis would be a better option and is more chunk up out of the problem rather than going to groups that fours on the problem, more find solutions than problems. Now Ester Hicks in the film the secret says the same groups orientated around problems keep you focused on the problem, so there not free of the problem and many have a cult style to them when they try to leave.

if you look at some of their quotes love to much, tough love these are not positive elementals, they are negative in their intent unconditional love and self-love and self-responsibility are what can be aspired to, tough love is just a way to try to control another's actions and the end result for them is they push everyone away rather than attracting positive people they try to control, anyone with any self-worth is going to run a mile from control freaks. All trying to control people does is fuel their ego, oh I got my own way, I got them to do this and that when they really didn't want to; that's not what life's about, it's about building a life for yourself that you can love and is about who you are not about what someone else wants. I feel moved to write on this because I see so many people every day living in this way the best part of their days seem to be about, or focused on what other people are doing, when people are buying newspapers watching television, news they are in effect for the best part focusing on other people's lives and having their thoughts and beliefs conditioned as well. If your allowing untold distractions in your life everyday then they're not focused on their own life so how can they possibly change their lives, they can't, they do not know how to, and because they do not know how to they take their frustration out on other by trying to control them. What has this got to do with hypnosis?

Well a lot actually because hypnosis and what the secret is; suggestion; the law of attraction is in effect, cause and effect, through suggestion this has to be applied, so where there is to a certain extent a stigma around hypnosis people are being hypnotised every single day every single person without them even realising it, the more we research the unconscious the more we know how information is processed and weather its accepted as a true fact or not, the thing is we can use these same techniques to our own benefit. Look at the similarity between a vision board and a billboard advert, so right off people know that billboard advertising works or billions of pounds wouldn't be being spent on it, so another keyway to change our own lives is to look at techniques that are designed to condition us or sell us something to our own advantage. After all these are all subtle types of hypnosis, and we can use these to benefit us rather than be conditioned by them; television is a very powerful conditioner so we could look at how we can turn this to our advantage, we could make our own news about what we want our live s to be and watch them every day for a couple of weeks there are a lot of very positive subliminal videos on you tube we can pick our favourites out and watch them every day instead of all the negative news imagine what a positive change that would be in our lives strait away your removing negatives and replacing them with positive's, in NLP and hypnosis, you will hear people say that it is a good idea when giving up something to replace it with a positive new one this takes away the dark void of just quitting something and feeling loss's this is the same principle, what are you going to replace it with.

When it comes to the question "how do we change" the answer to me seems to be scripts, everything has a script,)physics is the mathematical script behind how the universe works, and validates cause and effect, it cannot not); when we think to ourselves, we are in effect generating a script; so suggestion and scripts are what generates our daily life experience through synchronised scenarios; understanding this is the foundation block the bedrock to really turning our lives around in a very dramatic and positive way, obviously this takes a bit more work and planning than just one hypnosis session in fact it means carrying out a self-hypnosis session every day, my concept is creating daily hypnosis script's describing daily or future events, that we wish to happen in our lives, rather than just accepting a looped one; the first part of which I would say is learning to focus on what we want and would choose to do, to a certain extent it means ignoring what other people are saying and suggesting and only listen to your own suggestions and people who actually know what they're talking about in the fields your looking to work in; this is the part that for me takes the most time even when you know how to apply this, attracting the space and time you need to achieve this for a lot of people is a big challenge.

Not insurmountable but a challenge none the less. Family, friends and work can slow things right down if allowed, so we have to be able to set aside a certain amount of time to practice this every day and if you haven't got the spare time then make some, work out what you do at the moment that is essential and cut out what is not and what you have cut out will be your new spare time to do this every day. If you were given a magic want and told it would bring you all you want for yourself you would surely use it so this is your magic wand this will manifest all that you desire, for certain.

The principle of a hypnosis script is that it is dropped into the unconsciousness in exactly the same way as a single script for one thing, a daily or cluster script can cover more than one area pretty broadly, what I do is write out a life path that you wish to have and compartmentalise it then ad each component part bit by bit as you go along and build it up like a television episode or soap opera the difference is this is how your life is going to be. You can write in feeling great about what you have drawn into your life that you appreciate, you can write things in that will generate a feeling of feeling good which is apparently quite important, when you are composing your daily scripts, you are also building up an expectation also apparently important, so all these important things we are told about are being brought into the scripts; we can introduce a whole realm of different things in that will create positive end results. If your daily scripts take Fifteen minutes to recite well you can put a good deal in Fifteen minute script the positive ramifications of doing this though are infinite; and life changing, think of the metaphor "a picture can speak a thousand words", well a thousand words can change the picture which are you daily life pictures; so for me when I originally looked into hypnosis in some depth it was to learn how to change personal paradigm's, the concept of daily and cluster scripts and hypnosis sessions obviously does this and a lot more; we were never taught as children or when we were at school how to communicate effectively with our own unconscious, but those that understood this certainly abused it by using it to control us this is how we take back control over own lives/personal destiny, these are the paradigm's we are changing; and one of the main one's that were used was we have no control over our destiny we chose our life before we were born and were stuck with it being that way, which is of course untrue.

We have absolute control over our own personal destiny, with this knowledge on how virtually every aspect of our life plays out as our current circumstance, the trick is understanding that we can draw our present circumstance to ourselves by scripting it in to play out that way; in effect drawing the future we wish into reality; so could we consider this Meta hypnosis? When we hear people say you can visualise things into your existence most people would automatically assume they mean shut your eyes and daydream well that can have an effect and give you results however people who really transformed their lives did so by incorporating more than that, a script is a visualisation and when it is being played back as a hypnosis session the pictures the vision is being created by the unconscious.

Surely if there was only one piece of knowledge humanity had to understand then surely this is it. A key point here is a script is a programme as in, we are re-programming-ourselves, and re-programming our present perceived circumstances we can either perceive our circumstances as being how they are, with little hope of changing much or anything; or we can perceive it as something we can change on a day to day basis, as to what our will is, as opposed to allowing others to bend us to their will; Back to the future is a film most people love and what we are talking about here is exactly that because everything will have a de jar vous feeling as though you have already been there because you have, when you're in hypnosis with these scripts you feel them taking you somewhere, so when the experiences manifest in a sense you have already been there; in a sense taking you back to the future, If someone said to me who do you pity the most I would say the control freaks, because it must drive the insane trying to control everyone else, and 'keep failing'; I have a saying "you are not challenging me, you are challenging the universe", in effect turning their back on the universe as if to say they know better than the universe (totality).well that said in that instance their braver than me; I used to be a bit cocky when I was a lad, but not that cocky!

So as holders of the knowledge of hypnosis and what its true meaning is, well I'll tell you what the true meaning of hypnosis is not the adverts you see learn hypnosis in 7 days and make £260 a session, sure as a successful practitioner, you make a good living but that is fractional in the good we are doing, to benefit other people by coaching this, and so it's a case of both sides benefit with no lose to either, only gain that is what hypnosis is to me; earn a good living doing something that has always or for the best part interested me something I believe in and benefit others, surely there could be no better kind of job satisfaction than that. If more people are becoming aware of the so called "law of attraction and suggestion" then it stands to reason that hypnotherapy and life coaching skill's will be well sought after, and people practicing this may even experience a boom time, as more and more people become aware of their own free will and ability to change their own life's to what they want them to be; I feel that life coaching and hypnosis go cap in hand together as the objectives of both are the same, to help improve lives beyond what many would believe possible; from self-healing to manifesting a dream home or car or career, hypnosis and life coaching agree on the same principle that it is all in the mind everything that happens in our lives happens because of our mind set.

when we start to re-set our minds, we start to re-set our lives, our lives play out according to how are paradigms are set and this is how we change them with daily hypnotic scripts describing how our day has been as we would wish it. If we go back to Dr Mesmer and look at his experiments, we see the similarity of creating a type of ritual that built up expectation in his clients and the end result was the desired manifestation of health so if we compare that with writing scripts and reciting or playing them back as a hypnotic session, we can see that this script concept works he same, it builds up expectation and the end result of the session will be the desired manifestation and changing of paradigms. So the hypnotist is not bending the client to their will but acting as a conduit between the client and the clients unconscious; what hypnosis does is change paradigms in the client that the client has requested be changed.

An interesting spin off to this is the hypnotist being able to communicate directly with the clients unconsciousness and the client's unconscious replying through the voice of the client, (a form of channelling) this technique can be applied affectively in regression sessions. After a bit of research on this I kind of concluded at this point; that unconscious and the non-physical self are one of the same, for me the conscious self represents the physical world and the non-physical represents the unconscious so when we impress our thoughts on the non-physical sub-conscious, we create the 'structure' which then becomes perceivable in the physical consciousness. This is the concept of" reality shifting, paradigm changing," in which hypnosis techniques become the way we impress the conscious thought (imagined end result) into the non-physical subconscious, thus shifting our reality. Really all hypnosis is, is reality dimensional or paradigm shifting, the two subjects of hypnosis and reality shifting seem to be separate but are inexplicably connected. The areas of hypnosis that in general require a hypnotist are anaesthesia and regression, A point on manifesting goals is the relation between the Law of Relativity and the Law of non-resistance. The law of Attraction is applied through using the law of suggestion. And its manifestation is dependent on the suggestion being released, to constantly focus on the desire (without adding intention and action), in effect becomes like resistance.

The reason for example people become non-smokers through hypnosis is because of their acceptance that they are now non-smokers; this principle can be applied to everything in hypnosis. The scripts tend to work by association what we associate ourselves as being, having or experiencing can be realized through hypnosis scripts, which in effect are a visualisation technique possibly the most powerful type of visualization because it is easier to stick to a hypnotic visualization than eyes shut type of visualisation, where the person attempts to create a visual scene in the mind's eye the reason for this is, a script can be recorded and played back as a hypnotic session pretty much guaranteeing the person will be in a hypnotic state and if the session is required to be repeated daily until manifestation the visualization will not wonder off course, with visual visualisation (lucid dream) type visualising it can be difficult for most to keep the association and the projected desire the same without the mind wandering and creating conflicting objectives, the temptation would also be to carry the visualization on far longer than required, in my experience although I have had some successes with this type of visualizing it is hit and miss and many things I visualized in this way did not manifest. If we re-play a script, we may not see the visual images during the session the unconsciousness will make the visual associations to the worded script making manifestation easier to achieve with a certainty that if the script is properly formed.

CHAPTER NINETEEN

RESCOURCEFULL AND UNRESCOURCEFULL THOUGHTS AND ACTIONS

The importance of process! To change our mind-set ,"attitude" and what we experience in life, experience requires a process to be followed, what I am uncovering in my research is there is a definitive process of formula which creates what is viewed as a manifestation of desire, intention, action; whatever the desire is health or an inanimate object; on studying depth levels in hypnotic trance I have made a definite connection between level of trace achieved and the so called time buffer to manifestation if you read or view any programmes made by life coaches, they keep reiterating the need to feel good and that it has relevance in the manifestation process; note at this point, people questioned about how they felt in a delta state reoffered to a euphoric feeling! If we look at an affirmation repeated daily many times a day, when we look at the opinions of people on just affirmations then you find a very mixed bag of reply's, some say they work and have achieved amazing things just through repeating affirmations some will say it's a complete waste of time and affirmations don't work, then if we look at the nature of an affirmation in general they are recited in a full state of consciousness some may briefly close their eyes while saying the affirmation but this would only lead them into a hypnoidal state, therein lies a massive clue that the effectiveness and the time taken to achieve manifestation is in fact because they are in a full to hypnoidal state when repeating affirmations.

The conscious is far slower vibrational than the unconscious. so this tells us that the more influence the critical conscious has the slower and longer it takes to create a habituated belief that then manifest because the unconscious has updated a certain belief system and now tells the conscious that a new choice on this belief has been made. Now if we take a look at the depth scales in hypnosis, we see that the deeper into hypnotic trance we are in, the less influence the slower critical mind has. If we look at the so-called hypnotic delta state, then the experiences of people who have been put in this level of trance becomes fascinating, the most interesting comments.

I have come across about this state are the feeling of total euphoria (natural ecstasy) so in this particular state those tested and asked their feeing's on how they felt in this state were definitely feelings of feeling good. Interestingly when we look at the delta state of hypnosis, we find that suggestion is not possible physically which basically means the critical conscious is out to lunch, however non-physical suggestion is possible, so with all that is being said about the law of attraction and how to apply it, it seems to me the defining point is what level of trance the person is in when suggesting their desires to the sub-conscious. So the question that people constantly ask how long it will take to manifest seems to have the answer of, depends on what level of trance is being achieved when imparting suggestion to the non-physical subconscious. So after suggesting that the hypnotic delta "Esdaile state" would be the ideal state of mind to be in when imparting suggestions of desire written in the present tense, if this is indeed right then the inductions could be tailored for each client so after two or more sessions they are able to reach a somnambulistic state then when they can reach this state to then impart the suggestions this seems to me the quickest and most effective way to manifest suggestions and change belief systems that for most people block what they would really wish to achieve.

At this point I will introduce a quote from (June.G Bletzer) called. "Key to life;" its significance to this is obvious. "In balance with emotional stress every day, weather the stress is good or bad: 1: to have the correct attitude toward each experience that life presents, resolving any unpleasant experience that life presents at the time that it happens, to handle all emotions pleasant and unpleasant comfortably intelligently and satisfactorily in accord with one's belief system, to put each undesirable, subordinate or traumatic experience in its proper perspective, integrating it into a whole, as opposed to putting it aside without attitudinally resolving it; unresolved emotions are not put "aside" as supposed, but rather they go inside the body to turn up later in the form of disease or chaotic life structure; 2: it is just as important not to repress life experiences that are painful as it is not to dwell on the activity with resentment jealousy condemnation or pity. 3 Principle nothing in the world can hurt a person, no death of a loved one, no accident, no environmental catastrophe; no chronic illness, no loss of job or marriage, it is only the attitude one takes towards these experiences, which hurts the person".

Attitude is emphasised here, attitude is "mind-set "and can be changed through suggestion, especially, or more effectively in an optimised state of trance, such as the theta to delta state! Looking at the depth scale they have a resemblance to astral planes of existence which you would be familiar with, with any level of study on astral projection, (out of body experiences), what the depth levels represent to me are different 'non-physical dimensions' (planes) that are travelled through during the switch from lucidity to deep or ultra-deep levels of trance; astral projection would describe ascending to higher vibrational planes of existence, the depth scale describes descending to higher vibrational planes; if Euphoria is described as the feeling of being, in the coma state of trance, then they are saying, that they experienced being in a plane of non-physical existence with a higher vibrational frequency If something is different by one atom, then it is different by dimension, each level in hypnotic depth scales represent a different unconscious dimension; if one was to go from hypnoidal state of consciousness to a deep or ultra-deep state of hypnotic trance, then that person is shifting through different dimensions (of subconscious non-physical planes) possibly a reason for the phenomena referred to as time distortion.

A definition of this for example would be if a client is in a delta state for four hours, they would most likely say after, it felt only like a couple of minutes, because in that euphoric state, physical time ceased to exist. So the depth scales are evidence of this type of dimensional shifting of consciousness. They are showing the degrees of non-physical existence that the client is experiencing, in effect telling the hypnotist that they are moving to higher vibrational levels in non-physical existence, this becomes a very exciting thing to fully understand as if you listen to the speakers in the secret, and channel's like Daryl Ankar (Bashar) when they talk about changing anything, or manifesting a desire, they talk of alignment vibrationally, of the need to be feeling good at the time of visualizing, so it could be a fair assumption that if someone is in a deep hypnotic state where they are feeling euphoria, then they are in vibrational alignment with being able to manifest the suggestion of desire whether it be a car, or riding the body of a disease, this could clearly be what is being defined as the time buffer or the age old question of how long will it take to manifest a desire and intention.

If we go back to just reciting an affirmation in full consciousness which can be effective for getting back onto a positive chain of thought but the reported manifestation time of this technique is very long, months even, instantaneous manifestation seems to be more evident when a person is in a non-physical awareness known as a coma state or there a bout's, I once watched a video on YouTube where a person was in a hospital environment wired up to scanners for brain surgery no surgery was taking place but a hypnotist had put the person in to a hypnotic state that was clearly close to a Delta state a monitor showed a growth present in the brain area represented by a fairly large white blob, the hypnotist proceeded with the suggestion of the session and the white blob (growth) dissolved and was removed in '3 minutes'. This clearly shows a relative influence in manifestation time in accordance with what non-physical dimension the person perceives at that time of suggestion.

Stage 1: "Hypnoidal"–Very light stage of hypnosis in which most clients don't feel hypnotized. The majority of people feel completely awake to types of Hypnoidal states are Hypnopompic and Hypnagogic; Hypnopompic is the state by before waking up in the morning and Hypnagogic is the state right before falling asleep at night. A lot can be accomplished in this first stage: Weight reduction, smoking, withdrawal, and simple muscle control such as eyelid catalepsy. Stage.2: More relaxed state where larger muscle groups can be controlled and manipulated such as

Arm Catalepsy. Your power of critical reasoning starts to become impaired. Stage 3: You get reasonably complete control of your entire muscular system. Most people won't be able to articulate a number, stuck to a chair, can't walk and even partial analgesia Stage 4: In this stage you start to produce greater phenomena and is known as the beginning of the amnesic stages.

The person will forget items such as their name, number, address, and other items. Glove Analgesia and feeling touch, but no discomfort. Stage 5: This is considered the start of somnambulism. You get cool stuff like complete anaesthesia and experience the ability to neither feel discomfort or touch. A lot of different pain control techniques can be used in this stage as well. You can also experience what is called Positive Hallucinations which means you can see and hear things which technically are not actually there. You can also experience real age regression in this state and not just remembering the past. Stage 6: This is the next level of Profound Somnambulism. You can experience Negative hallucinations which means you won't see or hear things that actually are there. There are conflicting opinions on the relevance of the depth scales amongst some hypnotists there is a discussion on hynothoughts.com that shows this, I would say the depth scales are relevant and that more emphasis could be put on helping the client achieve delta or ultra-depth states of trance before the scripts of suggestion are applied. Even if someone were highly analytical there would still be a hypnotic process that would enable them to reach this state, in my further undertakings and experiments on self-hypnosis I would now view coma state as the optimum level of trance to ensure success, far more rapidly than a light to medium level. So, as I have said the significance of the depth scale are that they show a dimensional level of awareness in the non-physical sub-conscious, so the dimensional shift would be relative to reality shifting (manifesting desires and intentions). A note I would put here is nothing exists in the physical realm without first having structure (blocks of thought form) in the non-physical realm.

So a suggestion script delivered to the unconscious in a delta state is likely to have a different dimension than one delivered in a medium trance state, the dimensional difference would most likely be how readily the unconscious accepts the suggestion as true, bearing in mind the unconscious processes information different to conscious and will drop repeated negatives and process them as positive ones action to suggestions. like Boolean scrip in computing; True/False; only true actions are stored as a memory and creating a memory through suggestion is part of the manifestation process, so suggestion in the coma state could shorten or remove completely the so call "time buffer" effect, because the time distortion phenomena is experienced to a far greater degree than in a medium trace state. An induction built up of three stages first stage an induction of relaxing suggestions, second stage a deepener, third stage a further deepener in the style of an elevator or descending stairwell induction designed to take the person to the bottom floor of hypnotic trance, the floors are three in number to make the person go three times deeper, then in a coma state the suggestions are delivered. This would be an ideal procedure for self-hypnosis.

I believe that the time buffer, manifestation time is conducive of conscious interference and how deep rooted the belief is that's being changed, thus the delta state would suggest that the time buffers existence would be reduced when there is no conscious interference to the suggestions; if the same suggestions are delivered but in different trance states, then would there be a different time ratio of manifestation to the suggestions; we could put manifestation times as slow, in hypnoidal to light states, slightly faster in medium states, fast to instantaneous in deep to ultra-deep states.

The thing is with the delta state is that it's generally used for anaesthetic purposes, and suggestions for other hypnotic practices were viewed as only requiring light to medium trance states, to me this seems like a monumental oversight; there are many hypnotists that know the depth scales but say they have no relevance. I personally think these practitioners are seriously missing out. However as we are dealing with self-hypnosis feel free to experiment with different levels of hypnotics states and make notes to see if there is any difference for you. Time distortion describes awareness of existing in a dimensionally non-physical reality, where the concept of clock time and space do not exist; synonymous with theta or delta states of consciousness, the three ways in which we can travel to these non-physical planes are, deep meditation, hypnosis, and biofeedback training; when we use these technique's we go from a monotone view of life with just a physical perspective, and consciously trying to work out how to get what we want to achieve, to having a new partner who deals with all the how's, we do not have to do it all through the physical consciousness, the amount of power and control this gives us over our own destiny's is unlimited. So the delta state of consciousness could well be the optimum state to be in for post hypnotic suggestion.

Like a two way radio, or just receiving, the two are separate in terms of what can be achieved, if we look at a meditate state where the mind is cleared of any mundane thought, this state of being would best represent receiving intuitive thought and channelling, which both receive information through blocks of thought; the two way radio concept, would represent sending blocks of thought into the non-physical plane, and creating thought form through the structure of the suggestions which are then transmitted back as physical form experiences and events conceived in the non-physical and perceived in the physical.

The Eight Horizons I came across in one of the course lessons, are similar to an idea got for script's, the idea was to split the script into seven segments, aspects of a person's incarnation, i.e. Property, home life, career, ambitions etc. these ideas are valid as they show there are more than just a couple of dimensions involved, for example if you were to take seven to eight square sheets of clear glass, and label each sheet with a different aspect, then you put images on each sheet relevant to each aspect, then if you stand the first sheet in front of you and then stand all the other subsequent sheets, one behind the other, then looked through the first one; what you then see is your physical tangible reality coming from multi-dimensional layers. What I find interesting about the eight horizons is the survival of each set of aspects, the survival of each aspect being dependant on what the persons belief on each elemental is, for example someone's ambitions are dependent on the mind-set and the belief that the ambition is possible, because if the persons belief is it is not possible, then that ambition won't survive. So a can do will do mind-set is essential for the survival of that ambition. I often used to watch Grand designs what is great about it is the people who are building the house are asked how thy see it going, how long it will take, how much money it will cost, then at the end you see how the build went and more often than not the one who talked of potential problems mostly financial, experience through the build how they had perceived pre-supposed the build going. So, if the person is anticipating problems or potential problems they tend to show up, preferences are what the critical conscious mind is constantly making known as decisions, the decision of any prolonged thought is about what side of the preference is being focused on, if they focus on the negative preference which is the opposite to what they would prefer then they are choosing that as a preference because that is what they focused their thoughts on. In hypnosis this is the objective of the script is to create a preferred choice of habit than the one they have, relative to what the intended objective is; when someone goes to a hypnotist to quit smoking, they are simply changing a preference from smoking cigarettes to be free smoking them, choice of preference.

The art in writing the script it seems is to choose a preference of objectives, intentions, but not a preference on how the objectives/intentions will come about; when this is done some quite remarkable things start to happen; the critical mind no longer has to devise ways of achieving the objective, it no longer has to keep trying to figure out how to make the objective happen, if the conscious mind try's figuring it all out blocks start to come up, because the critical mind can only reason ways that it views as possible by virtue of what they believe, whereas the non-critical mind can find an infinite variety of ways the objective can be achieved, the critical mind can only see a few sometimes none. When a so-called miracle happens all, it is really is, is a change of preference, maybe from one extreme to the other but the change is quick and viewed as a miracle; all it takes really understand the way to communicate properly with the unconscious.

When we as Humans realise this then all that we wish, imagine to be we become, because that is our preference and because we understand the way in which to communicate it, the unconscious for most people is little understood let alone how you communicate to it, other than the haphazard way we were conditioned to, which for most is acceptance that their destiny for the best part is set in stone, fated, out of their control their understanding of visualization is distorted by believing it is solely about viewing something in their minds eye, so hypnosis is a channel between the two separate worlds of consciousness and unconsciousness, if we view the conscious as the creative and the unconscious as the receptive. A block of thought or the script of preference is the creation of the conscious that is being sent in a hypnotic state unconscious receives the instruction of preferences. The person then receives the communication as a visual perception in their conscious physical actuality.

It has now been scientifically proven that the majority of the population are making daily decisions the wrong way around, they think logically when they could be thinking intuitively, and they think intuitively when they could be thinking logically. This error in thinking effectively produces the effect of attraction and repulsion, repelling "pushing away" what they do want and attracting "drawing in" what they don't want and the key reason for this is, because most people are chasing an hourly, annual wage. Another way of putting it is they are trying to work out how when they shouldn't be, when it should be left to the unconscious" and not thinking how when they should be "doing it with the conscious." Logic is the realm of the conscious, intuition is the realm of the unconscious and super conscious, the ones who really get caught up in this are the ones who operate almost entirely in the high-beta brainwave state, those who have habituated ways of operating in more than one brainwave state have an easier time because they are more in tune with the intuitive unconscious, whereas those who operate on a near entirely high beta state can only view things in a logical physical way and are virtually cut off from their unconscious except maybe when they are asleep dreaming. Those who are seen as studious, writers, artistic, creative, operate on a more low-beta, alpha state which brings them closer to the intuitive unconscious, the deeper into the slower brainwave cycles we go the closer to pure unconscious we get.

Do we inhabit a planet which we share with eight billion other people, each one of those eight billion people has an individual mind of their own how many of those people understand what mind really? we do not know for certain how many of those people understand the way we manifest our life experience we are the minority at the moment. It is certain that more and more people have started to look at what the law of attraction is, what the seven universal principles actually mean, now days there is so much religious rhetoric so many religions so many manmade laws so much information so many truths and half-truths you could be forgiven for giving up even trying to sort out the wheat from the chaff; there are different civilizations on this one planet from the ancient tribal cultures, to multi-commercial metropolis's with over forty million people residing in a single city, cramped living conditions and small spaces being sold or rented for a premium prices.

Billions, billions of people chasing the hourly waged job or career, work pressures, peer pressure, cultural and religious pressure, people being pushed to do more and more, with little or no personal downtime to themselves, with the idea that we have our own personal free will becoming almost like a myth; lack of personal space privacy constant scrutiny on our actions and movements, the pace of life getting faster and faster barely having time to think let alone make decisions on what we think, and were is all this leading, eventually it will lead to total burn out, stress to such a degree that our body's become unable to heal themselves because the immune system cannot function properly causing disease and a spiral of negative reactions and confusion.

When everyone is focused on what everyone else is doing, people living virtual lives spending more time on virtual entertainment than growing food, mass areas of good agricultural land unused because they are all crammed into cities resembling ant hills, people quite literally losing their minds because they forgot the old ways, virtual worlds replacing the unconscious forgetting how to communicate with their unconscious, completely ignoring their intuition. For lots of people meditation is viewed as a bit of a joke allowing the mind to be quiet for twenty minutes a day as a waste of time and for some even being able to fit in twenty minutes a day quietly in their own space undisturbed for many is almost impossible. This is what a hypnotist will come across on a daily basis are people who expect quick fixes, a quick hypnosis session and everything changes like waving a magic wand, but it all runs a bit deeper than that and most people haven't got that depth of understanding where hypnosis is concerned, hypnosis is one name that can describe part of a formula that has been given many different sub-categories, reality shifting, quantum jumping, mind control all sorts of names have been given to what is essentially creating our life experiences intentionally. Belief systems, conditioning and involuntary decision making, as human beings we all have one thing in common when we are born, we have no tangible conscious (critical decision-making faculty) in the physical world we are completely dependent on others for our survival, in nature that makes us the same as any other creature on the planet. What makes us different from other creatures on this planet though is out incredible ability only found in humans to utilise our imagination and with words and pictures turn our focused thoughts into reality, actual experiences, in other words for those that know how, it means we can choose our mood and what kind of lifestyle we have, however before we undertake this kind of change in ourselves, up to now you have almost completely conditioned reactions not responses to what you think you have bean perceiving.

What I think holds people back the most from any kind of great transformation in life is weather people question what they believe, or even look at what they've been told to believe to see if that is actually what they believe, or whether it even makes any sense to them, when they scrutinise whatever belief their looking at, understanding what we believe and why we believe it and letting go of old ways of thinking to make way for new ways of thinking and doing things will be the deciding factor in whether people create major change in their lives that they want or not. People tend to have two one of two primary mind-sets compete or create, for the most part people are conditioned to compete, if your mind-set is predominately competitive then your decisions and lifestyle will be completely different from someone who has a creative mind-set. Someone who has a competitive mind-set will more than likely be caught up in some sort of rat race or find themselves constantly stuck in a rut, people who change from being competitive often find themselves being much more independent and self-reliant and experience amazing changes in their life, so looking at what we believe and what our mind-set is, is actually very important if they want any real change in their lives. People who compete tend to have an attitude of they must be able to do something better than someone else rather than doing something because they enjoy it and not worry if their better than anyone else. Creative minded people tend to have an attitude of doing something to the best of their ability, and focus on how well their doing rather than looking at what everyone else is doing; so what I'm defining here is one of two ways of doing things one gets you what you really want the other does not get you what you really want because they don't know what they really want because they have been conditioned to just accept what they get, when someone does something without question it means thy have been conditioned to do something without question, a prime example here would be a soldier, they are conditioned to carry out a task without question that is the definitive of conditioning, if you're not focused on what you really want to do then someone else is focused on what you do, so conditioning, the best way I can describe it a biased way of viewing things by what their paradigms are set to at that time, if someone had a belief that something was impossible, then they changed their paradigm to believing that something is possible then they shift the likelihood of that thing whatever it is being possible and actually being a part of their actuality. Everything that we view as a positive change in our lives comes from a shift in what we choose to believe or accept is true.

The only way we can make the impossible possible is to believe it is possible that in turn will increase the probability that it is possible to that person and the unfoldment will be something will show up that proves to the person that it is possible so then it goes from belief to knowing with certainty, so we need to start looking at the beliefs we have that benefit us and those that work against us.

An example of this would be someone who is diagnosed with a terminal illness, if they have a conditioned belief that the only cure lies in the hands of a doctor or some type of medicine and have no belief in self-healing or healing by affirmations, hypnosis or changing what they focus on then the only options they have and percentage of survival comes from the doctor, because they have the paradigm that, that is the only form of healing so most in that category would view self-healing as impossible; If someone was diagnosed with the same type of illness but looked at other types of healing or had already looked at other types of healing through testimonials of people who cured themselves of a terminal illness

through some sort of visualisation then the likelihood that they could heal themselves independently of surgery or
medicine would be far greater because their paradigm is set at this being possible,

    A belief system is a variable not a constant in other words all beliefs can be changed they are only constant for as long as you believe it, so if you have a competitive or creative mind-set you are still creating your own reality, the difference is how much of your reality is from focused choice and how much is from automated beliefs that are possibly in direct contradiction to what you are trying to achieve; this is exactly the reason why we have to look at what we want to achieve and look at the component parts of that i.e. weather money is required or skill sets, and what the beliefs are on those component parts like how do you view money do you view it as the root of all evil or as a tool to help you achieve your goals, do you view money as easy to come by or very hard work being involved these are all things that need to be considered when looking at changing your life, and your mind-set and weather your conditioning it, or your being conditioned with untold subliminal messages through television, computer, games politics or news, understanding the function of mind-set is key to changing your reality.

    If you cannot or will not change your mind, you will not change your life, Hypnotic states multiple dimensions and universes, physical reality, and co-existences. The majority of people probably think they exist on a purely physical level, a monotone singular existence which has time and space as a measurement of where they are in life, young or old rich or poor are all concepts of measurement; for most people this is the way they view their reality this is however potentially a tunnel versioned way of viewing things and very self-restricting and limiting. To exist with only a physical view point can put up unlimited obstacle's and restrictions because they always seek a physical solution to their physical problems, wanting to acquire something would generally require something considered to be equal in value to the object or service such as precious metals or money, a physical solution to a physical problem of acquisition which creates the problem of acquiring the precious metal or money, problems, problems, problems, and always looking for the physical solution. When people become ill they look for a physical solution medicine or surgery, which again for most people requires money depending on what type of operation or medicine sometimes vast amounts of money the person perceives as beyond their means which in turn creates more stress and anxiety on top of the stress and anxiety already brought on by the persons illness, the person may then be faced with being too ill to work and having to acquire money with no waged job, the bog standard way we acquire money; which in turn becomes the root of most humans decision making, which is essentially chasing the money with only physical action which becomes a cycle that people become stuck in so just having a physical perspective and viewing things from a purely physical dimension puts vast limitations on our potential to realise a reality which would actually be our choice, rather than making the best of a bad thing.

It's easy to get caught in the cycle of viewing things from a completely physical attitude and miss the non-physical structure that creates everything physical and the way the non-physical structure is formed. Which is from pure focused thought; Understanding that our imagination rather than being wishy washy daydreaming, is actually one of our greatest tools that we all possess, which brings in the different levels of astral or non-physical planes of simultaneous synchronised existence and the concept of multi-dimensional universes and the co-existence of everything running at the same time in the here and now, and the transformation of reality's through probability's, or potentiality. If we look at universe which is mind stuff itself and what we know of the world is the structure of the mind, which works in a way described as law of action and reaction, forming various levels of energy consciousness which is subject to "the law of thought."

These so-called laws are a way to describe the process of creation. So this could mean essentially that each different vibrational frequency is fixed to its own energy level the higher the vibrational frequency we give out puts us in a happier state of mind the highest state of mind being on the universal sub-laws so aspiring to that level of being. All other levels are varying levels in-between so the concept of multi-universes can be explained as a universe at every degree or vibrational level essentially billions of them. So when we vibrate on a higher vibrational level, we draw in that which exists on these levels into our physical conscious reality, so our physical reality is multiple layers of various things in our existence cut and pasted so to speak into our daily existences from different universes, also known as planes of existence, which exist separately in their own right but are all connected to create interconnected existences. So the way we use this and become the creators of the reality we perceive is through attitude, the connection between all this is hypnosis through hypnosis attitude can be changed, meditation, hypnosis is the way we open the channel to the unconscious the receiving and broadcasting counterpart of our physical conscious self the other handset of the two-way radio. In understanding this we understand the way of manifestation, the formula that is creation itself combining imagination with suggestion and impressing this on the unconscious, the simplicity of this is awesome you imagine what you want and when the unconscious accepts the suggestion as real it becomes reality then actuality, hypnosis is a tool we have to get the suggestions accepted by the unconscious as true, when the unconscious accepts something as true, it becomes true in our reality. It is about co-existing with a pre-defined big picture or personal platform to operate from, most people only co-exist with all the problems like cost of living, which keeps them bound to a day job, the only way out, is to create and associate to co-exist with your own big picture.

When someone goes into an hypnotic trance they travel through different dimensions of consciousness this is also signified by the difference in brainwave frequency's experienced at different levels of induced trance, the irony here is when we are in a lower brainwave state we are in deeper levels of trance so the slowest brainwave frequency is the deepest state of trance, but when in this plane we are in a dimension of highest vibrational frequencies, so the point of co-existence isn't just co-existing with other people and animals but we co-exist on different planes simultaneously the law of corresponding opposites doesn't mean just for everything there is an opposite but also all the varying degrees in between.

We co-exist on all the varying non-physical degrees as well, so when people are very negative those aspects of themselves from those planes connected to these frequencies dominate and those frequencies want to stay as long as they can, so you have to consciously shift them; for the person to shift their reality. When we are very positive then positive aspects of ourselves become dominant in our reality, these are the ones we have to practice shifting back to when our confidence takes a knock; the probabilities of every degree are being constantly played out and the ones that have the most focus on them become the ones that dominate the persons physical reality. So the stigmatisation of hypnosis NLP and esotericism and the positive end results it can bring are a bit of a pain in the neck to humanity in general. Not knowing the way to change paradigms and effectively reality of each individual cannot really be viewed as being in the public interest, as the media and politicians love to put it, what is in the public interest is educating people of the benefits it brings and the simple principles that make it work, the concept of hypnosis, and reality shifting, isn't understood properly by the majority of the population even with films like, the Secret, life coaches and philosophers writing books on the subject the key principles are still being missed ignored or just prejudiced against.

The problem most people have which really shouldn't be underestimated how big a problem it is for them is they seek physical solutions to physical problems, which keeps them focused on physical problems, so gives them more physical problems to deal with because they focus on the problem, everything physical contains a non-physical structure that comes before its physical presents so a physical problem requires an non-physical solution when you focus on the non-physical you focus on the solution. Visualization actually creates the non-physical structure which then becomes physical in reality and actuality.

Visualisation has different aspects to it, it can be mind's eye visualization, or it can be repeating affirmations or scripts, the depth of trance the person is in at the time has an effect of how many times it will need to be repeated before it manifests as physical reality. Hypnosis is a tool, to change a habituated way of doing things it is habitual when you don't know you're doing it otherwise it is a choice. Again this comes down to beliefs we have we can use hypnosis to change choices we make. Or make a new choice or beliefs that become dominant one over the old one, when we repeat something over, we are affirming the new choice and the new choice will be affirmed in physical actuality, therefore there are reports of so many incredible things having happened through hypnosis and NLP. Because we use it to re-choose what we would like to experience, that is about ourselves rather than being about others because we can only make our own choices not other peoples. You cannot look at another person's choice and say it is wrong because you are not that person you can only say your own choices are right or wrong, because you cannot exist as the other person and exist as yourself simultaneously, when people try to do this, it creates a negative paradox for themselves.

When a person goes to a hypnotist or NLP practitioner, they are making the choice of what they want to change not the hypnotist or the NLP practitioner, the practitioner just knows what the best type of intervention or script would be to achieve this, a person is not likely to say they are happy and content and want to be miserable and upset instead, they will consult a practitioner to bring improvements and benefits to their life. What these practices can do is bring into alignment beliefs that will help them achieve what they want by analysing the beliefs they have and whether the belief they have is their own choice or was inherited and made for them, when we see a belief as being something they don't believe then the old belief will fall away and be replaced with the new one, it's not until they analyse what they believe and why that they actually know whether they believe it or not, it becomes a part of getting to know the self through self-examination.

Most people don't like being laughed at so they often make choices that aren't going to bring them what they really would like for fear that their family or friends may laugh at them, when that happens you allow other people to influence your choice don't let them let them laugh because when you have what you want, and they are still stuck in the same rut the laughter goes back to where it came from them. So when other individuals are spending so much time on judging or criticising other individuals, they are in effect putting their own existence on suspended animation maybe not going backward, but definitely not going forward, they are watching a play on another stage stupefied but not playing a role on their own stage. People have a fear of being on their own but what they do not realise is that if they follow their own intuition and path that they are creating they will never be on their own or lonely because they

RESCOURCEFULL & UNRESCOURCEFULL THOUGHTS, ACTIONS

will draw in people who are on the same or similar vibration of loving their own life the same as them. These are two main inherent fears people have for not reaching their goal or full potential, being laughed at or being lonely, what they don't realise is that these fears will keep them in a box for eternity because they will allow other people to influence their choice because they want to fit in with those people or culture, rather than just be who they are accept who they are and allow the universe to match them up with like-minded people who will not mock or judge them, the people who mock and judge others habitually are on a lower vibrational frequency and cannot experience the same existence as those who are on a higher vibrational frequency, hypnosis helps us move up in the frequency we operate on and those on lower vibrational frequency's will drift off or fall away from the persons new reality.

If you haven't achieved or attracted things, you want it is because you have not scripted it in to happen that way. Unconscious mind needs clear commands, which in effect are what these suggestions in hypnotic state are, clear instructions to the unconscious mind, you do not have to worry why or how it is that way, it just is a universal absolute. Create new beliefs by "pre-dictating" them beforehand, look at the word pre-dictate, (prediction) to mean pre-state how your life is. Now re-frame the word visual, you don't have to have a full-blown lucid dream type visualisation, the visualisation is a perception, so if you're not seeing the picture that's alright because your perceiving it that is what brings the realness of realisation in, so if you close your eyes but don't see a visual it's fine because your perceiving it, and that's what causes the effect; the perception is always the prerequisite to the projection.

When we look at cause and effect (law of attraction) and we look at gravity; "what goes up must come down" and "what we send out must come back" (personal returns), this is the effect of gravity pulling the object back, now look at the cause and effect (law of attraction) when you send out sustained thought, cause and effect (law of attraction) works in the same way what you send out is what you are gravitating back into you existence, so without meaning to be mean to anyone, however if you are spending the best part of the day moaning and looking at what everyone else has with jealous eye's or your constantly opinionated on what everyone else is doing, then you seriously need to look at what you are gravitating into your existence via cause and effect (attraction); It starts on first dimension then second dimension, then out to the fourth dimension and gravitates into the third dimension. If you try tuning into a radio station and you have it set at a frequency that is different to the one the radio station broadcast on then you're not going to receive the broadcast of that radio station you're going to receive something else, the principle here is the same every time you think or send out a thought you are in the process of suggestion, which is cause and effect that is the power of attraction, it is sustained suggestions that become as I mentioned habitual beliefs that manifest.

There are natural phenomena reported with hypnosis, "time distortion", (the session feels a lot shorter than it is), anaesthesia, which happens naturally when a person reaches a certain depth level, the body switches from nerve feeling to sensory feeling, which is used for stopping pain; some have had hypnosis and reported psychic abilities they never had before like seeing auras, most people are for the best part seemingly disconnected from unconscious mind, when you start using hypnosis and understanding the "secret" language of the unconscious mind you open up a connection to yourself you never knew you had before, and adds to the whole concept of knowing yourself. We live in an information highway were we can go online and research information at our fingertips, with a bit of research we can find testimony's from top of their game doctors, who will say there are numerous cases now of people miraculously recover from terminal illness without taking the traditional modern medicine and the only explanation is self-healing we find the same with Quantum physics experts who point to a holographic universe and quantum entanglement, which is all telling us that our lives are what we think them to be by virtue of cause and effect.

Everything in the universe shifts perpetually this describes reality shifting, which equates to changing beliefs around values. When you change beliefs, you don't just shift reality you shift actuality. The three core concepts eliciting the three primary core concepts; "Wealth, Health, Relationships;" so, every humans wish, or desire has a root at one or more of these three concepts; (this is big picture building) Like the primary colours from which all other colours can be mixed. All desires and intentions can be affected in a positive way through working on creating positive perspectives in relation to Health, Wealth, and Relationships, and this will filter down through other values/beliefs connected to this and create positive change there to.

The first step with self-hypnosis as your medium/channel to the unconscious is to write perspectives on each of the three concepts that are positive and beer some kind of relation to the types of results you are looking to achieve and repeat the hypnosis sessions with these perspectives until you feel confident that the suggestions have been accepted by the unconscious; when the suggestions are accepted you can expect to see almost instant results in some cases, but they may not be what you may consider large to start with, although there is no rule that says they won't be large to start with there is a degree of feeling your way intuitively, you can repeat the hypnosis session every day when in an altered state of consciousness the unconscious will accept the suggestions whether on the first of thirty-first day, keep repeating.

Then at some point the suggestions will be accepted, it's an absolute that the repeated suggestion in altered state will become actualised. It is important to understand that in terms of mind-set and system of beliefs (with exception of universal absolutes) a truth is only a half-truth that is the truth your mind-set holds as true, which is the truth for you even if it's not a truth for others and these truths play out as your reality as life experiences so you can absolutely change the truth to what you believe from your true/self-perspective, opposite truths can both be true that is the paradox, getting money is hard is a truth, money comes with ease and less effort is a truth, you choose which one you choose to be a truth for you. A surface value thinker will tell you what they are experiencing in their life like the stress, illness, or all the things they want to have but have not got. The surface value thinker is reacting to not having, sometimes by jealousy, anger, even fear they may lose what they have got, a core value thinker will tell you how great they fell because their creating their reality by following a process that creates their reality so they enjoy life rather than react to it they understand that working on perspectives that support having the more positive things in life creates changes on a much broader scale than focusing on one surface value object, the surface value reflects the outer self, the core vale reflects the inner self, the inner self holds all the perspectives that are essentially held as memories. Creating your own perspective and delivering it to the inner self creates memories as soon as the perspective is committed to memory then it becomes part of your reality in a moment it's the conscious that works on a slower level the unconscious works on a much faster level this is why sometimes instant manifestation occurs, more often than not there is a time buffer because of how deep-rooted previous beliefs or values are.

These three areas of life cover everything in our existence as human beings everything we want to change is rooted in one of these concepts; Buddhists say it all comes down to "the way that we relate to everything" which is true. I put it in three concepts to make it easier to work with, but it is all essentially about what you relate to and the way you relate to things this gives the effect of drawing in or pushing away, NLP's relationship with hypnosis is that words used in a certain way have a certain effect creating hypnosis sessions with understanding of NLP can effectively make each session very effective, by understanding the way the mind is processing language that are becoming remembered experience. If you were planning on buying a house, do you jump strait in for a mortgage or find ways of generating an income that can enable you to buy without a mortgage when you start to apply these things at some point there will be the opportunity that arrives to do that, would you be prepared to let go of where you live and the associations that go with it; yes, no or to what degree either way.

Be aware that letting go of old ways brings in new ways, but what would you be prepared to let go of is something you should also look at when looking at what you want to draw in. When you find yourself to be very family or hometown orientated you have to look at whether the change you wish for is what you want and not influenced from the demands of others; you have to ask yourself searching questions to understand what you actually want, or whether what you think you want is still being influence by outside dominant personalities, dominant personalities are essentially outside opinion, family teachers and so on. asserting themselves over your opinion. look at a girl or boy from a family with a big professional history say an accountant, Solicitor or Doctor they say they don't want to carry on the family tradition, they will most likely to be under heavy pressure to follow the family trade, however what about when they decide to have a mind of their own and want to go down a different path, they may have a very strong family orientation, however what about the individual persons wants and needs, how much do you give of yourself to keep other people happy?

Does this actually make you happy? would you give up something you really love and want to do because of outside peer pressure? As you start "pondering" these questions you start to find yourself, proper thinking is about putting all outside opinion to one side and viewing it with you own opinion, we are often faced in relationships with to continue a relationship or finish with the relationship, or just keep the relationship at a minimum these are choices you will all come across and its part of the letting go and drawing in process; it's just something you get used to its part off the whole change process, as long as you keep focused on change for the better you'll be fine, it just becomes another part of getting to know your true self, and understanding letting go is part of the whole process that gets you what you wish to have and be.

The word self and all these other associations to self, examples are. self-actualised, self-directing, self-esteem, so you say to yourself. well how do I become more "self," the simple answer is to learn to become less dependent on outside opinion of you and more dependent on the natural recourses you already have, such as intuition, a working functional relationship with your unconscious mind, creates functional flow, most probably most of the population are brought up with a put other people first, which is a value right? Value other people before you value yourself. People are generally encouraged by a very well-integrated "manmade" system to be dependent and dependable; I am not going to go into all the rights or wrongs of this value, but it does act as a trap, not to be self-directing, because all these people will direct you, probably to a place you don't want to go to, but their all there directing you, why would you need to be self-directing, or self-motivating. Well the answer in short is because what you have is externally directing and externally motivated, which actually means you're not really going where you want to, you're going where someone else wants you to, you're not motivating yourself but being motivated, apart from working through this book when have you ever drawn up a list of the things "you want", not other people wants, just yours, it is not about being selfish, however it is about putting yourself first, what do you want your life to be and how big a margin of difference is there between the two, of what your life is now and what you want it to be; the process of learning and practicing self-hypnosis, puts the "self" back into actualised, directing, motivated and esteem, the main focus of this book through various chapters and subject areas is to know thyself, know thy craft, know thy craft literally means have a craft or ability's you use to generate an income that is doing something you love to do, which benefits others as well as yourself.

You don't have to do stuff that benefits others, but you get no return, just as long as it benefits the person more than the money exchanged. Our actuality's are the result of the complex meta-programmes we run, and the response or reactions to those programmes running, we can tweak individual parts like changing a habit, or put a cluster scripts together, and start shifting things on a more wholesale level, we are programmable from within, where you are at now and where you are going to be in the future will be defined entirely by the programmes you choose to keep and the ones you choose to change, by the values you choose to keep and the values you choose to change, one thing is for certain though, no change means the same old same old. There is a quote from a series of book written by Terry Goodkind, called The Wizards first rule; "People are stupid, because they believe what their told either because they want it to be true or because the fear it may be true" so it becomes a matter of being discerning and more thoughtful about what you believe rather than reacting out of fear or blind hope, what do you thing they use propaganda for to misdirect people so ask yourself before you believe one side of the story without knowing the other side for certain, is it even relevant to you and are you being misdirected.

Every person has their own free will, or what they will or won't do, when a person is in hypnosis the persons will cannot be changed unless it is the persons will to do so, i.e. desire and intension both have to be present, so any fears that a hypnotist can bend someone to their will,

RESCOURCEFULL & UNRESCOURCEFULL THOUGHTS, ACTIONS

against their will are unfounded, outside of deliberate destructive brainwashing, covered in psychic self-defence, the person is always in control even in hypnosis, an example I have stated before, someone takes their kid to have hypnosis so the kid stops sucking their thumb, now the kid may show the intension to stop sucking their thumb, and say alright Daddy, I'll stop sucking my thumb, but the child has not got the desire or intention to stop sucking their thumb, a hypnotist might hypnotise them to stop and they may stop for a couple of days but they will revert back to sucking their thumb because of desire and intention and will, most hypnotists wouldn't do a session for the kid anyway because the parent wants the kid to do something they haven't got the desire of the outcome for and most practitioner will tell the parent that strait off, they won't do it because it's against the kids will..

CHAPTER TWENTY

AFFIRMATIONS AND AFFORMATIONS

From thought to thought form to thought physical thing or experience the thing with affirmations is most people never finish the process, the reasons are; affirmations are done in full conscious awareness which means the veil between the two consciousness's is closed, so you have to run the I' am and whatever the affirmation is, literally thousands of times a day for a long period every day until you convinced conscious mind consciously that what you are affirming is actually actual, eventually conscious mind will relent and send the instruction to unconscious mind that it is reality. So generally speaking affirmations do work however repeating them hundreds of times a day becomes slow and cumbersome, and most people give up after a week. They are alright for shifting mood states repeat a few dozen times that you feel happy and grateful and sure enough you'll find something to feel happy and grateful for; you can run affirmations in hypnosis every day and the one session with an affirmation in will count as a thousand repetitions consciously, for the simple reason the affirmation in hypnosis has at least some of the conscious veil open, so my advice with affirmations is do them in a light to medium hypnotic state until actualised.

Affirmations are a planned grouping of words affirming a truth as you desire it to be, repeated daily silently, verbally or written out; to stir up the divine spark of perfectness within the human seed and change outward manifestations; instigated by the conscious mind but aimed at the unconscious mind to change ones belief system; brings words of truth into being that are not manifesting in their life at the time; can be designed

AFFIRMATIONS AND AFFORMATIONS

for any aspect of one's life, harmony, abundance, health or education; verbiage should not be lengthily; more effective if used for one's self, and decreed with emotion or after meditation.

So what is hypnosis, well it's basically a collection of affirmations, but has long been a debate on whether affirmations even work, the whole principle behind an affirmation is to make the quote stick and manifest in to the persons unconscious reality, however affirmations are presented in different ways but they are all designed to draw in positive end results and hypnosis scripts are affirmations but they are presented to the unconscious directly, whereas others are not; the other methods are to repeat an affirmative statement over and over daily until it has become an habituated thought believed to take around twenty to thirty days, but with hypnosis we can place several affirmations in one daily session and bring about so much more than the result of one repeated affirmation. If we work on the theory that the unconscious creates the pictures to the narrated script; the believe it when they see it attitude becomes self-defeating, in as much as you have to believe it before you see it then surely this would mean that whatever you recite through a hypnosis session you will be viewing or holding like it is in your actual life experience even if you ae not associating mind's eye visual to it; affirmations that are linked to the script, then become more powerful because they are bringing the focus back on the desired end result. For me this is the most exciting thing about hypnosis. We are in direct communication with it for long enough to set down the affirmations in the sub-conscious mind, without the critical conscious blocking any information in the script. Anchoring which I have mentioned is a better way to use affirmation than just repeating thousands of times a day, is basically what I saying, affirmations are a collective of instructions, directional linguistics, to be suggested to the unconscious with anchoring you only need to repeat the affirmation while actually anchoring it in a conscious awake state, the anchoring strategy is repeated four to five times.

When we look at it, when we shut our eyes and visualize what we want this is still an affirmation you are affirming on the unconscious mind what you want, now in a brainwave state where you can visualize with eyes shut is the same as in hypnosis, the brainwave's have slowed and the person is in a hypnotic state like lucid dreaming so for those who say they cannot achieve visualizing something in their minds eye then the same thing done in a hypnosis session achieves exactly the same thing. You will hear people say they just used to shut their eyes and visualized it, and indeed they did manifest using this technique but I feel that repeating a visualisation through a daily hypnosis session is actually more powerful than just the eyes shut visualization, now in most cases of eyes hut visualization problems can arise they can't conger up anything visual or fall asleep before they had chance to, or their mind wanders, a hypnosis session however incorporates having the eyes shut but the difference is even if the client or yourself can't see the images to the script like a visualization the script is creating the images from the script if you said a certain type of car for example and you know what the car looks like and associate the words with the car, then the subconscious can create the image from that. I think if you mention the word visualization to most people, they will describe eyes shut seeing pictures in their minds eye scenario; but wouldn't consider reciting or repeating scripts as a type of visualization.

Essentially, we write out what we want to visualize as though already living it then when played back as a session everyday has the same, or more powerful effect of drawing the visualization into reality; the effect is the same we conjure up our reality. To quote conjure up (magic ceremony) a ritual and focused thought used to bring etheric world intelligences into action for a desired task; theory: to become involved with real entities who are brought to life by personification of patterns of the psychics collective unconsciousness which comes from inside and outside the mind; it is sometimes more convenient to acknowledge the existences of an angel that performs this function than to recognise possession of spiritual power within one's self that could be awakened by an invocation; "beings" within and "beings" without. Invocation: Formulaic thoughts, incantations or affirmations used to stir a shift in consciousness defined as "reality shifting."

The art of attention and awareness; both "conjure up" and "invocation" sums up the hypnosis process perfectly; so where quantum physics gives us the math behind this, hypnosis gives being spirit in physical form, experience of living, it's the visualisation that creates the structure of what is being manifested; by holding the structure with focused thoughts; Forethoughts; so being in a hypnotic state can be associated with the physical being , being in a time dimension that is not linier, but being in another time dimension simultaneously, and builds the structure on another astral dimension that will manifest into the physical dimension. So if someone in a hypnosis session said they felt like they were in two places at the same time I have had that feeling for sure in self-hypnosis sessions, Generally Hypnosis consists of Induction. A highly suggestable technique used in the beginning of a hypnosis session which puts the subject into a hypnotic state of consciousness, in preparation for prescription, (suggestions) takes from around five to twenty minutes depending on the subject's hypnotisability, performed by narrated guidance.

Induction is generally split in two parts, inductions for non-analytical, who are more open to suggestion, Inductions for analytical, who are less open to suggestion; basically non-analytical find it easier to go into trance and let go than analytical, Inductions for analytical are instant, or centred around giving the conscious mind a task to do, non-analytical are more rapid/progressive relaxation scripts. Induction is a process most commonly known in hypnosis that heightens suggestibility and leads a person from beta state of consciousness to alpha and theta states of consciousness, which are known to be most effective for delivering suggestions to change behaviour, or to manifest desires and achieve goals, gain confidence, and remove phobias.

To induce trance usually a visualisation is used as a means to relax the person into a hypnotic/trance state, also with people who are more analytical an induction is used to give the conscious mind a task to do to suspend conscious activity while the suggestions are prescribed, such as counting down from one hundred to zero, or telling them to repeat a lounge twister in their mind while the induction is taking place. The point of an induction is to reduce or remove conscious/critical mind interference; inductions range from five minutes to half an hour it's dependable of how suggestable the person is and what level of trance is being induced. The levels of hypnotic state are: Hypnoidal, Light state, medium state, and deep state; with varying degrees of depth in each level, other known state are Hypnagogic state, a short time span just before sleep takes over.

When the conscious and unconscious mind are changing dominancy in their roles; the conscious mind becomes passive as unconscious mind take over the thinking; this process sets up an equilibrium of mind activity when the two minds are on the same level of activity, lasts from a few seconds to a few minutes, in relation to profound somnambulism when this level is being aimed for, however without going into actual sleep but keeping the state on the cusp in a deep theta switching to delta state. Hypnopompic state, (Count out), the opposite to hypnagogic state, when unconscious gives over dominant thinking to the conscious mind, a count out generally from one to five replicates or induces this switch in state as a soft way of bringing someone out of a hypnotic state. Induction in NLP is the use of linguistics sentences not "statements constructed in a specific way; it isn't so much an induction as using sentences in a way that sends a command to the unconscious mind without conscious mind blocking it, this can be done by confusing the conscious mind, and while conscious mind is trying to work out what has just been said the command or instruction has got through to the unconscious, a simple example is, "what is the problem not", chunks the person up out of the problem by forcing the unconscious mind to focus outside of the problem and spin for solutions. So if you find yourself stuck on a problem and all you can think of is the problem ask yourself what's the problem not.

A common technique is pre-suppositions, suppose you do this first then that after, induces the suggestion of doing this first then that after, a pre-supposition is an induction to the effect of the action of the pre-supposition. Don't sit in that chair now or you will go into trance to quickly, induces the idea that when they sit in that chair they will go into a hypnotic state, statements like this are designed as a primer for rapid induction, then the work the client has instructed for change in behaviour, habit or some other meta programme takes place, the induction is a means to an end, to open a direct link to the unconscious and deliver instructions.

Milton Ericson used linguistics to great effect; he created inductions for putting people in a hypnotic state that sounded like pure gibberish, however embedded through the statements of gibberish were direct commands, "embedded commands" cause and effect statements, you will be in a trance at the count, of twenty, while the conscious mind was going frantic trying to work out the meaning of the gibberish was, the command passed strait trough to unconscious/subconscious mind unhindered by the conscious mind, which was very busy.

You can create inductions that sound like a normal induction, i.e. a forest walk and ad embedded commands in the induction that will work like a deepener, for example you could write an embedded command that says as you listen to the sound of my voice, you can feel yourself going deeper into a relaxed state." You don't write it in as one sentence like that quote but split it so it fits in the induction un-noticed, just emphasise the embedded words when they appear, and split them into a few words at a time, this works on a kind of subliminal level where you can be reciting an induction, and embed another command disguised as part of the induction, it is a bit of an art mastering this and you have not got to worry about this when you put your first sessions together this is just an example of how linguistics can be used to send direct commands to the unconscious.

The more you focus on this and realise it's true, the better the understanding you will have on the way to communicate with your own unconscious mind to become master of your own destiny. Human beings live in a "mental" world and everything in it is held together by their thoughts and emotions; Humans co-create life forms, inanimate objects, atmospheric condition, their bodies and the earth proper; the invisible electric impulses that emanate endlessly from their heads direct the course of the cosmic atoms; these impulses are influenced by peoples daytime thoughts, speaking, reading, inner dialogue and their dreams and sleep thinking, bringing about three dimensional manifestation; one can deliberately co-create what he or she desires to manifest by using, affirmations hypnotherapy, and focused directional thinking. We can create our own opportunities, perspectives with self-hypnosis, part of which involves learning to let go of the situation you think you're in and create, perceive the situation you want to be in, "nothing happens by chance" and that includes change, it's all pre-dictated, the desires that are focused on most are the ones that manifest. Believe it or not when things constantly go wrong for you for the best part you have desired it and intended it by what you were focused on most especially if you are constantly talking about things going wrong all the time you activate the desire and intention, at least that's the way unconscious mind receives it. when working on mindset and scripts or visualisation you are creating and increasing the probability of it manifesting through the focus being more on the new probability than the old or other ones, manipulation of probability's then changes your reality thus changing your actuality in real terms.

The highest probability is the final stage before actual manifestation. The non-physical structure prior to any manifestation is the possibility that it exists; so when you create the probability of an opportunity the opportunities will percent themselves. The Statements of intention create the possibility when the focus is held and repeated it then builds enough substance, form to go from possibility to physical tangible reality; so for example like the hypnotic sandwich; I want to have, I can have, I will have, I am able to have, followed by the desire and intention creates the possibility that it is possible, and in Universe every possibility already exists, this is the way to tune into and manifest the possibility's you prefer rather than the ones you have had to endure. A change in perspective of a concept changes the possibility related to the concept; a negative possibility of a concept changed to a positive one creates the possibility of a positive result for anything related to the concept with a new positive perspective, it is literally like flicking the switches of possibility. The primary fundamental objective of any script of suggestion is to create, generate positive change; either in the persons behaviour, attitude, belief systems and their perspective of their current reality which in turn leads to the change they actually experience.

The primary areas of a person's life that these areas refer to are ambition, health, finances, relationships, habits, pretty much any script that has ever been written for a hypnosis session would fall in to one of these categories; I would imagine the vast majority of people go to a hypnotherapist for one off sessions like quitting smoking without looking any further into what hypnotherapy represents in terms of what could be achieved if hypnotherapy was used on a regular basis; with a little research it becomes apparent that this can open up doors and possibility's into our lives that we could previously only dream of, it can give us a whole new perspective and outlook on life. The stories are abounded of an incredible array of achievement's healing in all areas regeneration of human organs returning to healthy ones, eyesight being restored, cancers and trauma's being reversed the list is endless of what can be achieved when we apply a script of intention, suggested in hypnosis. Even quantum physics and some mainstream science now conclude, you cannot have universe without mind entering into it, so when we put hypnosis further under the spotlight, we find that hypnosis shows us a way to communicate with our unconscious mind very effectively; and with effective communication with the unconscious we manifest by choice rather than chance. Then we are no longer dis-functional and develop functional flow in a real sense of the word because we become whole again (Holistic) when this communication doorway is opened.

On the other side of the coin hypnosis also comes under the umbrella term of the psychic, esoteric as altered state of consciousness is four dimensional; hypnosis's original roots of origin, it's well-known hypnosis has been in use for a very long time, we also know that the ancient Egyptians knew of affirmations, and re-framing, so in various forms or style it's probably been around for as long as Humanity has, spell-craft holds the same principles as hypnosis, desire, intention, focus, meditation or holding the point of focus before reciting the script or spell, traditions were then added to this to apparently add power to the spell such as burning incense casting specific spells at times of specific planetary aspects or phases, candle colours and all this kind of thing were added to create an atmosphere and expectation for example.

If a specific herb were required then the collecting of the herb and enchanting it all built up the expectation that the spell would work, weather they viewed this as actual magic, or they understood the communication connection between the two conscious minds and how things manifest. They must also have known not to cast a thought on how it will manifest just that it will, so weather planetary aspects played a part in anything or not, the whole exercise was about building the intention and focusing on the end result, so witchcraft was in essence understanding the way words work and their power in statements. Hypnosis is as much a wise craft as the term witch in witchcraft has an old English meaning of craft of the wise, well I would say understanding this to the point of being able to manifest is indeed wisdom; It was also said that when a person could manifest at will they had the power and were called a 'witch' to mean wise.

The concept of a spell and hypnosis script are essentially the same. How far back can we trace this, well there is a theory I quite like that the cave paintings of early stone age man could have had a specific purpose, like vision boards before they went out on a hunt, they may have painted the animal they were hunting and in essence visualised the animal manifesting, we can only wonder if that is true or not, it's certainly an interesting idea. Man has always had the ability to 'create' a concept or idea and so I wonder just how in tune early man was with intuitive thought, I was talking to a friend a few years back and we got onto the subject of tribal cultures shamanism, and I said these people are famed for their incredible knowledge of plants and their uses, now when they had no library or even books for that matter how did they have such a good idea of plants and healing, we both drew a blank under that one I thought about it later and it dawned on me that they were asking what they perceived as the universe, or unconscious questions, and receiving the answers intuitively, after thinking on it for a while it made absolute sense, when you think of different cultures cut off from each other, yet when anthropologists studied these cultures they found that some had belief systems so close, and healing rituals so similar that it baffled them as to how this could be so, the only logical answer would be they habituated ways to ask questions and intuit the answers. So people were practicing at least some form of hypnosis thousands and thousands of years ago, the connection we all have whether we call ourselves Shaman, Witch, Wizard, Psychic, are all representative of people who could in effect reality shift, using techniques to induce a hypnotic state and communicate suggestions to the unconscious, giving them the ability to change events and circumstances in their life.

So hypnosis's connection to reality shifting becomes apparent and reality shifting probably better defines hypnosis than hypnosis does as in shifting reality in the realm of the unconscious and this is where we can really start getting creative. So when we look at reality shifting and start to piece the puzzle together the clues start to emerge that everything in our existence is about caused and changed by our mind set. If we set our mind to receive an answer intuitively then we acquire the answer intuitively, because we set our mind to believe that this is possible, hypnosis is about mind re-setting, changing old beliefs and values with new ones. when we take the (im) out of impossible then everything is possible, and when we start thinking possible that is when we can start to manifest what others would say is impossible; if you said right, I am going to live in this incarnation for three to seven hundred years still have the energy of a twenty-year-old, and look and feel youthful, you wouldn't have got to the end of the sentence without cries of impossible!

There is obviously a plane of future probabilities, most things are stated in terms of probabilities; The people who would scream impossible to living for more than a couple of hundred years, are conditioned to perceive it as improbable that anyone could live for too hundred years, and the reason people don't live to Too hundred years is because they haven't challenged the probability they have been conditioned to expect or anticipate. Every hypnotic script is a new probability; rather than an acceptance of an old probability, this surely shows how much scope we have to play with where hypnosis is concerned. So let's look at this a bit deeper. There is an overwhelming amount of evidence and testimonies backed with professional observers reports, who will say that the body will regenerate every tissue every organ, cell, every aspect that is the Human body, back to the condition mind-set is set to, so when we create a mind-set of health and vitality that is what the body becomes; every other idea is a conditioned thought. What we learn through hypnosis and the formula of applying scripts of focused thought, is how to change and develop a new mind-set, the unconscious can regenerate the body by default to maintain perfect health indefinitely, our bodies can last out for an eternity because the unconscious runs all bodily functions by default, hypnosis is one way we can re-set the default.

I read a commentary from the seven universal principles, it said that when we understand this and we apply these principles or formula to our existence, then people would look on that person as if they were God like because of what they have achieved, which to the other people's pre-programmed, conditioned minds would seem impossible; when we have looked at this again and we ask is it possible to live in the same body for three to seven hundred plus years the answer then becomes yes; if the mind can conceive it then it already exists. The possibility already exists we just have to apply the knowledge of how to create new habitual thoughts and beliefs, which for everyone with a bit of practice is relatively easy if you want something to exist in your life and can conceive that it can exist, then you create a script that makes that thought a habituated thought, then the existence of that thought comes into your existence. So how this is the way we create new habituated thoughts.

Script it out play it back in a self-hypnosis session daily until the suggestions manifest, which can vary with different people depending on how much they believe this formula, process will work. I would say anything from days to weeks to months I believe it is really down to whether you do this with background thoughts of this is really stupid, or if you do this with background thoughts of this absolutely works they say belief is all well I absolutely believed in this before I started, and that's what I put out to the Universe (Faith) if you constantly resist the idea that this works then obviously your unlikely to carry it on for long or when you persevere, then when little things start to change or manifest then the belief starts to come around it just takes them a bit longer, the established idea of how long it takes to habituate a thought is twenty one to thirty days; This obviously varies from person to person. "When a thought becomes habituated, it becomes a belief, and manifests with absolute certainty." What it is saying is beliefs manifest so question what you believe and only believe what you want to manifest. Everything that is logged in the unconscious is a truth there are no non-truths logged in anyone's unconscious; everything is a belief that something is true.

when you call on the unconscious to bring you something you do so by making it a belief, the Universe does not say well you never did the washing up this morning so no you can't have that, the universe shifts to manifest what you asked for without condition. conditions are manmade to control people, you cannot have tough love because you cannot impose conditions on love without the intention to be to control that person; tough love is the corresponding opposite to unconditional love, so anything that is hooked up with a condition is nothing more than a control mechanism, so once you are just focused on yourself and what your drawing into your life with free, will those who try to control you will dissipate from your life because they are powerless over your free will to live your life as you choose not even good old threats or intimidation won't work on someone with universal confidence. So after a week two weeks a month their attempts to get a reaction from you fail because you are focused on yourself, and their frequency's don't match up to yours, so the universe removes them out of your experience that's the beauty of this there is never any need for retribution because you handed it to the universe. you can only attract into your experience that which you give the best parts of your thoughts to, so when you give the best part of your thoughts to what you are wishing to attract that which you do not wish to experience falls away because you switched the best part of your thoughts to your life no other people's option's, other people's option's become like subordinates that you give no mind to, if you give none or little mind to something then it cannot exist in your experience.

Even if you're at work all day and work colleagues drive you up the wall, as long as you can switch your thoughts back to what you are manifesting then they have no effect because as soon as your focused on yourself then your frequency's shift up a couple of gears and they cannot drag you down to their frequency unless you allow it by giving thought to them in your designated time to focus your thoughts on you. At the end of each day only focus on that which you desire or events of the day that have pleased you erase all the other ones from your mind and before you know it, you're shifting your reality.

The key part to reality shifting is be focused on what suggestions you accept on a conscious level you can have everyone in your life tell you can't do something ,a job, skill or self-healing you don't have to accept their suggestions you can decline that on a conscious level without actually pushing against them the law of non-resistance is to just decline people's views not push against them, and allowing them more leverage, they are just opinions of others and if you suggesting to yourself you can do and decline the options of others then you will do what I do, is if someone says something I decline I think of an opposite affirmation to cancel out the negative comment it works better than you might think for example if someone insults you say I'm perfect as I am if someone threatens you then say the only thing that can harm me is my own attitude and my attitude is good if you look at the story of the man dubbed the miracle man that says it all, one of his quotes is when you get your mind you can rebuild yourself and build all other experiences in your life. "Man becomes what he thinks about most.

CHAPTER TWENTY-ONE

EXAMPLES OF INDUCTIONS, DEEPENERS AND SUGGESTION CLUSTER SCRIPTS

Examples of inductions and deepeners; Note: feel free to edit or play around with the scripts to suit yourselves; before using a self-hypnosis session turn your phone off or on mute, and be as certain as you can that you will not be disturbed, deep state induction and deepener. Note, this induction and deepener is a very deep theta/delta cusp hypnotic state, you should not attempt to drive or use machinery after this until you feel fully awake. Countryside and Garden Induction: As you walk into your garden which encompasses acres of land---you look out at an abundant countryside around you---standing in the garden there is a fresh gentle cooling breeze---the air is full of the scent of flowers growing in the garden. You pause for a few moments and feel infinite connection to nature----the plants---the trees---the sky above---the ground under your feet. You feel the brilliance of the sun shining down its warm healing life giving glow. You now focus on the light from the sun over your right arm; and move it gently back and forth from the tips of your fingers to your shoulders, until you get the sensation of the warmth penetrating your skin---and then the muscles----and then the nerves---and then the bones---until the light from the sun touches every nerve----every cell---every sinew---every consciousness in your right arm. And you find yourself letting go and drifting deeper----and deeper. Move the light now gently to the left arm, from the tips of the fingers to the shoulders, just move it back and forth until you can sense and experience of the warmth of the sun penetrating through the skin---and the muscles---and the nerves---and the bones----until the light from the sun touches every nerve----every cell---every sinew---every consciousness in your left arm---until both the right and the left arm become---very---deeply---relaxed;---easily---gently--effortlessly.

You move the light of the sundown to your right leg now. From the tips of the toes all the way to the hip joint, a light will focus and move, just move it back and forth until you can sense and experience of the warmth of the sun penetrating through the skin---and the muscles---and the nerves and the bones---until the light from the sun touches every nerve----every cell---every sinew---every consciousness in your right leg which becomes deeply relaxed---because with each word that I utter, with each breath that you take---this feeling and sensation of letting go and relaxing increases moment by moment, breath by breath. Focus the light of the sun now over the left leg from the toes to the hip and back and forth, up and down just move it back and forth until you can sense and experience of the warmth of the sun penetrating through the skin---and the muscles---and the nerves---and the bones---until the light from the sun touches every nerve----every cell---every sinew---every consciousness in your left leg until both your right and left leg---relax---deeper---deeper---deeper. You move the light now and bring it into your stomach---focus it there like a ball of energy, feel it begin to warm and glow and to soothe every organ---every system---every cell---every atom every consciousness in your body. And just relax---release---and let go---and go deeper---deeper---and still deeper. You bring the light now bring it and focus it on your chest and experience the light from the sun entering your blood stream---feel and sense and know that the energy is vitality---the life the light the love from the sun is surging throughout your entire body---through---bloodstream to heal, to soothe and re-vitalise, as you go deeper---still deeper into a hypnotic state.

You bring the light from the sun now into your head and move it down your spine until it touches you tailbone, when it touches your tailbone it will light your entire body like a florescent light bulb, from the tip of your tailbone to the top of your head. And then the light begins to move and shimmer and vibrate as it pulsates through every nerve in your body---you are aware of the energy of the light moving down to your pelvic region and down your legs, from the small of your back around to your stomach---and between your shoulders---and around your lungs and your heart---across your shoulders---and your neck and your head, your entire body is relaxed---more---and more---your shoulders relax---as does your neck---your scalp relaxes---the right and left lobes of your brain relax---your forehead and the little muscles around your eyes---and cheeks relax---your jaws relaxed and open and finding saliva, you will merely swallow it and go deeper---and deeper---still deeper---into a relaxing hypnotic state.

As you walk further into your garden which is abundant with plants and trees of all kinds you walk over to the beds of roses and I crouch down and take in the smell of a rose in full bloom you breath in through your nose and take in a sweet fragrant smell of the rose---you stand up again and look at the different colours of roses shades of---purple---red---pink---yellow, and white---all in full bloom and beautiful to the eye. As you look around the rest of the garden there are other flowers and herb beds and vegetable patches with a variety of different blooms and plants growing, you feel so alive and living in the magic of life---the abundance of the universe all around you—the birds singing in the trees---the breeze gently rustling the leaves on the trees.

A group of squirrels are running up and down the trees, all around you is teeming with life. As you walk along you feel the unconditional love of the universe all around and within you---you are relaxed and calm as you walk towards a wooded area of your garden---there are of different types of trees some bear fruit--some nuts, some are tall mighty and wise---some are shorter and younger. As you walk along the path that goes through the wooded area of your garden---on the ground away from the path is a carpet of small flowers ferns and shrubs, you stop briefly to listen to the sound of the birds calling to each other in the trees. You continue walking along the path and come across a large oak tree with centuries of wisdom---as you look up there is what looks like a hole in the trunk of a tree, a wise looking owl's home, it looks out hoots and goes back in the hole. As you come towards the end of the woods the path leads to an open field, you look out across a large rectangle shape field enclosed by rows of trees.

The unploughed field resembles a carpet of green, with yellow and white specks, which are daisy's buttercups and dandelions-you walk a while in the field then sit down you take a few breaths then lay out-stretched feeling the warmth of the sun on you---take a couple more breaths and relax. You are surrounded by the great presents of Universe---only good do you give out, only good do you receive, you are now completely aware of your breathing---you count to four as you take a deep breath in through your nose---you then hold your breath and count to four. And count to four as you exhale the breath through your mouthy and count, to four and hold and you can repeat this effortlessly can't you.

As you continue to do this, you feel the leading edge of air through your nose, moving in through your nasal passage, down your throat and filling the inside of your lungs---you follow and sense the air passing through the inner parts of your body your mind is now empty of any mundane thoughts. You have can now let go and release any negative----burdens---emotions or feelings back to where they came from---and you feel totally relaxed---feeling relaxed and light as a feather---as you relax all contractions in your body become absent your body is loose and motionless---your muscles offer no resistance you feel loose and relaxed just as if you were a rag doll.

Complete relaxation means the complete absence of movement---it means the complete absence of holding any part of my body rigid---so as you are lying completely relaxed---all the muscles attached to your bones are relaxed and loose. If you make any volunteer movement, you can only do so by contracting a muscle or group of muscles---when you allow these muscles to become completely relaxed---your nerves to and from the muscles carry no messages---there are only sensations---your nerves are completely inactive--and it is certain that complete relaxation---in any part of nerves means simply zero activity in the nerves. It has become physically impossible for you to feel nervous---in any part of your body---when in that part you allow it to be completely relaxed. You feel very calm and peaceful---you are feeling better than you have felt for a long--

-long time. Any outside music, taping sounds or other noises will only function as a trigger in assisting you in relaxing---more and more deeply. So deeply are you relaxed---that you can actually feel a physical experience---in feeling yourself relaxing---deeper and deeper---enjoying all the wonderful feelings of relaxation---love----joy---happiness---being completely relaxed, relaxation. Being so intense---so much so that should you try to resist-consciously---the more deeply relaxed your body will go automatically.

There is a peacefulness you feel in my mind---and a calmness your experiencing throughout your body---it becomes stronger and stronger--- you continue to relax—even more soundly--- and more deeply---with every breath you exhale-Enjoying all the sensations---allowing yourself to relax without any effort whatsoever---your whole body just giving in---letting go----loose---and relaxed---Very loose--and very relaxed---as you listen to the sound of my voice---you feel yourself being guided deeper into relaxation---following my suggestions guides you into deeper relaxation---And the more You allow your body to relax the better you feel---and the better you feel---the more and more your body will relax---with good feelings going through your body and content thoughts going through your mind. You relax and let yourself go---you can relax and let yourself go---drifting as you will.

You now feel all tension or discomfort leave your body all your organs are functioning normally---your body tissues are mending as the blood runs freely through your arteries---sending healing to every minute pert of your body, and oxygen to your brain removing all impurities and letting your body become perfectly healthy. Even though you are now very relaxed-- there is a much deeper relaxed state you can reach---this is known as somnambulistic state of relaxation---this is perfectly safe---you can now choose to reach that deeper relaxed state. I will now count from five to one, in the transition of the count you will go into a deep---lucid relaxed somnambulistic, hypnotic state. To accomplish this level---all you have to do is just let it work---you can feel it working----as if you were going down an elevator---moving to deeper levels all the time---you know this is working---let it work---feel it working---you feel yourself moving further down---and down Five---you start to let go and slip into a deeper relaxed state---you feel yourself ascending towards a higher vibrational state of being---you just relax and let yourself go---this absolutely works. Four---you feel yourself becoming more and more relaxed and being guided towards a place of complete relaxation and euphoria---you just relax and let yourself go---this absolutely works.

Three--you are now feeling so relaxed ten times more relaxed---twenty times more relaxed---thirty times more relaxed---fifty times more relaxed---you just relax and let yourself go--this absolutely works. Two you are now in a deep hypnotic state and feelings of euphoria are starting to wash over you. You just relax and let yourself go-- this absolutely works. One---you are now in a deep somnambulistic hypnotic state and exist on a plane of complete euphoria---you have completely let go because you are totally relaxed---this absolutely works, Just let your mind go let it wander just as it will---for a short while you will not hear my voice, but when I speak again you will know that I have some matters of great importance to say to you---and your subconscious mind will listen---accept and act upon the messages it hears as they benefit you greatly, and are for the good of the all.

As you continue to drift in a euphoric and relaxed state you will stay in this deep hypnotic state until I count from one to five. With your eyes closed can you imagine being a child, as you're playing whether it be outside or indoors, walking in a garden or along a beach it can be where ever you choose, see yourself playing around or whatever it is you're doing, take on all your surroundings; what are the things you can see the things you can hear the things you can smell touch or even the things you can taste; you notice all of these things are giving you warm happy, enthusiastic feelings almost like you feel just before you open a Birthday or Christmas present notice the feelings of excitement and anticipation, take some time to explore your environment. Suggestion. Esoteric definition. The main factor in making thoughts manifest in the world is through suggestion by the spoken, written word or life experiences; this is done by the conscious mind, which perceives from outside stimuli, forms a concept or decision, then drops it in the computer mind, the unconscious mind; its then compartmentalised if there is a compartment to which the new suggestion can relate; if the suggestion is completely foreign, it will be spewed out until a new compartment begins to form, before thoughts can be manifest into mundane actuality, the suggestion must be accepted by unconscious mind; it then blends with the conscious minds ergs of energy that emanate from the head, with "meaning and purpose" which gives it the intensity it needs to manifest. In hypnosis either the hypnotist or the person doing self-hypnosis, is in essence acting as conscious mind, while conscious mind is put on pause, so it takes out the middleman i.e. conscious critical mind, so the suggestions aren't being re-processed by conscious before being sent to the unconscious. Two key words in this definition are meaning and purpose; when you are composing your script ask yourself what does this mean to me and what the purpose is, because the first thing unconscious asks is what is the meaning of this suggestion and what is its meaning and purpose. It is also the meanings and purpose that are changed by changing one single belief, can change the "meaning and purpose" of a whole array of things held in unconscious mind, the new belief interacts in a different way to the old one, values and beliefs give meaning and purpose to whatever their connected to.

As it suggests these scripts are designed to achieve an intended desired outcome, some scripts are designed to reverse pain; this is done by putting the person into a deeper level of hypnosis that induces anaesthesia, the nerve end feelings are switched to sensory so there is no sense of pain. Suggestion is the cause of manifestation, groupings of words that direct the focused intention for an outcome/purpose. The design of the script is to work on a specific area say pain relief in a dentist, the objective of the hypnosis script is to have the person to be in a deep enough hypnotic state to achieve anaesthesia, which causes the nerve end responses of pain to switch to sensory and the person is completely anesthetised, you don't have to be in a very deep level of trance for hypnosis scripts to work, light to medium is generally fine; the main objective of being in hypnosis though is to be in a hypnotic state, so as to have the effect that the conscious critical part of the mind is essentially paused while the scripts are being narrated to subconscious mind.

With this in mind it is easy to see the true potential with hypnosis, for working on everything from changing beliefs and values, to cancelling out recurring phobias and traumas, to changing habits, working with self-hypnosis will give you a massive positive resource; everything we have and experienced in our life has in some way shape or form comes from suggestions; the art of hypnotic suggestion is to suggest the desired outcome. Suggestions of this type of fall under clinical hypnosis as they are directed toward a specific outcome or purpose, so that is one set of hypnotic suggestion, the other type is a little more abstract using suggestions that are ambiguous or vaguely specific, the purpose of this type of suggestion is that it contains all the specifics however you allow unconscious mind to script in the specifics-and just guide it with ambiguous statements.

The three core concepts Health, Wealth, Relationships, elicitation. First off Health, Wealth, relationships are all nouns, so look up in the dictionary the meanings first write them down, then on each one continue to think of a s many meanings as you can for each concept, then when you have done that keep what you have written, and write down for each concept how you relate to each one in the here and now, not how you want to relate to them that comes next, just as many things as you can on each concept as you can, this includes any metaphors you can think of that you use now in relation to each concept. So around wealth if a metaphor pops up you find yourself using like money doesn't grow on trees, then write them down as well. Take your time on this a few days if you want, just let the meanings pop up and write them down. Then when you feel your done look at each list of each concept, and all the meanings you have that aren't in alignment with the type of meaning you want to have, use the meanings you don't want as a springboard to write out the meaning you do want, including any metaphors, simply switch the metaphor from a negative one that isn't in alignment to what you want to a positive metaphor that aligns to a meaning you do want. You see how much easier it makes it by using the old meaning as a springboard to create new ones.

Now you have three lists of meanings corresponding to the way you want to connect to the concepts of Health, Wealth, and Relationships. Now look at each list and put the list in order of what you think has the most importance to you and the ones that you feel are more likely to come first, so try to look at it like a time line, short, medium and long term, say for wealth, you decided you want to master a certain skill or craft, so this would be long term, so you could put I am in the process of becoming a master of this skill or craft, then think of the things you would be doing after mastering it, and write these down as having in the here and now, it sounds counterintuitive but in the process of becoming means you are also in the process of adding value to yourself, and if you need things to help you master the skill then unconscious mind can script those in, it also keeps it real so put a couple of things in each script that you do already have or do. In the process of becoming also announces to unconscious your desire and intension and its purpose and meaning; now turn these lists into ambiguous/vaguely specific statements.

Try to leave out amount of money it's to specific put in that which you want to acquire as having then unconscious mind can spin in how the money comes, with relationships focus on the types, personality, attitude, or characteristic you're looking for not specific people you know. With health keep the associations to being or in the process of becoming healthier, leave out any mention of illness, and not to give the pet name of any illness, make sure your statements are defining a positive meaning/purpose or outcome. You now have three lists of suggestion statements that correspond to each concept ready to put together, now look through the list you can record just Wealth, Health, Relationships, separately or you can mix some Wealth, Some Health, some relationships, personally I find this works best. As you cover various concepts in one session, so when playing back every day you have one forty or so minuet session not three forty-minute sessions each day, in terms of how often do I play them you can do it every twenty-four or twelve hours as long as the focus is kept on the session every day, don't worry if you miss a day but as far as you can play them daily and edit as an when things are manifested. Remember thought when focused on for a period of time becomes thought form, which then become physical form.

Here are some examples of "ambiguous/vaguely specific", statements and "cluster" scripts "Your ability to communicate with language is far greater than the value of money" statements like this put you above money drawing it in as opposed to money being above you, chasing it, You own a very large house and a very large area of land, which has a beautiful garden with many different varieties of trees and plant with beautiful scenery in the background. Our values and beliefs can be as powerful as medicine designed for illness and values and beliefs can re-right genes, placebo is one example of this, this suggestion script is orientated around health mostly, and sends instructions to the unconscious mind that through repetition will be accepted by unconscious mind! The script is an example of vaguely specific (abstract) which in itself contains the specifics without being specific.

The script is a post hypnotic, although you can change it to affirmation if you want to, "You" is post-hypnotic, "I" is affirmation, you are or I'm, you can use either in self-hypnosis. Cluster-Suggestion script: You're every organ, blood cells, genes are functioning as an organism in a body that is in excellent condition---and you have robust health., you have the vigour and youthfulness a healthy teenager. You are an energy being infinite in nature and aware of your own true self.--Your eyesight is continuously improving toward perfect sight.---Your hearing is continuously improving toward perfect hearing.---Your body can constantly regenerate and you are in an excellent state of spiritual and physical and mental health.---Your genes and stem cells work perfectly in healing and keeping your physical body healthy.---and are directed by your thoughts, beliefs, and actions.---Your body is continuously happy and at ease.---Any outside interference of your choices and decisions, belongs outside and returns to where it came from because it reflects and belongs to others.---as you have total free will of choice given you by the infinite spirit within.---Other people's negative opinion of you is none of your business. You can exercise and weight train regularly every week, to keep healthy.---You can always have a feeling of appreciating wellness and being alive.---Your skin is in the process of improving and becoming more youthful, Your head of hair is in the process of improving and becoming full and its original colour.---Your relationships are co- creative and co-existing.---your meals are well balanced and nutritious that sustains your whole body.---You have continuingly exiting, things to do and be interested and enthusiastic about.---your life is a continuously euphoric experience.---you can do as you will an it harm ye none.---you have an attitude that protects you and keeps you safe and happy.---You have and can feel love and happy emotions, continuously.---You are eternally youthful, curious, you can do anything you choose-You have only to choose to, and you are able to do.---Your life is really exciting and fun.---Your genes are programmed to keep your body in perfect physical health continuously. You have a life that is abundant easy and effortless.

You are continuously physically active and energetic ---you have a constant, continuous flow of energy through my body---you are self-generating. ---self-organising---your spiritual and physical self is infinite. ---All your bodily senses function in perfect harmony to each other. You radiate good health, wellbeing, abundant energy.---your chakras are clear, allowing free flowing energy throughout your being .you have mastered your destiny allowing, free-will to be the way you choose to live.-you always sleep soundly and wake up happy and full of energy and enthusiasm,---You have an excellent memory and perfect recall.---You read books and aspire to learn and keep gaining knowledge and wisdom.---You always speak and talk out loud in a clear confident manner; you are happy and great full that all these things are true of your reality---For the good of all, Still feeling good about myself and relaxed, I start to gradually come back to full lucid waking consciousness feeling very relaxed happy and experiencing the reality of these perspectives: Awakener 1: gradually coming back to full lucid consciousness, 2: feeling calm and contented. 3: Coming back more and more. 4: almost back now feeling fine in every way, 5: eyes open fully awakened and refreshed.

It now becomes like a quest to find and create our true selves and choose who we are with awareness that the whole of our reality as we see it has been programmed, and with understanding of the way linguistics really work and the profound power of words we can re-programme it and bring our reality/actuality into alignment with our deepest wishes and desires; we can and already do project outside actuality from within. This is essentially what is meant by self-activation, in other words a person's belief and value system the biggest chunk of which was formed from birth to, which essentially means our entire set of beliefs and values, both perceived as good or bad, came almost entirely from outside stimuli; so now we can not so much re-live from birth to six but re-create that which was dropped to our unconscious mind back then. Self-actualisation starts to happen when you actually start to question and elicit our values and beliefs that associate to the value, there will be many you think are valid and are happy with, and there will be a lot that when you say to yourself well do, I actually believe that, or do I want to believe that's impossible, that becomes the first step in changing our belief systems, which is our unconscious minds view of reality which happily is not absolute, it is variable.

Actions and linguistics that move toward pro-creation which is the only bias of infinite spirit/vital life force, the opposite being toward disruption and destruction. Which leads into the idea of self-healing and self-sabotage, which ever one it is defined entirely by the way we are thinking at any point in time; the upside is vital life force the energy that exists in everything throughout universe, is completely neutral apart from this one bias, which of toward pro-creation; which means there really are no rules no limitations only the ones we impose on ourselves, the best wisdom I have come across as a guide for this is "an it harm ye none do as thy will" if you follow this would you need rules anyway? Part of what learning hypnosis is about Is learning that the makeup/structure of the language we use every day is defining our experience as a Human being on the planet and start to understand that words cause end results which are in line with what will manifest as a result of what's being affirmed in the conversational statements or hypnotic suggestion both with others and self-talk; hypnosis is essentially a "strategy" for conscious communication with subconscious mind.

The conscious is Aladdin, and the unconscious is the Gennie in the lamp, which says your wish is my command. When we sit down consciously and decide what it is we really want our incarnation to be we can decide that consciously, when we record to repeat play the hypnosis session we are the "I" conscious self that is commanding the "you" unconscious self to manifest what we desire and this is the way it absolutely works, this is why hypnosis works very quickly in comparison to affirmations, with affirmations the "I" is trying to convince the "I" that so and so is true, with hypnosis the "I" is telling the "you" that this is true, want to live for hundreds of years in this incarnation fit and healthy, then make it a reality in unconscious mind first that at the very least that is possible not impossible. Suggestions can be used in other ways as well, if you want to feel more confident or motivated, close your eyes and remember a time when you felt really confident or motivated then hold yourself in that feeling state wrap it around you and when you break the state as you would with anchoring you will be more confident or motivated and that all happens by suggestion: PTSD's, phobias all manner of things that were problems for people are being reversed everyday with this knowledge and application of suggestion in a structured and strategic way.

That's directly tied in with the three absolute Universal laws, If you're not generally a patient person then then I have a metaphor for you about a boy who planted a seed and dug it up every day to see how it was doing; obviously it didn't do very well being dug up every day, what I mean by that is be patient enough and allow things to unfold of their own accord so to speak, you know you're using the right suggestions in the right way then you know it will happen just repeat until it manifests. This process is the key to realising and utilising that which is known as the law of potentiality most people never come close to achieving this because they don't know how to and aren't aware of the things I have shown you in this book, many people who all have inner power look to other people as having the power which is actually lying dormant within them, when this is realised you become like the President or Emperor or God of your own incarnation, you are the boss of you. How's are the realm at least in this case of unconscious mind, as I mention in conversational linguistics, the more you understand what the words are doing the more direct access you have to sending commands to your unconscious that are actually coming from you not outside hacking.

Some people are more visual some are more audio some are more kinaesthetic, hypnosis and minds-eye visualisation are both done with eyes closed and in an altered state of consciousness, I personal think through experience mostly that hypnosis is best although you can boost the hypnosis sessions with relevant mind's eye visualisation, the reason I think this is you have the hypnosis suggestions set and can repeat them exactly the same every day, whereas with mind's eye, it can be difficult to keep to the same theme without drifting or the theme changing, although this depends on each individual, and I would try both although to my mind all you need is the hypnosis session as unconscious mind is the realm of metaphorical imagery and can match the picture to the words, it is very smart, however if you are looking at specifics like a certain type of house or car, or type looks of person you would like a relationship with, then ad visualisation i.e. mind's eye or vision boards, keep the scrips as vaguely specific as you can, don't write in I want or have a BMW, write in something that pre-supposes being in the position to own one without mentioning money directly, as I showed you in the example of vaguely specific scripts.

As I said be open to experimenting a bit as well sometimes you can get an intuitive nudge to try something, and it innovates what you were doing before and comes up trumps so to speak. Sometimes what will manifest will be an intuitive idea or nudge of an action to take that will get you the outcome, sometimes it will just manifest, trust your intuition, or information of what to do will just pop up in your head, intuition is real and it is worth connecting to it, like the gut feeling, how many times had you had a gut feeling or hunch about something and you went with it and it was spot on, and how many times have you had a gut feeling about something and ignored it only to wish you hadn't. words are given to mean the same thing but they are not the same thing in hypnosis to surrender to a hypnotist would be to allow and accept the hypnotists choosing what the person is changing in their life obviously no one in their right mind would surrender their will of decisions about their desires to another in hypnosis we let go of mundane thoughts and relax but we do not surrender our will the hypnotist has put together or uses a script of suggestion in accordance with the persons instruction.

Hopefully now you can fully appreciate how effective and powerful introducing self-hypnosis can be for personal achievements and overall wellbeing, not to mention that this actually puts you as the driver not the passenger in your own incarnation, I could write a book just on the benefits of hypnosis from testimonies from people in general, practitioners and even GP's, from freeing themselves of negative habits to terminally illness being reversed through hypnosis and NLP interventions, and I think that now the old stigmas of hypnosis are falling away and people are starting to see that these things are not fiction they work and hypnosis

EXAMPLES, INDUCTIONS, DEEPENERS SUGGESTION SCRIPTS

and self-hypnosis can and will be an action towards your personal big picture. So when you act through self- hypnosis and action that are moving towards those goal the you start to synchronise an alignment and association to your big picture.

CHAPTER TWENTY-TWO
ESOTERIC INFLUENCE

Esoteric is defined as a deeper knowledge and understanding of specialised subjects like universal principles, hypnosis and NLP, the way everything in universe interacts by virtue of the universal principles driving it. The comparative form of Esoteric is the Greek word Eso which means "within." It is also synonymous with hermetic, which is the foundation of the seven universal principles and the way we relate to them. Esoteric is that which leads to knowledge of self. And recognition of intuitive thought, out of body experiences and a whole array of subject matter that covers spirituality, subtle energies, multiple planes of existence and inspired actions are coming from within through connected consciousness. And of course understanding the way things manifest is defiantly Esoteric. Universal principles and applying them, hypnosis and applying it, NLP and applying it, are essentially esoteric in nature by the subject matter and that which is defined as Subjective or that which is "within", when you walk along a road going to the shop or whatever it is and you are thinking, planning things in your mind, inner dialogue, self-talk, you are consciously performing the subjective action of inner dialogue, and unconsciously performing an objective, walking to the shop.

The point being we create our experiences to a large degree by this process of subjective thinking, intuition is subjective, though the information is objective; we are talking on a level of subjective cause=objective effect, objective effect, subjective cause, and that's the loop of manifestation. Esoteric science then becomes the explanation of how and why we manifest our reality what were actually experiencing is always pre-destined through subjective interaction. Also religions in all its facets all have this esoteric influence as a root. Areas of mainstream science which years ago would have mocked a lot of definitions around "psychic, esoteric" subjects, are now actually becoming the solid foundation underneath the "psychic/esoteric" definitions in as much as quantum physics has proved quantum entanglement to be real in nature, they are actively looking for the fifth force of nature or vital life force/infinite spirit and looks like they found a particle that behaves in a way that they think belongs to this fifth force.

They fired of two elections in opposite directions from a specially designed cannon, each electron traveling seven miles before exiting the cannons at either end expecting them to move around independently thus proving disconnected, however when they exited the cannon they moved in perfect synchronicity to each other, proving connectivity, so scientific proof that everything is connected is there in multiples this is essentially proving what a lot of us know because it becomes self-validating, that the esoteric definitions many of which are in this book are real in nature. The concept of this in as much as we all inhabit a universe in a connected and independent way it isn't too hard to understand given that everybody believes their unconscious to be exclusive to themselves, so every creature has an unconscious that is taking care of the things we don't think about body temperature, heart rate the day-to-day function of our body, so with that in mind we are vital life force in physical incarnation. It has been believed for a long time that most of who we are comes from our parent's genes! But on reflection of this viewing past life regression, it beggars the question how much of who we are now is influenced by our past lives and is any of our ingrained belief systems influenced from memories values and beliefs even strategies of past lives. We tend to have the belief that anytime the sub-conscious is referencing information to see if it is in alignment with the persons true self or beliefs we assume the sub-conscious is referencing from our belief systems in this life it is certainly possible that the sub-conscious may well reference past beliefs as well if it can't find a believe that corresponds to the reason it is referencing a belief in the first place, then past life memories may well be used, this would also help us understand why past life regression is so effective with things like phobias.

The conditioned human can be very resistant to change, for several reasons; which range from fear of the unknown, outside opinion, it's a lot easier to be critical of other people than it is to be self- criticising, how many people do you know that will tell everyone else what they should change about themselves however they never actually change themselves, if you have known these people a good few years and you look at their values and beliefs years ago and compare them now, exactly the same values and beliefs which implies they haven't changed on any deep meaningful level. Hypnosis creates change. So looking at the cynical perspective of hypnosis, often these people are happier trying to change everyone else to fit in with them rather than change themselves and will often shun hypnosis as a kind of subconscious resistance/avoidance to changing or moving out of their comfort zone, because they know what to expect in their comfort zone outside of that scares them, so they stay in their domestic cat like comfort zone, never straying too far, and always going back to the same place.

Their minds are more focused on other people's aspirations rather than their own, for these people it is like their own mind is playing tricks on them. Suggestion and permission; Scripts of suggestion used in the technique of hypnosis, are the same as what is called permission slips, you are giving what you understand as sub/nonphysical conscious permission to create a change that will manifest as a desired intention. A line of script is a permission slip to the unconscious to manifest that which is in alignment to what you are giving permission for, you never ask you sub-conscious for something you give it permission to deliver the intention, which maybe a type of relationship, money, or other. Lucid consciousness gives permission, higher vibrational or subconscious gives approval, and the subconscious will give approval every time to the permission.

ESOTERIC INFLUENCE

This perfectly explains the idea of the, I (I am, I will) sentences of I am a can be a permissive statement in relation to the here and now in the moment, I will is a permissive statement of intention. The more a person's attention is focused on themselves and what they do want, a side effect of this is to naturally repel that which is unhelpful or which they don't want.

The more proficient a person becomes at this, the more their life becomes their own with less burdens from other people, this is a profound effect of the reality shift, a person can have a life they fell is terrible and unhappy and hard, and switch it right round to being happy confident free from previous burdens and restrictions, just by being aware of and choosing what they put there at the idea/concept that the mind can be reprogrammed or remodelled, and the understanding of personal orientations, neuro the brain/mind, linguistic the language we use that influences our life/reality, programming the way the mind processes information, through sound, sight, touch, smell, spoken and written words. Our likes and dislikes are defined in each individual by orientation of preferences, the influences that decide our preferences become the programming that shapes and changes our lives.

Understanding personal orientation gives us the power to transform our lives by looking deeper at what mind and reality actually are, orientation and preferences' are perspectives that are defining the way our lives unfold, these make up belief system/mind-set that are our personality's. In the same way that there is a left and right brain hemisphere there are effectively left and right orientations an example would be someone who works better on their own has a different orientation than someone who works better in a team, their orientations in the way they prefer to work are opposite, this comes under a category of inner or outer orientated. These may be the persons preference, or they work in a team, but their preference would be to work on their own or in smaller groups rather than being employed by an organisation, many people may think their orientated in a certain way but when they look at it properly may find they would like to change something that they would prefer to do differently, whether it be a job or cloths our choices come from our orientation towards a conditioned or self-taught choice. NLP is also about stings of words/instructions being delivered wrapped in gibberish or some other form of communicating but the communication has been pre-scripted with knowledge of what the instruction is causing, the idea is staged around trance induction being very quick/instant transition into trance and by-passing any analytical block the person may have, the key to this process is timing and rhythm, rapport and delivery are the key to this.

The too defining differences in induction of trance is progressive relaxation give the person the experience of visualisation and feeling the physical experience of trance instant inductions are useful for example for creating an overall local anaesthesia as a pain killer in emergencies, and for calming the person. To some degree there is an element of ESP involved here or rather understanding of ESP when communicating with others there is a certain amount of telepathy involved though sensory perception is something we live with everyday though most are oblivious to it and what it is, most people believe the only way they give and receive information is by written, verbal, or visual communication. If you have the view that we are physically separate individuals but non physically connected, then understanding the way this works becomes much easier than if you perceive everything as solid physical everything that appears solid and physical has a corresponding opposite of non-physical non-tangible substance with no weight or density.

What people would describe as invisible or spirit this opposite side of ourselves is an information conduit intuitive nudges or ideas or feeling derive from this aspect of ourselves, when you have an idea or intuitive answer to a question it has happened because you asked a question and intuited the answer this form of telepathy is in everyone but only a few understand it to make any good use of it NLP and hypnosis are very small words for the information that they are an umbrella to there are things that are attributed as psychic that are connected to all of this in fact hypnosis is classed as a psychic subject. It's a close relative of astral projection for example, often if you mention the word psychic or a subject attributed to psychic such as mediumship you will in the main get an adverse or hostile reaction to it; everyone has the same connection to the psychic but as I said before only a very few study it and only a very few study and practice or apply it to their lives others may have a perception that any psychic study or practice means their trying to summon demons or devils which obviously is slanderous heresy of the subjects surrounding the psychic. You can read a couple of books on hypnosis NLP and think you have the whole picture but in reality, understanding it properly is as much an unfolding path as any other you aren't going to get a PHD with one or two books this is the same the more you study and the deeper you go the more you understand knowledge is power actually it's how much knowledge and understanding of the knowledge you have on a deeper level.

ESP Our intuitive side areas of perception that every person experiences but few recognise or acknowledge it Carl Jung famously extended his research and study of psychiatry and incorporated knowledge of ESP into his work. ESP is also another way to describe the psychic mind which every human without exception has it's not a dark side as in bad, the definition of good or bad is if the intention/action is designed to harm others or benefit them; It comes down to orientation, direction of thoughts; suggestion directs thoughts, a string of words is a suggestion which creates direction/orientation to something, Where are the suggestions that you mind process is directing you and is it influenced more by you or more by outside suggestion, this is what advertisers understand which is why advertising is so successful because they understand the use of suggestion, and the way it directs people; if someone has a product they think would be useful or I some way financially successful then they often produce a large amount of the product first then use advertising to direct people to their product. NLP is the art of changing perspective; which follows the process of becoming that which is words and the way their portrayed as an example the phrase though shalt not; gets processed the equivalent to thought shall because shalt not does not exist it hasn't happened it's not I the past present or future, so it has no place In existence don't want processes as wat because don't; doesn't exist it has no definition of being past, present, future.

What happens when a statement is made such as I do want, or I don't want the whole statement Its ignored and only the focus word to what the statement was directed to is processed. The way a worded structure of a string of words is portrayed and knowing what the right way to word suggestions, this is the difference between something manifesting from it or not, this explains why peoples reality and decisions are the way they are at any given moment. A lot of people make daily decisions out of avoidance so are constantly focused on what their avoiding and adding thought to what their avoiding with the negative emotion of what there avoiding then the highest probability of what will manifest is what they focused on avoiding because they were sending so many messages to the mind of what their avoiding that it became a physical reality. When I was studying hypnosis, past life regression, we apparently find out what that incarnation was about I thought on this a while and it dawned on me, that it's all about the perspective you're viewing that life from. So the non-physical aspect of ourselves is like the perspective from which we are looking at things from; pre-defined preferences are what constitute most people's mind-sets; orientation of Shepard or sheep.

Years ago I read a book called the artists way, there was a statement in the book that I decided to put to the test to see what orientates people and why the statement was if you were to say to friends family colleges at work your ambitions live abroad study or set a business up that they would in general look for ways to talk you out of it or stop you or hold you up; could this be true?

And if so, why? Interesting thing on the way to writing this it turns out to be true! Why would other people try putting others off achieving their dreams; the answer is a little long winded to be fair but there is an answer, what the other people friends etc. are focused on and their mind-set if you just announced that you are going to do something that their not and they focus a good deal on what they haven't got then you will likely get some form of jealous reaction this is because if someone is more focused on what they haven't got, then other people having what they haven't got can trigger a negative response because their response is something they haven't got, people often get so caught up in what others are doing they literally have not time to focus on themselves and just carry on focusing on everyone else except themselves, they can tell you about everyone else but they couldn't tell you anything about themselves because they are always focused on what everyone else is doing; Non-physical solutions to physical problems; what is a non-physical solution to a physical problem? Agreements: the orientation of mutual agreements do you actually agree with what you agree with or agreed to? Opinions are what generate our moment-to-moment reality self-opinion or unified opinions, opinions that help, opinions that harm. Remember the saying the best intentions towards others often cause more harm than good, but when people focus their opinion in a positive 'have now' context on themselves this then creates future 'have now's NLP, hypnosis, creative visualisation, and affirmations are all ways of applying this; these become the non-physical action required for physical solutions. Take the story of cry wolf the girl keeps crying, wolf! Wolf! so everyone comes out looking for the wolf, but there's no wolf, the girl does the same thing again later and everyone comes out looking for the wolf but there's no wolf, the third time the girl does the same thing again crying wolf! Wolf! Only this time there really is a wolf, and she cry's wolf but no one comes out to look for the wolf, so the wolf cobbles her all up.

The story implies that the girl continually created on opinion that there was a wolf so sure enough the wolf turned up only there was no threat from the wolf until she created the opinion of one, even though there was no wolf the focus on wolf drew the wolf. What your opinion of what you focus on is what you draw in; remembering this really is the start to personal change and growth, the focus word/words/images are the key to this. Optimum health focus on the opinion of optimum health and you gain optimum health putting yourself in the picture of your self-opinion these processes become self-optimisation the same as optimising a website using keywords, meta-data; Meta meaning above and beyond. So you in effect create your own met data of yourself with understanding of the opinions you are creating that are defining your life.

You either do this with conscious knowledge of what you are doing or with little or no understanding of why your lives are defined the way they are, self-meta-programmer; What we are talking about here is above and beyond what is considered in most of society as normal, utilising perceptions that are extra to physical sight, smell, hearing, touch and taste, the concept that is called reality shifting or quantum jumping is a reference to the same thing that is hypnosis and NLP changing personal reality with conscious awareness by process creates the impression of reality shifting/quantum jumping. God "good, ordered direction" of thoughts non-

THE MIND KEYS

physical spirit that resides throw-out and within everything that exists in multi-dimensional universe, non-judgemental in nature is directed by thought, the collection of all humanity's thoughts are what is directing all human physical reality.

You see then the way people are often group orientated by likeness of thought that's the way people attract and repel each other by thought orientation for example someone who supported a football team would be more orientated to someone who supported the same team and less someone who supported a rival team, but they both like football, people orientate themselves to people by what their dominant thoughts are on, dominant as in what they think about the most, most often. Can you monitor your thoughts and if so in what way? If you said to someone describe your life and they came back with a pretty negative picture, then that persons is directing their thoughts mostly to that reality because they are holding their focus on that reality; you monitor your thoughts by choosing the reality to wish to focus on rather than the reality you feel compelled to focus on.

Self-control of inner states, by self-opinion, this is basically a key to what most life coaches and the content of the film the secret are describing countering a negative opinion of you from someone else, and neutralising and over riding the negative outside opinion with positive self-opinion thus manifesting the positive self-opinion not the negative outside opinion; no one on this planet can make you believe something if you choose to believe different it all comes down to orientation of the opinions you focus on most, which for the best part need to be your own. So in what way do you view yourself what you can achieve and manifest, and what percentage of that is outside opinion of group's friend's family and media? There are two ways of thinking that define every person on this planet and whether they are poor and ill or happy and rich the two mind-sets are success or victim you can have a mind-set of victim and change it to success or have a mind-set of success and change it to victim what people are self-talking whether through conversation or in their own mind is what defines which mind-set their orientated to if the glass is half empty they focus on empty if the glass is half full they focus on full there are no half measures, just full or empty, rich or poor happy or sad is what they are telling themselves they are by affirming it over and over in their minds. I am creation causation to the effect of. Success creates more success victims create more victims, victims victimise people so if your family and friends are predominantly the victim you need to find a way to separate yourself from outside opinion of poor me or people who always complain.

"Self-control of inner states; by inner dialogue", is the way I would sum up what the Secret, NLP coaching, hypnosis, are rooted to; your inner state creates your outer state which is your perceived reality, you are literally talking yourself into your reality; whether you are talking to yourself which is OK by the way or talking to others you are talking in your reality it's a process of drawing things in when you are talking even through the medium of writing you pull a trigger of causing what you are talking about to be in the process of becoming when the same type of talk is repeated and the focus is held on that subject it becomes real, by virtue of becoming the highest probability and then real. So someone who scores as being more outwardly orientated would probably be less likely to be influencing their own inner states as someone who scores more inwardly orientated, inwardly orientated people still have circles of friends but the friends they have, they have drawn by adjusting their mind-set/attitudes which requires looking within, communicate to the within/self. The very important thing to understand here which has probably kept people from achieving or having things is the transition between being outwardly directed or inwardly/self-directing understanding this or not is the difference between failure or success no matter how good your magic wand is if you don't understand the differences of these mind-sets then you're up swan creek without a paddle because to achieve anything the Secret says you have to move to being self-directing many people look back on their live in horror when they have the realisation that their whole life up to knowing this was organised by other people and most just went along with it because they knew no better way.

Let me explain this in a bit more in depth. Outer directed people are in general spending the best part of their lives trying to organise other people's lives most often against the other persons own will, which in itself works against the law of nature/universal principles themselves, that which works against the law of nature will be removed by the law of nature those that work against these laws that reverberate throughout universe create attitude that will destroy them, man was meant to be self-directing not dictated to by those who claim an office and say they can direct others by their own opinion of what is functional but is this in the best interest of the masses that follow this conditioned way of thinking it certainly benefits whatever group is involved but does it benefit the individual person or does it subtract from their own free will and decision making. The group orientated person is more likely to be directed by the will of the group or set of groups than being self-directing in many cases they have almost no self-direction at all.

It all, comes from outside the self which means they are being directed, herded almost entirely by outside stimuli, little or nothing is coming from within although they have the perception that they are making their own decisions but there really not, their decisions are made up almost entirely by outside opinion and how they will be viewed by so called peers family friends etc. "peer pressure" by the decision they make. The group orientated person has the problem of trying to be themselves and keep everyone else happy, so they spend their lives trying to keep everyone else happy but never experience real happiness themselves because there far too busy keeping everyone else happy, the conundrum is they are not self-orientated enough to be happy; self-orientation, self-direction, self-opinion, self-belief is the prelude to self-esteem. If they haven't got a positive self-view then their self-esteem is seriously weakened to the point of disease, clinical depression even suicide, so creating and holding a good self-esteem can be a life saver.

CHAPTER TWENTY-THREE
INSPIRATIONAL THOUGHT

Inspirational mediumship, Asking a question, painting a picture, writing a poem sketching a picture writing a book taking photographs making jewellery, these are just some of the ways we can channel through inspirational thought, it really isn't to be underestimated just how powerful this is the reasons for this are because when you focus on these type of things you are creating you shift you awareness to something positive which causes a positive effect. Often Art, writing, playing a musical instrument are used as therapy's because they shift your focus to something you are interested in and enthusiastic about which scores at the top of the Human mood table, Apathy which is at the bottom is depression low self-esteem thoughts of suicide can be reversed very quickly by not focusing on what you see as a life of poverty or sickness and Improves mood drastically, providing you keep yourself in a mood of optimism, enthusiasm, Interest, you can lift yourself out of a dark depression into a state of joy because you take yourself on a trip of being absorbed in what you are doing that you can enjoy, when you focus on a painting writing etc. You move into a light trance state when you are in this state the door is open to inspired interests, that is the difference between watching TV and being in a light trance state and taking in multiple outside opinion or focusing on something that's about you that's positive and being in a light trace state, many people are living a life of absolute boredom because they aren't cultivating their own interests so they spend the best part of their lives looking at what others are doing and criticising almost competing with other people's lives instead of creating their own; their the expert on another's life but not an expert on their own life. Ah but their doing this their doing that, they're not doing this they're not doing that, they should do this, they should do that.

OK fine but what are you doing while you're telling them what to do and picking holes in their lives, and who asked you in the first place to direct yourself you first have to find who you are, and you won't do that by spending you're lives spinning a yarn about other peoples. To move up the mood table and gaining self-esteem means focusing on the self and not on other people. Relationships with other people are one of two things co-creating by mutual agreement or co-depending mostly not by mutual agreement, this is a very fine line with NLP it's about orientation between two opposites and the line in the middle; people who are more or mostly co-creating have a good knowledge of self and work well with individuals and groups who have similar self-knowledge, they draw people and are drawn to people who know themselves and are focused on creating their own life they add to each other's experience in a positive way, they value themselves so they can value others, they work co-operate together in a way that is give and take that benefits the self and the others without interfering negatively with each other's personal life design and by mutual consent.

This could be called additive relationship; they are alike by positive mind-set attraction/repulsion is not all physical by any means we attract/repel by likeness of mind-set many people think attraction is all physical it's not. When someone works, and it does take some effort and work on their self-opinion and self-perspective other things about their physical reality change, it's a non-physical causation that creates physical change in relationships and circumstances, without this causation nothing changes to any noticeable degree and people stay stuck in a reality loop. The thing to remember with co creating relationships is where the line is in terms of benefiting each other or harming each other for example unwanted help is negative interference remember you are going to be getting back what you are giving out a kind of holographic response sometimes it can be difficult to gauge whether you are helping or hindering. Good intensions when directed at others can be very beneficial or very disruptive and that's why it's such a thin line, if the good indentation are imposed on someone this will more often than not cause harm the person has to be permissive of help offered, if is forced it I not help, because you can never know-someone as well as you know yourself- if you know yourself at all, so initially hold focus on the self-first then allow the other relationships to unfold as you get to know yourself better; the irony is most people think they know someone as well as or better than they know themselves, or try to understand others better but spend little time trying to understand themselves better.

The better you understand yourself the better you can understand others if you don't understand why, you make the decisions you make how you can possibly understand the decision's other people make; harmony in relationships is part understanding your relationship with yourself, Often charity's that are set up to help actually increase the problem because they hold focus on the problem and attract more of the same problem. That which benefits the self; this is the job if you like of the sub-conscious mind to manifest in physical reality that which benefits the person, self-organises self by virtue of the perspective the person holds on various aspects of life, concepts, ideas, beliefs there are the template of individual reality's. Working with elementals, Elemental's what they are what they do, and the way things manifest through them.

They are of one of two things 'positive/negative' in orientation and effect, I am I have, are creations of the string of suggestion; constant persistent thoughts on the subject/object, repetition creates form, it's this "opening two word quote" which is of utmost importance it directs elementals to create the end result of the string of suggestion as positive or negative, The "I" in the quotation is constant and refers to the self the next word if it's have then it will produce /manifest having the same would be true if the quote was have not, each one is attached with a corresponding emotion defining the feeling of which ever quote has just been instructed to manifest for example to say and repeat I have a new house will manifest the house because that is what you stated as have so you must have it because you built the emotion of having around it; I have, I have not, I can, I can't, I will, I won't, I love, I hate. All generate a vibrational frequency unique to the quote and defining positive or negative. The opening quote is the 'clause' in the suggestion string, the agreement you enter into with yourself is the suggestion, word and expression of words are defining/creating their experiences in relation to weather words/expressions are of love, hate, will or won't are all linked back to the experience their having the way this is changed is creating feelings of having by focusing on what you want to behave and portraying as emotionally having.

Whether the mind is focused on chasing away or drawing in, is what pushes away or draws in the object or objective, I want to have is chasing away, have is drawing in. It's the expressions of wanting or having whether thorough hypnosis, NLP, meditation, visualizations, affirmations, gratitude; to express having give's having, "like attracts like, have attracts having." As Henry Ford said if you think you "can" or think you "can't" you are right." The opening quote and statement of truth then become like a metaphor, metaphorically you have so then in actuality you have, you write it as true you state it as true, true = true, "you state your physical reality before you experience/manifest it." You experience what you have stated as having. Part of NLP and hypnosis is understanding the condition that runs a statement/affirmation exactly like computer code only in this instance we are the computer, the affirmation, group of words which is always a truth is run like computer code with the result of the statement being processed as true or false, this is decided by the condition of the statement i.e.

I have is true I have not is true the statement to the condition is always true so to state not having or the implication of the statement is not having then it manifests as not having so to state not having is to state having not having; the statement always implies 'having in the moment' or doing/not doing in the moment. Just to point out that everything that exists physically only exists in the moment not the future or past anything attributed to past or future only exists as non-physical, if it were possible to travel like time travel then it would only be possible to travel to locations in the here and now not past or future because one has gone and the future does not exist yet only as a probability, it is the conditional statements that are focused on then become the highest probability and manifest. For most Humans on this planet their understanding of this principle of conditional statement has been reversed they think they are stating what they are experiencing as they experience, it but they are reacting and responding to what they experience and then re-manifest that experience because they in some way stated it, so what they state is what they intend to manifest without realising they are intending it first. Think! Would you state to yourself that you are grateful for everything going wrong or being poor or sick?

When you state something as having it, it is the same as stating being grateful you bring it into the percent moment continually; stating/affirming I have, I am grateful for, or thank you for, are all statements that it's in the here and now it affirms having now in physical experience. Science has already run experiments on the atom and whether a conditional statement affected the atom in any way the answer was yes conditional statements do affect the atom, which is proof that thoughts become things the conditional statement is the thought. This means the thing comes after the thought not the other way around. Relationships to the conditional statements; the condition equals the value of the suggestions the suggestions are always true and manifest in accordance with the value attributed to the suggestion. Imagine sitting in front on a computer before anything comes on the screen a command statement is run which then is shown on the screen you don't look at a blank screen and get what your wanting on the screen just by looking you press a key or instruction that runs the command it then manifests on the screen the command is made up of blocks of conditional statements, physical manifestation is the same the command of conditional statement runs what then manifests.

This subject and all the things I am and have covered comes under the umbrella of parapsychology which sets out to understand that which comes under psychic phenomena this includes hypnosis, astral projection, and the realm of nonphysical influence in physical life. The terminology of manifestation and what causes manifestation is what I have spent many years looking at through self-observation and observation of others I look at behaviour why people do the things they do and why most people think everything is fated and they have no personal control over it I watch many people live a rout routine life influenced almost entirely by the ideal and mind-set of the set waged day job. what started to become obvious to me before and after completing my hypnothcrapy diploma was words have substance they are creating and doing things so this became a study for me of what people are saying what they are listening to and the way lives are shaped by this, how much of what would be called psychic or magic is actually no more than the effect of statements that act as the cause, although I keep my work religious and politically free they probably would prefer people did not know this and that include companies that employ people as robots for a pittance of a wage.

That is the only time in this book that I mention politics and religions because this is not a religion, nor should it be politically orientated. This focuses on people as the individual self and developing self-esteem rather than have a metaphorical Achilles heel and be bound to pleasing and running around at the whims of their perceived peer's, the conditional statement and the condition/value that runs it literally has the power to move the metaphorical mountains like computer coding the conditional statement works as a command the must create the effect it is causing, there is no exception to this rule because cause and effect is an absolute principle, even scientist looking at the so called big bang are now saying there could not have been nothing and then a big bang because a big bang needs a causation, you cannot have an effect without a cause. The reason why human beings have created things on this planet way above and beyond any living creature on this planet is because we have a sophisticated language that is more than all other physical life on this planet, the only things other creatures focus on is food shelter reproduction we take that to a whole new level both good and bad, the only reason for this is we have and use conditional statement hence the phrase conditioning, the conditional statement is all that separates us from that which we would call the beast and in some cases used unwisely puts some bellow the nature of the beast because the beast does everything by instinct a bird does not have a smart phone with GPS to navigate its way when migrating it does it by instinct, so it stands to scrutinised reason everything we manifest above base instinct comes from the conditional statement before the manifestation can occur because that is cause and effect. So how much of what is perceived as psychic phenomena is actually nothing more than the effect of the statement and being in tune with the non-physical counterpart of the physical self, I have often mentioned hypnosis to people to see their reaction most have a negative response, yet they sit in front of the television and are being hypnotised, yet they say hypnosis doesn't work well if it doesn't work why do companies spend billions of pound on advertising on television.

Within an average of fifteen minutes someone watching television is in what is known as light a light to medium trance state (open to suggestibility) which is the primary goal of an hypnosis induction the more engrossed in the programme the person is the deeper in trance they go, it is possible to be in deep trance state while idly watching television there are good and bad sides to television most experience the negative side and allow themselves through complacency to be brainwashed and have their decisions and opinions made for them. We live in a multi-dimensional universe which is electromagnetic which means everything is made from a simple root which is the atom which when impregnated with thought become elementals, positive or negative in what they produce in physical reality as object or experience. So people are faced with a reality/actuality that feels like a dream or a nightmare by virtue of these things, people have been stupefied and dumbed down to the point of spending virtually all their time wanting what other people have instead of wanting for themselves from their own efforts and creativity, many people lie before telling the truth and only tell the truth if it's their only option what kind of a civilisation are we now living in?

Predominantly a dumbed down stupid one, they allow themselves to be treated no better than slaves or prisoners because they have no understanding of the basic universal principles (laws of nature) by which everyone and everything is bound to, if we were not bound by these principles we would not exist, someone said once about what I was working on mind over matter huh they said rubbish, if it was not for mind over matter you would not exist so by virtue of their belief if that manifested for them they would not exist in any area of the universe. So if you don't believe in mind over matter you are talking yourself out of your own existence, mind produces thought, thought produces and directs matter, the reason everyone's a critic as they say is because they are trying to live other people's lives not create their own while I've been working on this I have had people that oppose this knowledge, insult me threaten me slander and lie about me say I should settle for a crap day job and I say to them if you weren't so bone idle in the head you would be off living your own life rather than telling me what I should and shouldn't be doing, interfering meddling and basically making a bloody nuisance of themselves, my life is for me to live not them, one of the so called universal sub laws is non-interference.

The most amusing thing for me is how rigorously they defend the conditioned beliefs that keep them in a constant state of dis-satisfaction jealousy and grumpiness, their behaviour and comment a constant reflection of their own self-loathing projected outwardly at other people if you listen in on an average conversation most of it is talk of what other people are or are not doing very little is about themselves because they have nothing to talk on about themselves because they're not doing anything to advance themselves most people seek attention from discussing other people they have become shallow almost hollow of their own personality in fact most people are someone else's personality; Personality for many people is probably about 95% borrowed from other people a personality with real self-esteem is probably 95% their own true self-personality people seek constant approval from others rather than constant approval of themselves, the more people seek outside approval the less they are themselves and the more they are the product of another's opinion, and become an altered ego of others this is the difference between self-esteem and the ego, many people have absolutely no idea who they are or why their doing what tier doing they have forgotten how to be themselves and have no idea that every negative intention or action against another will cause a negative manifestation in their lives more than the intention or action sent against another.

So on reflection of terminology of sane and insane and what relates to either one comes back to self-esteem or the alter-ego, alter-ego being a mind –set that is a majority outside orientated self-opinion self-worth etc.

they will focus more on others and direct attention at other peoples perceived shortcomings and flaws as a way to keep the focus of themselves their this they're that is an avoidance of looking at themselves in an attempt to stop others looking at them to closely this relates heavily of the way people feel about themselves, I have known people who exhibit an outwardly confident, exuberant, extrovert personality, but in their own company are the opposite and any long degree of time alone they start to focus negatively on themselves in some cases causing self-harm even suicide, they project self-esteem.

However it's all superficial on the surface those with a good or high self- esteem can be very happy in their own company find things they like to do an art or craft even talk and joke about to themselves but they are aware they are doing this and is a reflection of being happy in themselves and their own company as well as other people's company, if your good company for yourself then your good company for others, if your depressive or critical company for yourself then you are depressive or critical company for others, the true inner self portrays the outer self in this way. Obviously, there are more complexities to the make-up of individual personalities, but these are the basic principles behind people's behaviour patterns. The bully is the weaker personality they to project strength by bullying yet this shows insecurity's and actions out of fear of other people's opinion of them they view a kindness as a weakness but when the shoes on the other foot they become the poor me merchants. Effectively making the bully not hard and strong but weak the biggest cry-baby is the bully that gets bullied back, the critic that gets criticised, the reason I have put it like this is to show that orientation of the negative or positive elemental directed by thought is that which creates reality, personality, and behaviour.

Past life regression is a phenomenon of hypnosis, it has often been said that when a person passes from one life to another their life flashes before their eyes and they learn the lesson of that incarnation, could the lesson in every case be perspective of mind-set (beliefs), even the perspective of having to die carries with it the corresponding opposite perspective of being able to live in one incarnation indefinitely. What is the deciding factor of living indefinitely happy health and wealthy or getting old and dying is the belief that one is definite, and the other is impossible possible cannot ever be possible if the person's belief is that it is impossible; belief can only manifest the belief not the non-be.

It seems to me that this then makes the God and the Devil concept not something that is religious but something that is individual mind-set The God concept being that which creates and adds to life, Devil being that which disrupts and takes from life, it is our mind-set that adds to or takes away from our own life reality's and experiences, the realisation that the God or the Devil are not entity's that float on a cloud dutifully hurling lightning bolts or miracles around, every miracle comes from within, we are all and all our experiences are products of our own mind the will of God becomes the will of the self, universe gave us free will the non-physical substance that is within and outside of everything that exists anywhere in any Universe is free willed when you understand the way to ask, spirit non/physical substance will deny no one anything that would sustain and enhance their life the only thing that denies them these things is their own mind.

We are energy beings that can evolve into that which we would not have thought possible or devolve into something we would never wish to be, we have the choice in this it is not fated beyond our control but well and truly in our own hands, there is no Gods will, or blame it on the Devil, it is all in our own mind and hands, we are all responsible for our own thoughts and actions there are no excuses anymore we no longer live in the dark ages of being able to say this information is not available or only available to those who studied Witchcraft (wise-craft) that was shrouded and dubbed evil to keep people from finding the truth, there are no more excuses what you do is because you choose to do it, we have freedom to go anywhere on this planet we choose to others do not have the freedom to say we cannot, you only have the freedom to make choices and decisions for your own life another's choices and decisions are theirs alone. You can rest assured that those who spend all their time working and attempting to bend others to their will and challenge another's free will, will go through what they have done to others because that is the law of nature, by which there is no escape no matter how far they run how deep they hide universe knows where they are and universe is balance, we are bombarded with manmade law after manmade law. There is only one law and that is the law of universe/nature;" to quote something I read somewhere once "beware the law of man." You can live within the law of man and against the law of nature and die anyway, you can live within the law of nature and live and live and continue to live indefinitely no matter what law man makes to restrict and bind people. So getting back to the elementals that which becomes experience and form from though, it appears now that the conditional statement we create about ourselves is that which is formulating our reality for example from infancy if a child I told their bad then this can continually trigger beliefs about themselves that they are bad so the child goes into adulthood continually believing they are bad that they are not worthy of good things, so it I difficult/impossible for them to manifest good things because their opening condition of themselves is they are bad, other opening conditions like 'what if, what if something goes wrong is likely to manifest something going wrong, other self-statements like I can't be rich because I am poor, so it appears most likely that every adults reality manifests in accordance with what they are told they are and what their situation is from one, two, three, four years old and these self-beliefs play out for their entire life because they are unaware their self-belief can be changed. So from year 1 a child's profile of themselves emerges in their conscious mind entirely by outside stimuli this then creates a trick in the mind that their life is fated in the way it unfolds this however in most cases is a false belief.

CHAPTER TWENTY-FOUR

PSYCHIC SELF-DEFENCE FROM DESTRUCIVE BRAINWASHING

What leaves you most open to a psychic attack or being manipulated against your will is assumption that something someone has told you is true, so an easy technique is to ask yourself why did they say that, why do they want me to do that, why don't they want me to do that, what your being told may be true, or a lie, a good lie always has an element of truth, to make it plausible, the trick is to ask yourself why not them, when you say why to another person i.e. why did you do that you are challenging their sense of self or their view of the world. If someone's putting up a smoke screen or has an ulterior motive, this is a good line of defence form them, Mmm. that's interesting, why do they want me to believe that. Another favourite with people who are trying to mislead or dupe you is to add a metaphor to their allegation. A good example is "there's no smoke without fire" that's true but that doesn't automatically mean what their saying is true. We see the way linguistics can work for us in this book now we look at the way linguistics can work against us from deliberate techniques to a casual comment, from groups with heavily ingrained social clue to keep the group together to people just trying to sell you something you just don't want; being able to recognise whether something is not quite what it seems or just being more aware of all these potential commands floating around us every day, In an attempt to bend us against our will in some way. At birth we all inherit a few things one of them is free will to make our own choices and master our own destiny: however there are quite a few things out there that will quite happily try to do that for you and to some degree may already be doing that. Being aware of what we're observing and whether we want to interact with it. Outside stimuli designed to suggest to you what you want, so you must become clear in your own mind what you want.

That's easier to do when you put your focus on what you want as opposed to all the other things you don't want, so avoid things that start making you think and feeling a negative way; we correspond by observation and interaction. We can take in a lot of information that isn't really relevant to us and it gets messed up in processing and becomes relevant. The way I have put the book together is so it's possible to see almost in real terms what reality comprises of, and how it plays out. And what degree of inner and outside stimuli, are influencing that reality, which we experience in the moment; the self-deity that we are creating as in the male or female characteristics, personality, personality types. The point here being within, rather than an external deity aspect, directed outwardly, but creating our own self by choosing the persona, personality types we want to adopt and keep, the process becomes like creating our own self-deity. In a way that acknowledges the interdependent self and the connection and co-existence with everything else; our awareness is also our defence, as you apply different parts of this book and build personal history of success, from small to large things, and you realise not from book knowledge alone but through experience, the realisation that we can be, have and do whatever it is we focus on the most, repeatedly over various timelines, if you were a deity what personality traits and personality, behaviour, world view would you have?

The point of the exercise is to project forward, future pace to how you would like to be as a person, and have moving towards actions lined up with it, by working through this book you have already been doing this creating your sense of self and going into it with an attitude of "everything's possible." So keep the direction you're thinking on focused on, what I want to do and how I want to see myself, in one, two four years from now. Ask your self-deity questions like does it have the ability to live for hundreds of years in one incarnation. "Everything's possible." The psyche psychic development being the divine part of the deity; the reason people who go on diets and put the weight back on is they don't see themselves in any way as being different or slimmer, this exercise which is all so what the best part of this book is about, is about seeing yourself in the way you want to see yourself and push the boundary's with "everything's possible". Sometimes for something you want to happen, it is happening can come from just believing it's possible! As far as the concept of psychic self-defence, attitude is one thing which is to some degree obvious, less obvious is hereditary beliefs, also a less obvious form of psychic self- defence is preventing unconscious self-sabotage, which is extremely common and way past pandemic proportions, Self-sabotage "through self-referencing" not self-harm which happens with conscious awareness, but sabotage that's happening without conscious awareness that can be changed to success. Self-referencing is a process of conscious and unconscious mind literally deciding what to manifest as your experience through this process which ties in with the 1-8 though/values levels, a kind of question-and-answer process between the conscious minds.

The point here is as I've mentioned a couple of times in this book you can have a windfall of millions, but if your self- referencing apart from having that money stays the same, then without having that coping system that comes from self-referencing those people are over 80% more likely to blow the money in two or so years and be in pretty much the same environment they started in, so part of psychic self-defence are the parts in this book that show you how to change the way your self-referencing. Outside stimuli designed to suggest what you want so you have to become clear in your own mind what you want, or outside stimuli will surely do it for you. We correspond by observation and interaction. We can get to the point that we become so focused on problems that the only thing that keep coming along are problems, mainly because people in general focus on the problem not the solution, and when they do focus on a solution it's all about object objectivity in a physical sense, which is a problem for them, because until they install in their strategies a subjective approach to an objective problem then it becomes for them very difficult even impossible to shift their reality much because of the process their applying. So adding subjective interventions will in itself create the solutions.

PSYCHIC SELF-DEFENCE FROM DESTRUCIVE BRAINWASHING

Something as simple as self-hypnosis defining what you want as already in existence in your life, and literally writing down questions to no one in general, just write them down and somewhere along the way, the answer will present itself. Self-sabotage becomes defence from the self, and all the information we are being bombarded with every day, which is sorted through our filtering system, but with all this information there are commands that are getting through to unconscious, which are manipulating your decisions and not necessarily in your best interest.

We can become so obsessed/absorbed in what other people are doing and other opinions that we get side-tracked from what we are doing and what our own opinion is, we can be tricked in to running around trying to please everyone else that we never do anything that pleases ourselves. Be aware of this because there are those who will quite happily have you running around and get nothing in return for it.

Being able to recognise language patters that are constructed to be highly manipulate, and controlling, apologies followed by it's just that, or statements like that I only want what's best for you, are highly manipulative statements, another particularly Important thing to have clarity on is association, what your thoughts and language patterns are associated to. Also look at whether a statement implies scarcity or abundance/plentiful, Swish language patterns and swish actions like what I would call NLP overlays, so someone says to you I only want what's best for you, overly in your head/mind it is not for me to want for others or others to want for me six to seven times, these strategies become like batting away balls trying to get your stumps, like their pee rollers, People often go to groups orientated around a problem, and often, very often it becomes like a swish pattern in as much as the swap dependency's and become dependent on the group, whereas when you master these techniques to the point they work for you can with a bit of patience and effort and maybe some help, but pretty much be able to sort thing out for yourself because you are more than capable of doing this, you know that now don't you. Language patterns are important and have great value to them because we run language patterns in our head so to speak all the time as well as in conversation and writing. Our language patterns are literally creating the blueprint around the three core concepts Health, Wealth Relationships.

Pattern: a blueprint or design surrounding all systems, thought patterns, language patterns, Strategy patterns, action patterns, patterns of choices., This I think would also imply that things we associate to as habits/addictions are actually choices, preferences, the choice may have been made a very long time ago, in the imprint or modelling period but is a choice, as it's in the values and belief patterns.

This becomes very empowering when we realise everything, we are doing is actually a choice, so we can change our choices. These patterns are effectively creating or updating blueprints that are destiny defining, our chain of thought and the language patterns we employ in various stages of conversation and self-talk. Our thought and language patterns appear to be the mechanism we use to as they say, "manifest our reality/experiences. "so when we master our thoughts and language patterns does that give us self-mastery effectively control of our own destiny's, the answer has to be yes.

And also is directly related to what thoughts/values level anyone is on at any point in time. So up or down the values level ladder is really being defined initially by thoughts and language. Which makes the process of creating a blueprint ourselves or updating an existing one a lot easier just by being consciously aware of the way we exist in universe and the experiences we draw in; this is all tied in by universal absolutes so it's kind of tough if you don't like the process or believe in it this is one instance when human belief doesn't have an influence. Essentially knowing this and applying it is also a form of psychic self-defence, not knowing this leaves people wide open to all sorts of mind manipulation, to be perfectly blunt about it. The more aware we are of the type of messaging we are constantly being bombarded with, is doing, as in people who talk in a way that is predominately necessity, be careful because that will rub-off on you, necessity doesn't define abundance in any way so look for the kind of language patterns that are more in line with where you're going and what your path is. As it turns out we have more choices and freedom to make choices and cause effects from choices that can improve health, wealth, relationships. We are talking on a level of "I think therefore I am" is pretty true, and now you have the tools to use exactly what that metaphor is saying. If you look at Humanity, and it's social structure you will see that people align to groups and how much choice they have in what they do every day, or how much choice they believe they have is part of what attracts different people to different groups.

This becomes more about understanding our own infinite choice system we have to work with as opposed to protesting about human rights, or governments etc. it's much more about creating choice from within not so much almost depending on other people or groups to make choices for you, it's a bit like breaking free from a dependency rather from working with and on yourself mostly by yourself without need to be dependent on groups or governments from everything and looking to blame everything everywhere else, it's actually about this, understanding this and applying it, , a mind-set of self-sufficient isn't just about the idea of grow your own food, though that's not a bad thing, it's more about being capable of doing as much as you can by yourself, not entirely but more than probably now. There may be some things in universe that are truly random, maybe; but our reality our in the moment actuality is not random it is all preconceived, synchronised, and the system it's synchronised through is in this book and is the way choices are made, trough values, beliefs, strategies, thought, language, this is our inherent toolbox to create our own reality with. Although not generic, we all inherit this incredible ability to choose freely, pretty cool eh. So understanding why we make certain choices and n being able to change or re-frame choices is pretty much the key to personal transformation in all areas of life. And with practice becomes self-defence.

The point here is we have unconscious choices going on that we can change consciously but although it's not a secret it's still not all that well know about, certainly not to any point of being mainstream thinking yet, that may follow in time though. Creating paradoxes, when unconscious mind holds something as true, and is presented with a variable or opposite of that truth it creates a paradox. Also what I would consider not just psychic self-defence but for wellbeing in general is the concept which is actually immutable so is an absolute and that is natural law where so called justice and personal returns are concerned, the natural law states that-predictable consequences based on the way things or conditions appear to behave, having no exceptions or deviations (if an exception appears to occur, it is because one does not understand the law in its entirety for that particular exception.)

This means that there is a natural law of balance. This process of manifestation seems to be tis create a paradox, then continue to follow intended desire, which in turn is operating thought a system of correspondence and compensation, another point of self-defence could be talking less about random irrelevant topics and being let's say more discerning with where our conversations are directing us to. The way this plays out on a global scale were tis is putting people on the thoughts and values level, which also defines being wealthy or poor, happy, or ill; "talk only of what you desire" wouldn't be a bad metaphor as it happens, obviously achieving that, takes some practice, Talk only of what you desire as in choosing to have or as in already having, do you think that would make a difference to humanity if everyone did that, without intending harm. This will obviously effect relationships, the point is if you analyse the direction your conversations going in company, are they affirming that you are in a negative position financially or otherwise, if you need to put that under the spotlight because is having an effect on whether you're manifesting what you want or not. There is also a balance between deciding what degrees of sameness and different you want to have, looking for a balance between extremes, is finding yourself.

Absolutes and function

Everything in universe functions by virtue of the three immutable universal laws, so we have the concept idea of absolutes and function, and where some things are stated as law, like law of attraction, but tested on its own as an absolute it is not an absolute, but a function that is absolute by virtue that it functions that way because of the three absolutes, which is why law of attraction is called a law it's not in the true science sense a law but a function that's absolute in nature. So these things and techniques we can apply are because we know why and how without needing quantum physics to tell us this, because when we start to apply these subjective interventions and look at our linguistics thing will and have to change by virtue of following things that cause things to function in a certain way. Here we can define functional flow and dis-function and what they are and why they work that way. Conscious awareness or not is the main issue, in as much as how many people are who are effectively following blindly, to coin a metaphor applying what I have put in this book and doing what they choose, and those A good question I have if we generate a more creative mind-set and less competitive on mind-set, would this be a form of psychic self-defence? The function to compete is to win or lose, so our bias orientation and why will help us understand ourselves and why we make the decisions we make.

Mind-set pairings that become biases, Creative/competitive, big picture/finer detail active income/passive income, abundance/scarcity, and self/group, this is where social science also kicks in, and the concept idea born poor or born rich where they start is where they will finish so to speak, because of these mind-set biases which we can alter. These biases also appear to tie in with law of association, and influence what we focus on most.

Then we come to hypnosis and NLP as psychic self-defence, and tools for advancement. To answer this we need to look at the concept of destructive brain washing, what recruiters that use these techniques are doing and the process they use, before I carry on with this if anyone and I think most people will be able to relate to having some kind of brainwashing or bending of their will, at some point, Hypnosis and NLP give us the tools to reverse any negative brainwashing. What do people use to recruit or bend someone's will to theirs? the fitting in mind-set, how much do we really need, have or desire to "fit in" which is also directly tied in with reptile mind, which means "fight or flight" but in relation to fear of not fitting in as opposed to Tiger, leg it, life threatening, and non- life threatening being the difference. People seemed to be obsessed with fitting in with a pile of external big pictures, but not really creating their own to fit in to. Are people in an apathetic or just above apathy most of the time by virtue of focusing so much time and energy into doing things they don't actually want to keep focusing as much time and energy as they can in achieving the things they want to do. The reasons people try to fit in and what there trying to fit in to, the ideals and values you have or want to change to, what are they describing as your ideals ideology s they follow.

Anyone seriously wanting to transform their lives will have to get down and dirty so to speak on ideology's, groups, associations, organisations, which ones have a direct influence on you via people you associate with, do the ideology's compliment what your trying to achieve, or behave like inner conflicts and seem to block the things you want to do., also looking at other people if you were modelling from Someone to become excellent at what they do what ideology's do they have and would they complement or conflict with what your about. Fitting in with the self and co-existing with others, though.

Building the big picture and neurological levels of change

Environment; When. Country, City (urban) or Countryside, Culture, traditions, Lifestyle, when constructing your big picture of what you would choose as preferences, focus on environment first it's important to have a clearly defined idea of the type of environment you are moving toward, then add focus to the other five as they tile off here. Behaviour: What, Lifestyle, in or out of line with twenty-one universal sub-laws, what would I have to believe for my behaviour to be in line with what I want. Capabilities: How, can do, can't do, objectives, which become your moving towards actions. Beliefs/Values, why our world view, what we perceive as possible/not possible, objects, objectives; Identity; Who, self-identity, who am I, how you see yourself and the way you would like to see yourself, one, two, three, four years from now. Mission, who else, we, others external co-exist circles, Family, Friends, business, intimate. Association is a big part of what's being suggested law of attraction is about, it's not that law of attraction doesn't work, it does, but they keep associating to things/ideals that virtually repel what there trying to draw in. So building a clear comprehensive set of self-ideals really comes after a bit of time working through the other chapters in this book, but the clearer the big picture is in your mind the bigger its possibility of manifesting. Integrating parts and ideas through process of defining self-ideas, ideals, ideology's, and choosing to integrate with that which is in closer alignment to the self-defining which is most in alignment with you by virtue of matching highest intensions. When you write down/affirm your ideals it has a it has a delete comparison effect so that which isn't in line isn't actually deleted but shifts down the hierarchy and the new ideal replaces it. Ideology: a manner or the content of thinking, characteristic of an individual, group, culture, or traditions. So in a manner of speaking our ideals personal or otherwise are like a way we direct thought patterns, which in turn direct our linguistics and actions, for example so called ideal lifestyles, the lifestyle of celebrity's, when you get down to meaning and purpose, even individuality, do you think the lifestyle of a celebrity is all its glammed up to be, or just more pressure and stress and to some degree loss of freedom. Look at the dependency's they have, from agents to a mile of other middlemen, or is it an ideal of perfectness that doesn't always turn out perfect. Ideal of perfectness: Also the same in definition as big picture, moving toward that which you think would represent and be you ideal of a perfect life/lifestyle, then that which is action toward it.

External ideals vs internal ideals

Free will of choice is by definition something every person has, however only a small percentage of the population are aware of it, because it ties in with the reality that everything is connected by a vital life force or infinite spirit; which gives us our very existence, and free will to have, be, and do whatever we choose to, we have an infinite right to make our own choices without interference from outside opinion, because outside opinion is none of our business; our big picture and what we want from the incarnation we have is our business, there are no rules only one wisdom that guides us toward what we want and away from harm, "an it harm ye none do as thy will" I would say if you have never come across this wisdom before, spend a bit of time meditating on its meaning and the consequences if you ignore it, do you ever ask yourself before you take an action on something, is this going to benefit myself and others, or harm myself and others, because to harm another is to harm the self. If you took that wisdom to heart, would you need a man-made law or rule? Would you need to be told," though shalt not," when you are not desiring or intending harm in the first place, we can have whatever we desire without causing harm to thy self or another. An infinite free will means we have the capacity to manifest our reality as we will, and whatever your life is at the moment you have manifested with your free will, but it is defined as if you're in control or not by your level of thinking and personal attitude. If you ever heard of the phrase "give Chi to get Chi" it is a reference to energy the give and take of energy and the Chi you give energetically is the Chi that returns to you, so give good energy give bad energy that's what returns, for example someone does something that causes someone else distress, the person says it wasn't their intention to cause distress, however the outcome defines the intention as one could say it was not for them to interfere in the first place, it really mean we should be focused on our own stuff not interfering with other peoples, " the best intentions can cause the most dire consequences" knowing this and being mindful of it is also a form of psychic self-defence. So what is free will? It's desire, intention, action.

From a person who knows themselves, which means they are aware of their beliefs and values, and how to change them; it's the ability to communicate with linguistics that causes a flux, from thought, to thought form, to physical thing or experience. It's the ability to form a concept idea, and bring it to fruition, it's the ability to transform our lives by changing the way we see ourselves, and not being so hung up about outside opinion of the way others may see us. It's about self- responsibility, and gives us a strong self- esteem and sense of self/our purpose in this incarnation; it's about having the courage to be honest to yourself and others about who you are, what you are about, one of the most courageous actions we make is being honest in relationships, most relationships crash at the first hurdle because one or both people in the relationship aren't being honest, or they create internal conflict which isn't good for either parties, which leads to deceit, anger and in general are bad Chi together, and eventually so called toxic relationships, the other is accepting people for who they are and not trying to change everyone that doesn't fit with your view of the world, that said if your faced with their way is the only way and it doesn't fit with you, then minimum contact or no contact may be the best option.

You have to decide as you go along. If honesty in a relationship is a big value of yours like it is for me, then why change others to fit in with you, when you are more than capable of attracting people who would already fit with you without telling them they have to change their religion or get a haircut to fit with you, it's the difference between having deep meaningful relationships and shallow sunny weather friend relationships, the who else in the big picture. In terms of finding what really fits with you, a good exercise is to look at the ideals you have and external ideals you may be interested in and ask yourself a question, would this be a moving toward pleasure or pain, the reason I say this is because most people in general are not future pacing with awareness/mindfulness, and a consequence of that can be they inadvertently find themselves moving towards pain obviously without intending to, I have talked about reptile mind the most ancient part of our brain, now reptile mind will like fight or fight act in the same way when your moving towards actions are not toward pleasure it will without you consent do all it can to keep you from moving toward pain. So it's a bit like swimming against the tide or worse a rip tide, when your actions are moving toward pleasure then you have the support of reptile mind as opposed to it trying to move you away from your objectives, and then you have more alignment towards your objectives with support of reptile mind. Is what you are doing serving others first but not yourself or serving yourself first and then others. External will. How I have come to understand this over the last decade is, free will with man-made clauses, the main difference is "and it harm ye none do as thy will" is permissive, whereas the man-made rules and laws are not, the problem really comes when the rules and laws are repeated over and over; this is because of the way unconscious mind processes our linguistics.

    Firstly unconscious mind learns through repetition repeat something over and over like an affirmation and it's going to manifest, secondly unconscious mind doesn't process negatives, so when you repeat an instruction like don't do over and over, unconscious mind processes it as do, not don't, if you give an instruction once like don't touch the door the paints wet, then they won't touch the door because the pains wet, and there's no repetition, however if you give an instruction don't touch the door the paints wet several times in a minute or so the person will touch the door. Have you ever told a youngster, not to do something, as in don't do that,

I told my kid a hundred times don't do that, it's like there deliberately going out of their way to do it just to any me, there not, you instructed them to by repeating do that, even though you said don't the instruction gets processed as do.

The point to this is to define instructions coming internally and externally, the free willed way is more internal the external will way is more external; the concept of know thyself, is really defining giving the self-instructions, as opposed to all the instructions coming externally. The process of finding the beliefs you don't know you have that influence your day to day life, if you were to ask yourself can you think of a time when you wanted to do something but didn't have you ever thought there is an automated trigger that kicks in on a reptile brain level, what if I fail and everyone laughs, pretty much everyone has done that at least once, so where did the belief, that caused reptile brain to kick in with being embarrassed: away from pain, so there must be a belief that you would fail, where did that belief come from? And ask it out load or in a whisper the point is the answer must come it has a cause-and-effect component to it, if the answers not in a book it will come intuitively as an example, ask the right questions and you are in the process of finding your true self. The way we individually relate to everything, and the way we relate and mirror with others; interactive relationships, includes interacting with the self, the way we interact relate to ourselves is key to who you end up attracting and repelling where relationships are concerned, when you change the way, you view and relate to yourself, you change the external relationships as well, awareness of this is self-defence when you look at it and change the way you relate to yourself. It corresponds to the constant message board of communication between conscious and unconscious self, there are those who have awareness of this, but most have a distorted perception of unconscious, especially the way it processes information, from within and from without.

This becomes the simple root that which controls our outward relationships, from Family, friends, and work colleagues, these are all defined by the way you see yourself, more so than the other way around. You are where you are, when you think to yourself "I want to change my life and be myself." So ask yourself or just ask out loud how you see your life and its meaning and purpose as being, yes this does relate to relationships, if you don't know your own meaning and purpose in life, then there are plenty who will tell you what it is and have you running at their command, When you have that down on paper if you don't like what you see then you start to create your own meaning and purpose in life and not just follow a pre-fabricated destiny, generally far more restrictive than when you know your own mind and why you are doing what you're doing, you then give yourself, self-direction, as opposed to being herded, following and chasing, the consumer mind-set or the investor mind-set, investment in the self, when you change the meaning and purpose of your life you change the way you relate to your life and who you relate to or choose to associate to.; relationships to family and occupation, organisations/associations are the key primary areas, of who we relate to and whether it induces, resourceful or un-resourceful outcomes.

For example most people keep the same occupation, or key worker status, and never change it through to retirement, work colleagues figure in relationships and the level of success, abundance or scarcity are defined from this The point is that we have free will, the thing is it takes, a fair bit of nitty gritty to get from where someone finds themselves when they choose to change their life, from creating a big picture and self-direction, the decision making and choices of moving forward actions always come down to the self/individual, too get from a metaphorical A-B, you have to make choices along the way hand have direction of outcome/destination. So the three groupings of relationships, family/inner circle, occupation, organisations/associations, have to be looked at and you have to be honest with yourself, or you will find yourself on a perpetual board of snakes and ladders, if any of the relationships are like having a bout or heated debate, then maybe you are just on opposite sides and best left alone, but the decision of personal relationships is always your own, then you will start to appreciate the way correspondence works. Look at the type of relationships you have and the type you want to have and find a balance between the two if that's possible if not you have to look at the relationships, you're prepared to let go of. These relationship groupings, ask yourself how much of your decision making is influenced by these relationships, and are they going to fit with the path you're carving for yourself. The skills, ability's, and strategy's for getting things done are often rooted in relationship groups, so you really must think, if the skills, ability's, and strategies actually give you any, or no chance of achieving what you really want, then to some degree you have to re-model from people who are excellent in the skills you want to learn, and these things are moving toward actions.

Creating options that may not have been available before, the better your skills and ability, the more option s you're likely to have, also with relationships, the type of options that people have can depend on the type of relationships they choose to keep. People with a scarcity mind-set tend to be low on options, whereas people who develop an abundance mind-set tend to have higher options and are more able to be flexible. There are groups within groups like a matrix, the organisations/associations people find themselves in from their upbringing, orientate around three groups known as Globalists, trade, capitol, investments, nationalists, who are about tradition identity of their nation, individualists who are more self-directing, more self-sufficient minded. Our personality traits come from a balance or imbalance between these three ways of thinking. So for want of a better description, finding the self means being able to operate on all levels to some degree, and generally end up preferring a more individualised way of operating in this matrix of relationships of interaction and observation.

Pretty much everyone's mind-set has degrees of bias toward/away from globalist, nationalist and individualist, in other words our belief, values and strategies, are taken from various aspects of each of these three ideals/ways of thinking which creates and overall way of thinking, they define our personal orientation, between self and others; one will be at the top of a person's hierarchy of parts and ideas, perspective which we view the world from, say individualist first then globalist then nationalist, but peoples perspectives will have a natural bias of on as the main one, which can be changed and generally will come from upbringing. In the same way people process information, one will be a top bias, like visual, then audio then kinaesthetic, or a variance on that. These are the things that are automatically making our decisions and choosing our preferences, and to change this you just must look at each part and decide which aspects of each part you want to keep or drop and thus create balance between these three ways of thinking.

We see this play out in the thought/values levels one to eight, four being the centralised way of doing things, through governments and established national ideals, which also incorporate and relate in some way to the globalist and individualist ideals, above and below the centralised part, are combinations of centralised and degrees of global and individual ideals people incorporate into their lives. This knowledge becomes self-defence in as much as being able to understand the "push and pull" effect it has on personal decisions, the more in command of your own decision making, the more in control of your own personal destiny, which somewhere along the line is what everyone is trying to achieve. How real or superficial something is, comes down to the meaning and purpose you give to it on an individual level, your big picture must be a part of yourself and come from within, becomes about practicing focusing on that which has real relevance to you as opposed to all the external outside stimuli, which claims to have relevance or impotence to you, but under scrutiny turns out to be superficial in real terms. Control of personal destiny is really about achieving levels of self-esteem by achieving the big or small moving towards actions, with a mind-set that is far more entrepreneurial, as in building something from scratch that you interested in and reflects who you want to be and developing ability's to become more self-dependant and self-reliant. People in general tend to be more externally reliant than self.

Motivation and direction

I spent a long time wondering why many people claimed to have tried things to do with mind over matter and claim it doesn't work, which puzzled me, because it should word, unless they are working on cross purposes to themselves, then I realized what it is or one of the key things which effects motivation direction and level of thinking and doing and puts people in a perpetual cycle of working on cross purpose to their true selves, the reason surprisingly was the mortgage, which is also related to a belief and value that the only way to buy a house is with a mortgage and that's perceived to be that, but then think about it, this creates a subconscious pre-supposition that you cannot build a business and buy a house in let's say four years, but the only way is through a mortgage and all the hurdles that come with trying to get one; which then lives as a value and belief, deep rooted from the modelling period, that creates a cross purpose value, which when changed to a belief and value that they can buy a house from working from their own efforts, brings them in to alignment with what they want to achieve which for most people would be to be free of the mortgage or having an alternative big picture that will get them their house without a mortgage.

The defining difference between moving toward a personal big picture and moving toward a mortgage is, one supports abundance the other supports scarcity in terms of mind-set; So creating your own big picture and just focusing on moving toward that as best as you can to start with, eventually flicks the switch from scarcity to abundance, but it takes a bit of time and patience the difference in the mid to long term outcomes and if your life is still feels fated or you feel empowered and have control of your own personal destiny ten years from now comes down to this, and building a deeper understanding of what limiting beliefs are and how to flick the switches, to create real personal change. The difference is the values and beliefs will be different to achieving your big picture, than if they are directing everything toward a mortgage creating the belief that anything that has a large price tag requires a loan or mortgage to get it, rather than getting it from living within their means and creating wealth from within and from their own efforts. This is a reason why there are so few Entrepreneurs in comparison to steady day job pay the mortgage options.

If anyone has researched subjects around Universal mysteries and may have come across channels or psychics who have quoted, you have to remember who you are! So how do we remember who we are, as it turns out we look back at humanity's origins, and eventually each person will have roots Northen, Southern, Eastern or Western hemisphere, that are Nomadic in nature, connected to nature and spirit, the evolution of Nomadic peoples where; hunter gatherer, herder, farmer, they did not want or need to depend on science to tell them they are connected. The vaguely specifics of this are Nomad is also the origin of herbalism and self-healing; and connection to spirit/life force, nature itself; Nomad are individuals and nomadic communities that have skills and abilities of being self-sufficient that the western mindset to a very large degree has forgotten. The western mind-set has become dependent on subbing everything out, and less able or willing to do things for themselves. Achieving Personal destiny and a semi nomadic lifestyle, the way to advance without falling into pitfalls and traps. Being more self-sufficient requires more ability to be responsible for their own decisions and being economically self-sufficient not just grow your own self-sufficient. So to some degree psychic self defence is also the ability to become self-directing to stand as an island or individual sone like stone henge, and also co-exist within communities, and maybe what is evolving now is exactly that, large numbers moving up to a more less dependent on leaders, able to manage their own destiny and co-exist with others.

The focus to be more independent needs, to be more inward on what abilities and skill you want to learn or add, however, not to fulfil an employer's needs, to fulfil your own needs, being more able to do this and be able to work remotely from home or in small communities looks like it could be the way forward, and getting from whatever Values level you are at now, to six, seven, eight, values in doing so you release yourself from self-restricting systems.

The shifts start to happen when you start to change direction in thinking, desire, intentions and actions. The content of this book gives you all the tools you need to achieve this. The more we replace compete with create, and being creative moving towards your big picture the quicker you get to a place called personal destiny, which is self-esteem and what you accomplished to get there. Making a list of what you associate to as Creative and Competitive, what creative things are moving towards your goals and what competitive things are moving against your goals, big picture. The more you cultivate an attitude of create your own personal destiny, the less the desire to compete with others personal destiny.

Now you have read the mind keys, any questions either chapter by chapter, or notes from the overall book please contact for quote.

THE MIND KEYS.

Life Transformation coaching

enquires@mindkeysinternational.co.uk

£14.99

Printed in Great Britain
by Amazon